AFTER INVOLUNTARY MIGRATION

AFTER INVOLUNTARY MIGRATION

The Political Economy of Refugee Encampments

Milica Z. Bookman

LEXINGTON BOOKS

Lanham • Boulder • New York • Oxford

LEXINGTON BOOKS

Published in the United States of America
by Lexington Books
A Member of the Rowman & Littlefield Publishing Group
4720 Boston Way, Lanham, Maryland 20706

12 Hid's Copse Road
Cumnor Hill, Oxford OX2 9JJ, England

British Library Cataloguing in Publication Information Available

Library of Congress Cataloging-in-Publication Data

Bookman, Milica Zarkovic.
  After involuntary migration : the political economy of refugee
encampments / Milica Z. Bookman
        p. cm.
Includes bibliographical references and index.
  ISBN 0-7391-0426-8 (cloth : alk. paper)—ISBN 0-7391-0427-6 (pbk. : alk. paper)
  1. Refugee camps—Economic aspects. 2. Refugees—Economic conditions.
3. Forced migration—Economic aspects. I. Title.

HV640 .B58 2002
305.9'0691—dc21

                                                                        2002005216

Printed in the United States of America

♾™ The paper used in this publication meets the minimum requirements of
American National Standard for Information Sciences—Permanence of Paper
for Printed Library Materials, ANSI/NISO Z39.48-1992.

For Karla and Aleksandra,
may you learn to love to learn.

CONTENTS

LIST OF FIGURES AND TABLES

ACKNOWLEDGMENTS

Many people have contributed to this book and I take this opportunity to express my profound gratitude to them. I would like to thank Nikoli Natrass, Tony Joes, and Ljubisa Adamovic for their helpful comments and suggestions. The staff at the Surplus People Project and the African Studies Library were helpful and patient, for which I am appreciative. I would like to thank Alphonso Olbuehi, Tommy Cohen, and John Luis for facilitating contacts in South Africa. Jim, Stormes, Rob McChesney, and Gonzago de Villa helped with contacts in Central America. Richard Bookman led me through cluster analysis, and Chris Dixon helped me with library resources.

I am grateful to Judi Chapman and George Prendergast for supporting my research in many different ways. Dori Pappas, as always, has been indispensable both as secretary and friend.

I want to thank the members of my writing group, who have been a part of my life over the past year: Eddi Ann Freeman, Jennifer Hurst, Anna Sadkin, and Elissa Vanaver.

Last but not least: Richard, Karla, and Aleksandra, you have contributed to this book simply by being.

1

INTRODUCTION

Throughout history, people have migrated. Some have moved voluntarily, in search of a better life. Others have been forcibly displaced from their homes. Some of those involuntarily displaced persons wind up in camps. The lucky ones are quickly repatriated or resettled elsewhere. The unlucky ones live out their entire lives in what become de facto permanent encampments. Examples include the Palestinians in Lebanon, Eritreans in the Sudan, and Saharawis in Algeria, all of whom have spent decades in camps awaiting resolution of their status and a return to their homelands.

Such encampments are different from the short-term relief centers that provide emergency aid in the immediate aftermath of a disaster. Indeed, they are unlike the camps portrayed by CNN cameras in which temporary tents hide desperate faces and starving bodies (such as the makeshift camps that housed Albanian refugees from Kosovo in 1999). Instead, permanent encampments are those concentrations of involuntarily displaced peoples that have matured beyond what relief agencies call "the initial phase"; they have graduated from the short run to the long run. They have transcended the mere satisfaction of basic needs for food and shelter. Their concerns have become focused on employment, education, trade, and capital accumulation. The goal of simply surviving has been superceded by the goal of achieving a decent standard of living.

At the turn of the new millennium, it is estimated that some 35 million people across the globe live in various kinds of encampments. In South Africa, over 3.5 million people were dispersed and then assigned to encampments during 1960-1980; Eritreans fled to Sudan over 30 years ago, and some 300,000 still live in camps there; Vietnamese boat people left their country in 1975, and 40,000 are still encamped across Southeast Asia; hundreds of thousands of Tutsi refugees went to Burundi in 1962, only to be joined, in the same encampments, by their nationals in the 1990s; and Native peoples of North America were resettled in the past century on reservations, and over one million are still there. Clearly, the number of people that live in encampments is not negligible.

Also not negligible is the number of countries that host encampments: at this time, over 90 countries have camps with over 1000 members. In Africa alone, only four states have neither gained nor lost over 1,000 refugees.[1] If we add to that list the countries that are home to encampment residents, namely the ones that have produced the involuntary displacement, then the total number of countries associated with permanent encampments rises to well over 100.

In addition to the number of countries represented on this list, their diversity and geographical breadth is remarkable and points out that encampments are a global phenomenon. Indeed, they exist in the new world (Canada, New Zealand) and in the Third World (Hong Kong, Costa Rica); they exist in highly developed states (Australia) as well as in less developed ones (India); they exist in democracies (the United States) as well as in authoritarian regimes (Sudan); they exist in market economies (the Czech Republic) as well as in command economies (Iran). As such, encampments cut across geographical regions, levels of development, and political and economic systems.

Given the number of people that live in encampments and the number of countries that are host or home states, encampments warrant the attention of scholars, policy makers, human rights organizations, and the media. This study represents an effort to focus attention on permanent encampments by asking some fundamental economic questions. How do encampment residents survive long after international aid dries up? How do they manage in the absence of a state apparatus? Specifically, are they employed? What do they produce? Are their economies monetized? Are goods and services exchanged in markets? How are prices determined? To the extent that residents engage in economic activities with their adjoining host communities, the following questions are relevant: what types of jobs can they get, how are they treated, what is the net flow of money in and out of the camp, etc. Finally, this study places encampments into the global economy by exploring the changing role of international agencies, the linking of aid with adherence to "universal values" (such as respect for human rights), and the crucial role of diasporas in representing encampment residents abroad.

The answers to the above questions differ across countries. In other words, the quasi-universal presence of encampments does not imply uniformity among them. Intuitively, we might expect that encampments in more developed countries are different from those in less developed countries. However, the reliability of intuition is limited, and, in its place, this study offers an exploration of why they are not the same. This study assesses the ways in which encampments in different economic and political contexts take on different forms, have different structures, and serve different goals. In that effort, this study looks at an old issue (namely population displacement and subsequent encampment) in a new framework (namely, the post-Cold War world). In the twenty-first century, so much has changed with respect to economic relations (including increased integration in the global economy, globalization, etc.) and so much is new in the political sphere (including democratization, liberalization, the spread of western values, etc.). How do these new conditions affect encampments and do they affect them all in the same way?

A typology of states according to economic, political, and social indicators enables answers to the above questions. Such a typology consists of two principal groups, one of which includes highly developed, liberal democracies that participate fully in the globalization process and the other of less developed, authoritarian states that fear international contacts. The principal hypothesis of this study is that democratic, market-oriented countries are preferable hosts to encampments than authoritarian countries with command economies.

This hypothesis is tested by studying encampment economies at three different levels: the micro, the macro-domestic, and the macro-international. At the micro level, this study observes the nitty-gritty of how people live out their daily lives. It observes the encampment as a quasi-closed economy. The extent to which a market develops and the way in which producers and consumers function are assessed. At the level of the host economy, the extent to which the encampment is integrated into its neighboring community is observed. Specifically, this study focuses on the nature of employment outside the camp, the extent of trade, and the direction of net financial flows. Finally, with respect to the international economy, the role of international organizations and diasporas is assessed.

ABOUT THIS BOOK

A book on population movements, *The State of the World's Refugees*, begins as follows, "Large scale movements of refugees and other forced migrants have become a defining characteristic of the contemporary world. At few times in recent history have such large numbers of people in so many parts of the globe been obliged to leave their own countries and communities to seek safety elsewhere."[2] Moreover, in 1995, the *UNHCR Annual Report* stated that "the end of the Cold War generated a strong sense of optimism about the international refugee situation. With the rivalry of the superpowers over, it was thought many conflicts would be resolved, large numbers of refugees would be able to go back to their homes and resources being used for relief could be moved to rehabilitation and development."[3] It then goes on to state that "precisely the opposite has happened."

Social science research responds to current events such as those described above. Given the increase in involuntary displacement in the post-Cold War period, coupled with the decrease in absorptive capacity in Western and non-Western countries, academics are beginning to respond by addressing the question of what happens to involuntarily displaced persons. The underlying goal of this study is to be at the forefront of the resurgence in interest in migration and refugees.

With respect to focus, the emphasis of this book is on the *aftermath* of population displacement instead of the more popular proximate source, such as ethnic cleansing. It focuses on *permanent* encampments, while most recent literature has addressed short term refugee camps, resettlement, integration, third country resettlement, initial asylum, and repatriation. It focuses on the *economic life* of encampments, in contrast to the legal, human rights, and political literature that has dotted library shelves of late. It focuses on an *international perspective* insofar as it places encampments within the global economy instead of viewing them as isolated problems to be tolerated by host states. In that way, while the story told in this book is about the political economy of permanent encampments, the super-story is about the world in the twenty-first century.

While method is discussed amply in chapter 2, two points warrant mention here. First, this study is based on the premise that world states can be divided into tiers. Cluster analysis is used to identify similarities among states on the basis of selected indicators. Second, since this study did not entail micro level field work in one or two camps, it does not contain the high degree of detail and subtlety associated with such research. However, by relying on secondary comparative statistics, it has a global perspective that enables large-scale assessments and comparisons. It reflects an underlying interest in exploring comparative complexities of encampment economies rather than seeking the laws that govern a single case.

This study adopts a broad definition of encampments. It lumps together all permanent housing of peoples forcibly removed from their homes, such as refugee camps, internally displaced resettlement communities, reservations, etc. Attributing such an umbrella property to the term encampment enables the comparative study of a large number of solutions to involuntary displacement.

The book is arranged as follows: the introductory chapter defines some basic concepts and develops the framework with which to study encampments. In addition, selected encampments are described with respect to selected characteristics. The world in which encampments exist is described in chapter 2. It is there that the two tiers (and two subtiers) are presented, along with propositions to be explored in subsequent chapters. Microeconomic aspects of encampments are presented in chapter 3, while the macro angle is explored in chapter 4 and international issues in chapter 5. This organization allows telescoping on encampments (chapter 3) to be followed with a gradually expanding view of their place in the domestic economy (chapter 4) and, finally, in the international economy (chapter 5). Given the crucial role of ethnicity in forced population movements and ensuing encampment, an assessment of the link between economics and nationalism is imperative (chapter 6). Finally, the concluding chapter synthesizes the findings and explores the ramifications and implications of encampment differences by tier.

DEFINITIONS AND CONCEPTS

In 1969, R. Chambers described the study of population settlements as "an academic no-man's land."[4] Since that time, there has been an explosion of interest in settlements, resettlements, reserves, reservations, and camps. Encampments have been studied by economists, especially with respect to their contribution to the host labor force, the loss of human capital in the home state, and the fiscal burden imposed on host states.[5] Geographers have focused on the spatial dimension of both population movements and encampments.[6] Legal studies have addressed camps from the perspective of what is acceptable within the international and domestic context.[7] Demographers have pondered the ramifications of population loss and gain on home and host states. Migration and subsequent encampment have been studied from the perspective of political science and international relations.[8] Philosophers, anthropologists, sociologists, psychologists, and students of human rights have all approached encampments from their discipline's viewpoints.[9] There have even been efforts to observe population movements simultaneously from a variety of academic perspectives, representing a positive step toward cross-fertilization of fields and views.[10] Outside the academic literature, the United Nations High Commissioner for Refugees (UNHCR) and the U.S. Committee for Refugees (USCR) have contributed invaluable reports and assessments.

Irrespective of the discipline, an understanding of each other's basic definitions is a prerequisite for dialogue. With that goal in mind, a short review of definitions, as well as concepts used throughout the text, follows.

INVOLUNTARY POPULATION MOVEMENTS

A study of encampments must begin with an assessment of how people found themselves encamped. While populations by definition had to relocate in order to be housed in encampments, the nature of that relocation process is crucial. The key variable in the relocation process is the freedom to choose whether to migrate. Failure to recognize the importance of choice in migration decisions has retarded much research and postponed our understanding of the nature of encampments. Hugo pointed out this deficiency, stating that initial research on population movements in the Third World was based "either explicitly or implicitly on the premise that population movement is a fundamentally voluntary process. This is due to an inappropriate transfer of concepts and models developed in contemporary Euro-American society."[11] Indeed, while most current migrations in the western world are based on free choice, this is not true across the globe.

The fundamental difference among migrants is the extent of choice that they have in their migratory decisions. Choice distinguishes the 2-3 million people who cross borders every year.[12] Choice distinguishes the 130 million people who lived outside their home country at the end of the twentieth century. Choice also distinguishes the millions of people who move within their own countries (a phenomenon most clearly evident in China, where some 200 million people have moved more than 1000 miles, amounting to more than the worldwide total number of people living outside their countries).[13]

There are two types of population movements, voluntary and involuntary. Voluntary population migration results from a personal cost/benefit analysis that indicates relocation will maximize utility. The choice to migrate is assumed to be rational; the process of assessing costs and benefits is assumed to be an informed one. Most voluntary migration is motivated by expected economic benefits, namely, a better job (including higher wages, improved working conditions, greater status, more possibility for advancement, increased job satisfaction, and so forth). Sometimes the voluntary migrant bases his/her decision on nonpecuniary considerations such as family bonds, political inclinations, and so forth. Whatever the motivation, the migrant exercises free choice in the migration decision and bears the responsibility for that decision.

During forced (or involuntary) migration, the decision to migrate is imposed on the individual or group. Involuntary migration includes both the forcible physical removal of individuals from their homes as well as the exertion of pressures that make survival in the present location untenable. Either way, people are evicted or transferred. They have no choice in the migration decision.

There are numerous reasons why involuntary migration occurs. These can be classified into two broad categories: nonman-made and man-made disasters (roughly coinciding with Rogge's distinction between politically induced refugees and ecological refugees).[14] The former includes natural disasters while the latter includes displacement for economic purposes and political reasons. When disasters such as floods, droughts, landslides, and earthquakes occur, people are involuntarily moved from their homes. While such calamities obliterate homes and destroy livelihoods, and thus create displacement as certainly as armed troops, the ensuing encampment of people is rarely long term. Once the affected area is reconstructed, migrants return home. It is the economic and political reasons for involuntary migration that are more likely to produce permanent dislocation.

Among the economic reasons, the most important is dislocation for the purposes of labor exploitation. When whites moved to the New World, they needed cheap workers to exploit the land and they turned to the blacks of Africa for their manpower needs. From the mid-fifteenth to the late nineteenth century, some 12 million Africans made the voyage to the Western Hemisphere.[15] Before and after, millions more had trekked by foot to the Middle East where Arab traders sold them on the market. Everywhere they went, slaves dug in mines, cleared land, planted, and harvested. Inside homes, they cooked, cleaned, washed, and tended to children. The transportation of chained Africans to the New World has modern parallels. Indeed, the movement of Jewish and Slavic laborers during Nazi rule in Germany and the forcible treks of Karen men in Myanmar for jungle clearance projects are all examples of the involuntary labor migration. They show that such forcible movements have occurred throughout history and across continents (indeed, involuntary migration continued to be a significant form of migration until quite recently. According to D. Eltis, it was not until the 1840s that annual voluntary European migration to the Americas exceeded the involuntary African migration.[16] In fact, fewer than 10 percent of the estimated 9 to 15 million transatlantic migrants before 1800 were free).[17]

Political reasons for involuntary migration include international and domestic circumstances. Among the former are wars involving armed intervention and/or political warfare (such as propaganda or a victorious new political system). War situations provoked Chinese population movements in Indo-China following the victory of North Vietnam; Jewish emigration from Germany, Poland, and Croatia during World War II; and residence exchanges among Greeks and Turks following the Greco-Turkish war of 1922. New political systems were responsible for the pressure on Germans to leave the Soviet Union and Eastern Europe following World War II and Asians to leave Uganda in the 1970s. Wars of liberation or decolonization provoked a mass exodus of Portuguese from Mozambique and whites from Malawi and Rhodesia. Another component of the international circumstances of population displacement is the redrawing of borders in peace when it puts national, religious, or racial groups on the

wrong side of a border. Indeed, mass population movements occurred on the territories of both the Soviet Union and Yugoslavia after their respective breakups.

With respect to domestic pressures on populations to involuntarily relocate, the most important is turbulence of various forms: i.e.,
a violent government change, such as one associated with a revolution or a coup d'etat that carries with it either policies adverse to a
given people or simply violence. In this environment, persecution
on the basis of religion, race, or ethnicity, whether by sporadic harassment or planned genocide, is apt to arise and result in displacement (for example, the Armenian exodus from Turkey, the Indian
flood from Guatemala, and the Muslim exodus from Myanmar).
When ethnicity is at the root of involuntary displacement of populations, then ethnic cleansing is the term of choice.[18] However, it is
noted that minorities are not the only ones suffering from what
might be a brutal, dictatorial government that harasses members of
society: the political opposition may also be a target, resulting in political migration (for example, the exodus of political opponents of
Pinochet from Chile or of Ayatollah Khomeini from Iran).[19] Alternatively, people may be the victims of a political experiment (such as
when some 90 percent of Tanzania's peasants were herded into *uja-
maa* villages and their homes burnt to prevent their return).[20]

In the twentieth century, there were numerous politically induced
population movements, many of which entailed forced evictions.
The communist revolution in Russia produced some 1.5 million displaced persons, while Turkish policies induced the movement of
some 250,000 Armenians and, later, over one million Greeks. During and after World War II, Hitler's government induced migrations
of 10 million people in Eastern Europe, while the partition of India
caused a displacement of over 10 million Muslims and Hindus.
More recently, the creation of Bangladesh uprooted over 10 million
people; Sudan accepted approximately 350,000 Eritreans; Somalia
took in 800,000 people fleeing the Ogaden Province; the Soviet invasion of Afghanistan sent two million people into Pakistan; Iraq's
invasion of Kuwait sent 380,000 Palestinians out of the Persian Gulf;
80,000 Cubans fled Cuba over the course of a few weeks; 100,000

Jews fled the Soviet Union in a few years during the 1970s; and some 60,000 Ingushis refugees live in squalor in Ingushetia after being cleansed from Northern Ossetia. The 1990s war in Chechnya displaced some 800,000 Chechens.[21] During the waning years of the cold war, namely 1979-89, some eight million people were driven from their homes by "superpower proxy wars," in places such as Afghanistan, Cambodia, and El Salvador.[22]

Such evidence of voluntary and involuntary population movements does not imply that there is consensus among governments or scholars as to what constitutes one or the other. Guilty governments all too often attempt to blur the difference (for example, after some 1-3 million Kurds were displaced from their homes in Turkey, their villages burnt, and their livestock dispersed, a Turkish official described the population movement as positive since "migration is an expression of freedom").[23]

Categories of Displaced Peoples

In his study of refugees, Aristide Zolberg emphasized the importance of clarity in definitions pertaining to displacement.[24] Even minor nuances in the way displaced peoples are defined and classified are important, not only because they provide a common denominator for academic discourse but also because they have practical implications. Indeed, definition and classifications are the basis for policy. In the recent past, the importance of definitions in setting policies was clear in Rwanda (where the international community was not compelled by law to intervene because the massacres were not defined as genocide), in Bosnia (where the international community was justified in intervening because it defined an administrative territory as a separate state), and across Asian states (where defining Vietnamese refugees as economic migrants rather than refugees justified their expulsion). Moreover, international agreement over definitions is also important because there is variation in interpretation from country to country. Indeed, the question of who is a refugee gets answered by the host country and, therefore, is subject to the whims of the country's domestic policy and the goals of its international relations. Jeff

Crisp, in his study of the politics of refugee numbers, points out that this results in the lack of useful information about the size of the refugee population.[25] That does not provide a good basis for compatible policies by home and host states.

In contemporary international jargon, several terms pertaining to displaced peoples convey information about their host destination, their international status, and the proximate push that induced them to move.

Refugees have been defined as those individuals that flee from man-made disasters. The most commonly used definition is that of the 1951 UN Convention on Refugees, according to which refugees are "People who are outside of their own country, owning to a well founded fear of persecution, for reasons of race, religion, nationality, membership of a particular social group, or political opinion."[26] Gordenker amplified this by defining refugees as "persons who have left their customary homes under the pressure of fear for their present or future lives, because of immediate, overt threats or—more comprehensively—clear denials of basic human rights whose enjoyment is required for continued life over a short or longer period."[27]

Irrespective of the precise reason for their displacement, refugees cross international borders. They then may also become broadly classified as immigrants, and, more specifically, asylum seekers and/or undocumented persons. Asylum seekers tend to be from countries where political repression or chaos force some people, with particular circumstances, to find life unbearable. While in the past, asylum seekers were mostly defectors from communist countries, now the countries of origin include Sri Lanka, Somalia, Libya, and the former Yugoslavia. This is the most nebulous, unclearly defined category of immigrants and, as a result, is the most controversial. Yet, Western countries are reluctant to repatriate asylum seekers for humanitarian reasons. By contrast, undocumented persons are those who have crossed a border but do not have the appropriate permission to establish residence.

Refugees, immigrants, asylum seekers, and undocumented persons are all terms used to indicate that an international border has been crossed. If displacement occurs within state boundaries, then it is called internal displacement. A large-scale study undertaken by Roberta Cohen and Francis M. Deng highlighted the magnitude of such migration.[28] Internally displaced peoples, they say, are forced to migrate but remain within the state and therefore within government jurisdiction.[29] The number of internally displaced peoples across the globe is significantly higher than that of refugees: there are some 30 million people across the globe, compared to some 23 million refugees. While China has the largest number of internal migrants, the Sudan has the largest internally displaced population. By some accounts, Turkey ranks second in the world, with 3 million displaced at the end of 1997.[30]

Despite their greater size, internally displaced persons fail to receive the world attention given to refugees. Indeed, international organizations, media, and governments focus their efforts on the plight of refugees more than internally displaced persons. This happens for two principal reasons. First, there is less information about internally displaced persons because they are monitored by the home state. Therefore, it is the home government that controls the information and its uses. Second, international law covers refugees but does not cover internally displaced persons. This second point is important and warrants further elaboration.

The comparison of refugees and internally displaced peoples pivots on one aspect of their definitions, namely, the existence or lack of a border crossing.[31] The reason why this detail is of paramount importance is because it determines the international protection and aid that people are eligible for.[32] According to UN covenants, refugees are entitled to specific protection and aid.[33] Thus, while international organizations can operate within a receiving host country to ensure that refugees get what they are entitled to, they have no comparable rights within the home state. This distinction is most evident when it comes to human rights. According to Luke Lee, "Although refugees and internally displaced persons are entitled to the same basic human rights, international protection of the latter poses the question of its compatibility with the traditional concepts of national sovereignty and non-interference in the internal affairs of a state."[34] In other words, organizations have

no legal basis for operation within borders of sovereign states, especially when uninvited by host governments (sometimes host
states allow operations but impose such restrictions as a tax on the
wages of aid workers or some proportion of aid supplies). This ruling applies to the UNHCR, the biggest, most experienced, and
most efficient organization that deals with displaced peoples.[35]

One subset of internally displaced peoples consists of so-called native or indigenous peoples.[36] These are long time residents of territory that has been claimed and settled by colonial newcomers. While
such occupation took place in several ways, the result was the dislocation of the native population (Malcolm Shaw described several of
these ways: effective occupation of *terra nullius* [when it is argued
that non-Europeans inhabiting territories had no sovereign rights
over those territories], cession [according to which European powers entered into bilateral treaties to acquire territory from local sov-
ereigns], and conquest [taking possession of territory through
war]).[37] As a result, there are currently several western democracies
that house native peoples whose descendents occupied the land before Europeans arrived. These are Canada and the United States
(home to the Inuit and other native peoples), New Zealand (the
Maoris), Australia (the Aborigines and the Torres Strait islanders),
Japan (Ainu), and Greenland (Inuit).[38] However, it is erroneous to
think native populations are limited to the New World. As evident
from table 1.1, indigenous populations exist in South and Central
America, South Africa, and Asia. It is also erroneous to think that
only whites displaced indigenous populations: for example, in
Rwanda, it is the Twa (Pygmies) who inhabited the land before the
Tutsis and the Hutus arrived.

To sum up, different terms for displaced peoples have different
connotations: "refugees" implies that a border has been crossed, "internally displaced persons" refers to a domestic situation in which
migrants lack international protection, and "native peoples" indicates
a population overcome by newcomers. Hence, when it comes to involuntary migration in the modern world, the answer to the question
"What's in a name?" is "a lot": a future, hope, opportunities, and,
most importantly, international support.

Table 1.1. Top Twenty Home Countries of Refugees, Internally Displaced Peoples, and Native (or Indigenous) Peoples, 1999.

Refugees		Internally Displaced Peoples		Native Peoples	
Palestine	3.931m	Sudan	4,000m	India	63.0m
Afghanistan	2.560m	Angola	1.500-2.000m	Myanmar	14.0m
Iraq	568,000	Colombia	1.800m	Mexico	10.9m
Sierra Leone	460,000	Burma	500-1.000m	Peru	9.0m
Somalia	425,000	Turkey	500-1.000m	Philippines	6.0m
Sudan	420,000	Iraq	900,000	Bolivia	5.6m
Yugoslavia	390,000	Bosnia & Herzegovinia	830,000	Guatemala	4.6m
Angola	340,000	Brundi	800,000	Ecuador	3.8m
Croatia	340,000	Congo-Kins.	800,000	Pap. New Guinea	3.0m
Eritrea	320,000	Russian Fed.	800,000	United States	2.0m
Burundi	310,000	Afghanistan	500-750,000	Brazil	1.5m
Bosnia & Herzegovinia	300,000	Rwanda	600,000	Russian Fed.	1.4m
Vietnam	292,000	Yugoslavia	600,000	Laos	1.3m
El Salvador	253,000	Azerbaijan	568,000	Bangladesh	1.2m
Liberia	250,000	Sri Lanka	560,000	Canada	0.9m
Burma	240,000	India	507,000	Malaysia	0.8m
Congo-Kins.	240,000	Congo-Braz.	500,000	Thailand	0.5m
Azerbaijan	230,000	Sierra Leone	500,000	Australia	0.4m
Armenia	188,000	Syria	450,000	New Zealand	0.4m
Guatemala	146,000	Uganda	450,000	Chile	0.2m

Source: U.S. Committee for Refugees, *World Refugee Survey* 2000, 4-5; A. T. During, "Supporting Indigenous Peoples" in *State of the World*, 1993, A Worldwatch Institute Report on Progress Toward a Sustainable Society, New York: W. W. Norton, 83 http://www.hsph.harvard.edu/grhf/SAsia/forums/Tribals/Tribals/M006T1.htm

To bridge the difference between refugees and internally displaced persons, scholars, such as Joke Schrijvers, simply called the latter internal refugees to stress their *de facto* fate as refugees.[39] The gap is also being bridged at the level of governments: U.S. Ambassador to the United Nations, Richard Holbrooke, claimed that, for him, there was no difference between a refugee and an internally displaced person.[40] They are equally victims. The distinction, he believes, is outdated, and borders should no longer be considered limits to international responsibility.

Categories of encampments. A plethora of names have surfaced in the post-World War II period to denote different kinds of encampments. These names are meant to convey information about their residents, their economies, and their political status. The simple ones are refugee camps, displaced persons camps, reserves, native lands, and homelands. There is less consensus on the meaning of settlements and *de facto* encampments and even less on state-specific terms such as welfare centers (the term Sri Lanka gives to its encampments), regroupment camps (as Burundi calls the encampments for displaced Hutus), informal camps (found in Papua New Guinea along the areas bordering Indonesia where Irian Jayans are housed), special settlement camps (for Chechens deported in 1944), and forced migrant camps (the term given by Russians for encampments with displaced Chechens who agree not to return to Chechnya).[41]

Refugee and displaced persons encampments are created for the purpose of providing involuntary migrants with food and medical relief and for preventing their dispersal. Those that survive beyond the short term acquire a long term emphasis, and they, like settlements, become focused on development goals and self-sufficiency. Reserves, reservations, and native lands are territories created by governments in the New World for the autonomous enjoyment of the indigenous populations. In some cases, the motivation for creating reserves had nothing to do with autonomy (for example, beginning in 1856, Aboriginees were put on reserves and given food and clothing. This was motivated by a view that they were dying out and pressure for humanitarian concerns led to the creation of reserves to "smoothe the dying pillow"). A homeland is the preferred term in South Africa to denote areas where the displaced black population was housed during the apartheid era.

De facto encampments are compounds in which populations experience conditions analogous to those in refugee encampments. Their residents are included in the USCR category of people who live in "refugee–like conditions." What are these conditions? They include such severe discrimination that their residents *de facto* lack choice in their housing, employment, consumption, and other economic and social activities. They might strive for greater integration into their domestic societies and economies but are shunned and find doors closed to them. As a result, they are poor and uneducated; they are marginalized and have few rights; they have few opportunities and little hope to reverse their conditions. Those that have no other choices are *de facto* involuntarily held even if *de jure* they are free to leave. Examples of Roma communities in Eastern Europe come to mind, especially in the Czech Republic where non-Roma residents in one town built a wall in the 1990s to isolate them from their Roma neighbors and in another, fenced in Romas in a settlement outside of town.[42] This is similar to neighboring Hungary, where some 40 percent of the Roma population live in "segregated rural ghettos" in small towns and villages.[43] Since there is much popular resistance among Hungarians about integrating the Romas, urban housing is rarely available to them. Also, black homelands in South Africa may be considered *de facto* encampments in the postapartheid era. While they were classical examples of encampments during the sixties and seventies, change in government broke down walls of discrimination and opened up possibilities for residents of black townships. However, it failed to increase opportunities sufficiently to significantly expand the choices open to residents. Similarly, the refugee housing estates established by the Cypriot government to house Greeks displaced during the Turkish invasion are *de facto* encampments.[44] Their residents, almost thirty years after displacement, have no other choices and are awaiting a resolution to their status.

Thus, *de facto* encampments are included in this study because they share numerous characteristics with traditional long-term encampments.

The involuntary nature of encampments.   Where do involuntary migrants go when they become displaced? While the lucky ones have family or friends whose hospitality they can enjoy, and the wealthy ones make their own housing arrangements, the majority are housed in encampments. While these encampments carry different names, they share a common denominator: they are not the residence of choice for their residents.

Indeed, most inhabitants of encampments would rather be elsewhere (even if conditions in encampments are sometimes better than those in their home regions). There are two ways in which encampment residence is involuntary. First, residents join encampments as a result of involuntary displacement. Whether they were internally displaced due to a change in government or they became refugees as a result of a war, residents did not choose to leave their

homes and embark upon encampment life. Second, residents of encampments also stay involuntarily. This does not mean that they are
enslaved in their encampments (with the exception of camps in Sudan and Burundi where some residents are held as captives and are
virtually enslaved). Rather, there are degrees of involuntary residence. Some camp residents have no alternative choices since the
host country refuses to integrate them; other countries refuse to ad-
mit them, and their home country refuses to repatriate them (such
as the Saharawis in Algeria and the Palestinians in Lebanon). Others are displaced within their own countries, and discriminatory
laws or practices prevent their integration into mainstream society
(such as the Romas in the Czech Republic). Others yet have freedom to move, but little realistic opportunity to improve their conditions elsewhere (such as Native Americans living on reservations).
Host governments, albeit rarely, attempt to create opportunities for
their encampment residents: they grant citizenship rights to encampment residents to pave the way for their integration into their
society (as Jordan did for the Palestinians) and even encourage their
resettlement (as India did for the Tibetans).

The temporal dimension.   The hope expressed by the UNHCR,
namely that the 1990s would be the "decade of repatriation," failed
to affect most residents of permanent encampments. While 40,000
refugees returned to Namibia at the beginning of the decade, and
the conclusion of the war between Ethiopia and Eritrea drew many
Eritreans out of their decades-old encampments in Sudan, other permanent camps were inundated with new migrants. Indeed, all too often an old caseload was mixed with a new caseload, changing only the
composition of the population while leaving the net size constant. W.
R. Smyser wrote in 1985 that the long lasting refugee presence in
many countries of asylum had "fundamentally altered the nature of
the global refugee problem."[45] A quarter of a century later, that statement rings even truer as the number of long term refugees increases.
Dona and Berry claim that before the 1980s, refugees spent short
periods of time in camps, but since then, increasing numbers of
refugees have not been able to repatriate or integrate in host countries.[46] The international community has called these people "long
stayers," their encampments "the neverending camps," and the solu-

tions to their plight "non-durable, non-solutions."[47] According to Rogge, "The least desirable option open to asylum states—to keep refugees in holding camps—is unfortunately being increasingly adopted."[48] Indeed, for lack of better solutions, encampments continue to survive over the long run.

Yet, their longevity ceases to be interesting to those who are most equipped to come to their aid. "Long stayers" are in contrast to the involuntary migrants that most often get on the western radar. Graphic images of hunger and despair are broadcast across western living rooms. The visual impact of ragtag shelters motivates individuals, donor agencies, and responsive governments to rapidly improve those conditions (or to remove the images from the screen). This "CNN effect" extends to temporary encampments. Permanent camps rarely make it to the evening news because, due to their permanence, there is rarely anything new to report.

Encampments become permanent either by transformation or by creation. In other words, camps may be intended as short term, but over time, they acquire properties of permanence and undergo a transformation. Alternatively, they are conceived as permanent and created with the long term in mind. These two types of permanent encampments, differing by their original intent, are described below.

Temporary encampments become permanent for lack of better solutions to the population displacement. At their inception, they are envisioned as holding camps and are equipped to address the most basic needs, i.e., provide shelter, safety from crime, food, elementary clothing, etc. When other solutions, such as repatriation, settlement, and integration into host society or third country resettlement are not feasible or have failed, then the short term becomes the long term. This process of camp transformation is due to the following factors: first, home countries often refuse to take back their refugees (for example, Morocco is content with the Saharawi population living out in encampments in Algeria and is postponing all efforts of the international community to repatriate them); second, host countries often refuse to allow resettlement and integration, preferring to serve merely as transit locations (as, for example, Hong Kong); third, third-destination countries often refuse to grant asylum (as West European states are increasingly doing); fourth, the international community often sends mixed messages because it supercedes domestic governments in resolving a refugee situation in some cases but not in others (such as the plight of the Kovoso Albanians but not that of the Kurds or the Palestinians); and finally, the goals and expectations of encampment residents are also relevant, especially when their negotiating positions are hardened and they demand repatriation and reject alternative solutions (such as the Palestinians who demand to exercise their right of return). Thus, permanent encampments are products of political inertia, indecision, and haggling over issues that result in the postponement of decisive action. As a result, the temporary solution gradually becomes the permanent solution, and encampments gradually transform to adapt to this reality. Joffee describes the process of transformation as consisting of the movement between three states: primary, transition, and maturity.[49]

How long must a camp be in existence before it is classified as permanent? In other words, at what point does a temporary camp become permanent? There is no clear demarcation point. Permanence cannot be measured scientifically. Its existence is identified qualitatively rather than in empirically quantifiable ways. Nevertheless, it can be said that an encampment is permanent when the basic needs of its population are met and when employment is sought and employment solutions are found. It is also permanent when children born in camps reach adulthood without ever having lived elsewhere. Finally, it is permanent when funding for the camp changes sources (Weiss and Collins have noted that short-term relief comes out of different funds from long-term development, so the source indicates the degree of permanence donor agencies perceive).[50]

By contrast, some encampments are designated as permanent at the time of inception. Often called settlements, such camps have been very popular in asylum countries in Africa, especially during the 1970s and 1980s. A camp that is *a priori* permanent, rather than becoming so *a posteriori* and by default, is one whose goals and economic activities are fundamentally different. In permanent camps, basic needs are met and residents have graduated to concerns about income–generating activities, education, working papers, and marriage. They have integrated into the neighboring community at least with respect to economic interaction.

However, irrespective of the original intent of permanent encampments, their populations continue to experience two sentiments. First, they continue to harbor the hope that their encampment will end one day. Even if they invest in learning the host country's language and laws, even if their children go to host schools, even if they earn incomes, they retain a hope of returning to their homes. This hope is found among the Palestininas, who dream that they will liberate the Israeli occupied territories; among the Tibetans, who wish to return to Lhasa; and among the Native Americans, who hope to roam their ancestral lands unfettered. The second sentiment follows the first: encampment residents have a sense of living in limbo. Despite decades spent in encampments, they are cognizant of their permanent impermanence. As a result, camp impermanence has become institutionalized as residents have learned to live with it and accept it. This combination of hope for return with a permanent sense of impermanence leads to ambivalence. Even those residents who have been born and lived all their lives in camps are ambivalent about investing too much time and energy in making the encampment successful and then having to move as their situation changes. As Allen Buchanan noted in his study of secession, when newcomers make improvements on land that they are subsequently expelled from, they are not owed any compensation.[51] In order to prevent such possible future loss, and also to prevent settlement that will obliterate the memory of displacement, some camp residents refuse to invest in camp future. Azrt describes this phenomenon with reference to Palestinian refugees: "Camp inhabitants in Lebanon would uproot saplings that had been planted, in opposition to even the most meager symbols of permanence."[52] In refugee camps along the Burma/Thailand border, the Thai government imposed regulations preventing the building of permanent buildings that might convey permanence.[53] In Turkey, the Kurdish internally displaced population lives in *gecekondular*, translated as "huts built in one night" and intended as no more than temporary shelter.[54]

Both the institutionalization of impermanence and the reality of permanence have important economic implications. They dampen dynamism; they dullen creativity. They provoke feelings of resignation, which in turn breed apathy (adding to the apathy associated with the experience of fleeing war or the stress of dislocation).[55] Under those circumstances, it is hard to maintain economic incentives and momentum.

The role of ethnicity. The African slaves, Jewish forced laborers, and Karen jungle workers mentioned in the earlier discussion on involuntary labor movements share a characteristic crucial to this research. Those who involuntarily migrate are of a different ethnic group (or race, religion, and language) from those who enforce the displacement. This reality underscores the important role of ethnicity in involuntary migration, and, by extension, to issues pertaining to encampments. Indeed, ethnicity underlies ethnic cleansing, as examples from Rwanda, Bosnia, and Turkey clearly indicate. Moreover, ethnicity underlies government policy towards refugees (for example, India welcomes refugees from Tibet but not from Bangladesh).[56]

Since ethnicity is relevant in the study of encampments, clarification of its definition is necessary. Ever since Vilfredo Pareto said that the term "ethnic" is one of the vaguest known to sociology,[57] research has attempted to clarify it. According to Anthony Smith, an ethnic group is composed of a people that share a cultural bond and that perceive themselves to share a common origin.[58] Ethnic affiliation is viewed as flexible and, in some instances, transitory, underscoring that ethnicity is neither primordial nor immutable. This dynamic view is based on evidence from across the globe of changing ethnic affiliations.[59]

The question of how to classify and define peoples remains unresolved and continues to dominate debates on ethnicity and nationalism. Possible categories abound, such as ethnicity, race, language, and so forth, and, despite their overlap and imprecision, they serve to group populations across the globe. For the sake of simplicity and convenience, in this study of encampments, ethnicity is referred to as the distinguishing characteristic even though it is not universally applicable. Indeed, sometimes race is the crucial distinguishing characteristic (as in South Africa) or it is language (as in Canada) or religion (as in Bosnia). Ethnicity is, therefore, used in the text as an umbrella term that includes race, religion, language, and nation, as the case may be. In that sense, this study heeds the 1997 proposal of the American Association of Anthropologists, suggesting the U.S. government use ethnic categories in federal data to reflect the diversity of the population and to phase out the use of race which is a concept that has no scientific justification in human biology.[60] Susan Olzak says that "since ethnicity is an outcome of boundary creation and maintenance, there is no obstacle to treating race as a special case of an ethnic boundary, one that is believed to be correlated with inherited biotic characteristics. Hereafter the term ethnicity refers to both racial and ethnic boundaries, unless otherwise qualified."[61] Finally, Van den Berghe also made a convincing argument for using ethnicity as an umbrella term: "While I still think that the greater rigidity and invidiousness of racial, as distinct from cultural distinctions makes for qualitatively different situation, both race and ethnicity share the basic common element of being defined by descent, real or putative. Therefore, I now tend to see race as a special case of ethnicity."[62]

Economic issues. The concept of scarcity is fundamental to economics. Indeed, economics is defined as the study of how scarce resources are allocated among competing ends. Encampments, by their very essence, are the epitome of scarcity. Given involuntary displacement, loss of property and income, economic and social marginalization, as well as the resultant poverty associated with encampment existence, scarcity permeates all aspects of life. There is a scarcity of employment, housing, food, education, land, and documentation. Moreover, there is also a scarcity of opportunities, hope, personal identity, and the like.

Given the pervasiveness of scarcity in encampment reality, the study of economics is at the core of a study of encampments. The question of who gets what, when, and how within the camp is crucial because it answers questions pertaining to consumption and production, the creation of markets for inputs and outputs, the role of barter in exchange, as well as the role of government in production and distribution. The question of who gets what, when, and how is also important at the level of the host macroeconomy insofar as it describes local employment and investment links to the encampment, as well as the nature of encampment participation in the host state's growth and development. Finally, the question of who gets what, when, and how in the context of the global economy is also relevant to this study because it shows the extent to which international trade and international financial flows (such as investment and aid) affect encampments.

Selected Permanent Encampments

This study is based on some thirty permanent encampments across the globe (see table 1.2). These encampments were not picked by physical size, nor were host countries picked by the size of their displaced populations. Had those been the criteria for selection, then all encampments under study would be in Africa and the Middle East. In an effort to have a broader representation of countries, smaller encampments were included. Whatever their differences in size, condition of encampment, official designation, all thirty encampments are contemporary. In other words, all are in existence at the time of writing, even if they underwent significant alterations since their inception.

While there is variety among the camps, there are also several common denominators that justify inclusion in this study. These common denominators emerge from the descriptions that follow which focus on similarities and contrasts between camps and their host and home states. None of the selected encampments are *sui generis*; in other words, they are not anomalies that teach us nothing, but rather they lay the groundwork for the identification of patterns and construction of frameworks for study.

A word of caution about names of countries and ethnic groups is in order. Some countries under study have more than one name, each of which has symbolic meaning. For example, Burma is currently referred to as Myanmar as well as Burma.[63] Since the government that introduced the name Myanmar no longer has legitimacy, some have preferred to use the old name, Burma. However, I have followed the example of the United Nations and use the term Myanmar, with no political preference indicated. Also, the Congo had been called Zaire under Mobutu's rule. When Kabila came to power in 1997, he reverted to the use of the old name. Today, it is called the Democratic Republic of Congo or Congo Kinshasa to distinguish it from the neighboring Congo Brazzaville. Similarly, some ethnic groups have multiple names. Israeli Arabs are sometimes referred to as Palestinian citizens of Israel or Israel's Arabs or Arabs in Israel.[64] Romas are sometimes referred to as Gypsies.

Host states. Countries that host encampments are spread across the globe and they are spread over several levels of development and

Table 1.2.   Basic Characteristics of Encampments

Host Country	Home Country	Ethnic Group	Type	Date of Encampment	Condition of Encampment
Algeria	Western Sahara (Morocco)	Saharawi	R	1975	EW (Spain) Morocco invasion
Australia	Australia	Aborigine	N	1920s/1930s	ED (colonizers/ natives)
Azerbaijan	Armenia	Azeri	R/IDP	1988	IW/EW (Armenia) ED
Burundi	Rwanda	Tutsi	R	1950s, 1960s	IW (Hutu/ Tutsi) ED
Canada	Canada	Native Americans	N	Early 1990s	ED (colonizers/ natives)
Congo (Zaire)	Sudan	Christian/ animist Black	R	1980s	IW (north/ south) ED drought & famine
Costa Rica	Nicaragua	Indian/ indigenous	R	1981	IW (insurg./ counter insurg.) ED
Cyprus	Cyprus	Greek	IDP	1974	Invasion (Turkey) IW ED
Czech Republic	Czech Republic	Roma	IDP	1945 1991	Change in govt.
Hong Kong	Vietnam	Vietnamese	R	1975	EW (US)
India	China (Tibet)	Tibetans	R	1959	Invasion (China) ED
Iran	Iraq	Kurds/ Iranian origin suspected	R	1980-88	EW (Iraq)
Iran	Afghanistan	Afghanis	R	1959	EW (USSR/ Afghan.)

Table 1.2. Basic Characteristics of Encampments (continued)

Host Country	Home Country	Ethnic Group	Type	Date of Encampment	Condition of Encampment
Israel (West bank; Gaza)	Israel (Palestine)	Palestinian Arabs	R	1948 1967	EW (Israel/ Arab neighbors)
Jordan	Israel (Palestine)	Palestinian Arabs	R	1948 1967	EW (Israel)
Lebanon	Israel (Palestine)	Palestinian Arabs	R	1948 1967	EW (Israel)
Mexico[65]	Guatemala	Mayan descendents	R	1960s, 1970s 1982	IW (insurg./ counter insurg.) ED[66]
New Zealand	New Zealand	Maori	N	1872	ED (colonizers/ natives)
Pakistan	Afghanistan	Afghanis	R	1978	EW (USSR/ Afghan.)
Papua New Guinea	Indonesia	Irian Jaya	R	1984	EW (Dutch) Indonesia invasion
Russian Federation	Russia	Chechens	IDP	1944 1990s	IW (Russia/ Chech.) ED
Somalia	Somalia	Various clans	IDP	1970s, 1980s	EW (Ethiop.) IW (inter-clan) famine, drought
South Africa	South Africa	Blacks (Zulu, Lhasa, etc.)	IDP N	1913, 1934	ED (colonizers/ natives)
Sri Lanka	Sri Lanka	Tamils	IDP	1983	IW (Tamils/ Sinhalese)
Sudan	Eritrea	Eritreans	R	1962, 1969	IW (Eritrea/ Ethiopia)
Sudan	Sudan	Christian & animist Blacks	IDP	1984, late 1980s	IW (north/ south) famine, drought
Tanzania	Burundi	Hutu	R	1972-1974	IW (Hutu/ Tutsi)
Thailand	Myanmar	Karen, Mon, Karenni	R	Since 1959	IW (insurg./ counter insurg.)
Turkey	Turkey	Kurds	IDP	1925-1965/ since 1975	ED (Turks/ Kurds)
Uganda	Sudan	Southern Christian Blacks	R	1955 1965	EW
United States	United States	Native Americans	N	1830	ED (coloniz./ natives)

Note: R=refugees; IDP=internally displaced persons; N=native peoples; date of initial encampment is followed by date of subsequent inflows into that encampment, if there was one; FW= war with foreign power; IW= war internal to state, including insurgencies; EW=external war, namely war with foreign state; ED= ethnic displacement, involuntary displacement, associated violence.

political systems. Three are in North America, two in Central America, two in Australia and Oceania, six in Africa, three in the Middle East, ten in Asia (including Turkey) and three in Europe. The absence of South America from the list is glaring, especially in light of significant population displacements in Peru and Colombia,[67] as well as some one million refugees from Cuba, post-1973 Chile, and, more recently, Haiti. These involuntary migrations are not included in this study because none of the displaced peoples live in encampments. They have dispersed or have become integrated into the receiving regions.[68]

The host states under study often contain various types of encampments. Some house both temporary and permanent camps (for example, the United States has temporary refugee camps, such as the Guantanamo military base,[69] as well as permanent native reserves; the Sudan hosts refugees as well as internally displaced populations; South Africa has native reserves, as well as Black homesteads).[70]

Sometimes, a single host state experiences several types of displacements (for example, Tibet had an exodus of Tibetan refugees and a forced inflow of Han). Some host countries are simultaneously refugee generating and refugee receiving (for example, Mexico houses Guatemalan refugees and loses migrants to the United States).

The experience of two host states is unique and warrants highlighting. Iran is host to the largest number of refugees in the world, yet only a small number of them live in camps. Similarly, a large number of Palestinians live in Jordan, but fewer of them are housed in encampments than anywhere else in the Middle East.[71]

Home States

Home states are countries where displaced populations originate. In the case of internally displaced peoples, home and host states are the same (for example, the Sudan, Australia, South Africa, etc.). Refugees by definition find themselves outside a home state. The countries that are home states to the encampments under study span the globe, as all continents have produced involuntary migrants.

Sometimes displacement within one country produces encampments in several countries. For example, Palestinians displaced from

Israel live in encampments in Lebanon, Jordan, Gaza, and the West Bank. Similarly, displaced Afghanis are encamped in Pakistan as well as Iran.

Two home states have undergone political transformations since the displacement of their peoples, thus complicating the choice of terminology for this study. For example, the territory from where the Saharawis were displaced was called Western Sahara, but today it is a part of Morocco. Similarly, displaced Palestinians left the territory of Palestine, which today is the sovereign state of Israel. In order to accommodate for these changes, Morocco and Israel will be designated as home states. That choice is due in part to the availability of data and in part to the crucial role those states play in determining repatriation and compensation policies.

Ethnicity.   As mentioned earlier, ethnicity is used in this study as an umbrella term that includes race, religion, and language. While most displaced persons in the encampments under study are in fact distinguished by ethnicity, in some cases (like South Africa), race predominates.

For the sake of simplicity, ethnic groups listed in table 1.2 are not disaggregated. In other words, South Africans in encampments are merely listed as black, without distinguishing between different groups or tribes within the general racial group.[72] Similarly, displaced peoples in the Sudan are listed as southern black Christians/animists rather than the Dinka, Beja, Fur, and Nuba groups. Also, native peoples in the United States are lumped together, as are those in Canada, New Zealand, and Australia. No distinction is made between clans, bands, or tribes (in the United States, there are over 300 tribes in the adjoining 48 states, and some 500 if we add the communities of Alaska, while in Canada there are some 542 Indian bands).[73] Such seeming disregard for the particularities of smaller groups may be viewed as unscientific. Indeed, Walter Williams has claimed that the term "blacks of South Africa" is as meaningless as "whites of Europe."[74] Nevertheless, such aggregation is justified in this study because encampment/host country relations rarely differ by tribe or by clan. If they do, then disaggregation is warranted and is included in the text.

The ethnicity of encampment residents always differs from that of the titular majorities in their home states, and usually also from that in their host states (Cyprus is an exception). Indeed, Iraq has displaced Kurds because they are Kurds, the Han Chinese displaced the Tibetans because they were Tibetans, Jews displaced Palestinians because they were not Jews, northern Arab Sudanese displaced the darker, southern Christian and animist populations because they were non-Arabs, and so on.

Type of involuntary migrants. All the categories of displaced peoples discussed above are included in table 1.2. The majority consists of refugees or internally displaced persons. Indigenous peoples are selected in only four states, despite the fact that they constitute a larger group in other countries such as India (see table 1.1). In those states, they were not displaced and are not encamped, therefore there is no basis for including them in this study.

The selected indigenous peoples have different official designations in different states. In the United States and Canada, they are called both Native Americans and American Indians (in the latter, they are sometimes designated as Status Indians [people legally defined as Indians are known as Status Indians while those that gave up their status or intermarried are Non-Status Indians]). In Australia, native peoples are called Aborigines, and in New Zealand, Maoris (incidentally, the literal translation of the word Aborigine is: the people who were here from the beginning, while the name Maori, chosen by themselves under pressure from white settlers, means normal).

Some countries have no designation or term for their displaced populations since they deny their existence. In Turkey, displaced Kurds are not recognized by their governments as displaced peoples. Despite the fact that by some estimates Turkey contains the second largest number of internally displaced peoples, the authorities do not acknowledge them as a distinct, and, therefore, do not have an official designation for them.[75]

De facto encampments are usually not recognized as such by their home governments. Instead, the blame for *de facto* encampment is placed on the residents who are viewed, at best, as poor and uncooperative and, at worse, as lazy and criminal. This has been the case for the

Romas in the Czech Republic. The Cypriot government is more generous and sympathetic in its description of the displaced population living in the *de facto* encampment created in government housing estates.

Date of initial encampment. The date of initial displacement of some encampment residents under study ranges from the mid-1800s to the 1980s. The oldest displacements and encampments took place in the New World. The remaining encampments were formed at random times, corresponding to local events and with no discernable geographical pattern (see table 1.2).

Among the displaced populations under study, the Tutsis from Burundi are the longest exiles in modern African history,[76] while the Greeks in Cyprus are Europe's longest internally displaced population.[77]

An explanation of displacement in the former Soviet regions is in order. Since the break up of the Soviet Union, Azeris have been displaced from Armenia and Chechens have been displaced from Chechnya. However, those are recent refugees. Azeris and Chechens are included in this study of long-term encampments on the basis of their post-World War II dislocation rather than the more visible and publicized displacement associated with the war of independence fought in the 1990s: in 1944, there was an *en masse* deportation of Chechens, as they were accused of collaborating with the Nazis. In late 1948, they were sentenced to remain in areas of "special settlement," which they were forbidden to leave for life.[78] While all nationalities were officially rehabilitated in 1957 and allowed to return to their homeland, many did not, and the current displaced Chechen population represents a new caseload added to the old.

Condition of initial encampment. In all the cases under study, man-made disasters caused population displacement and subsequent encampment. These include wars (both internal and with a foreign state), colonization, uprisings and insurrections following colonial withdrawal, foreign invasions, etc. While natural disasters, such as droughts, floods, and earthquakes, may compound the necessity to relocate, they are never the primary reason.

Some camps were set up as a consequence of penetration by newcomers (such as in the United States, Canada, New Zealand, Australia, and South Africa).[79] Others were set up to house populations displaced in the aftermath of colonial withdrawals. These tend to be in Africa and Asia and include Western Sahara (that produced refugees currently in Algeria), Irian Jaya (that produced refugees currently in Papua New Guinea),[80] and Vietnam (that, upon the exit of the United States, produced refugees currently in Hong Kong). In other cases, peoples were displaced as a result of invasion by foreign powers. This includes Palestinian displacement following the arrival of Jews and the establishment of Israel,[81] Tibetan displacement following the mass arrival of the Han Chinese,[82] Afghani displacement following invasion by the Soviets, and Greek displacement in Cyprus following the Turkish invasion.

The most common proximate reason for displacement and subsequent encampment is interethnic conflict in which one ethnic group stands to benefit from the decreased presence of the other. Eviction of a targeted ethnic group is then a way to consolidate power through what has been called the demographic struggle for power.[83] Examples include Armenia, Rwanda, Eritrea, Burundi, Sri Lanka, etc.

All too often, a combination of reasons for displacement and encampment coincide. In the Sudan, for example, some 5 million people have been uprooted due to a drought in the early 1980s, followed by a famine, and, finally, a civil war.[84]

Table 1.3. Demographic, Social, and Economic Characteristics of Encampments

Host country	Encampment Pop. (E) Displaced Pop. (D) Estimates	Geograph. Character. (#camps; location)	Free. of Movt.	Citizenship	Principal source of funding
Algeria	(E)165,000	4; Tindouf	N	N	UNHCR Polisario
Australia	(E) NA	scattered	Y	Y	Public Funds
Azerbaijan	(D) 90,000	15; border areas	Y	Y	UNHCR, Public Funds
Burundi	NA	NA	Y-	N	UNHCR, NGO, RG
Canada	(E) 227,500	2,250; scattered	Y	Y	Public Funds
Congo	(D) 200,000	border areas	Y-	N	UNHCR, NGO, RG
Costa Rica	(D) 40,000 ('89) 75% Nicarag. 1/4 live in camps	2; Tilaran, San Jose, Limon	Y	N	UNHCR Public Funds

Table 1.3. Demographic, Social, and Economic Characteristics of Encampments
(continued)

Host country	Encampment Pop. (E) Displaced Pop. (D) Estimates	Geograph. Character. (#camps; location)	Free. of Movt.	Citizenship	Principal source of funding
Cyprus	(D) 200,000	Southern Cyprus	Y	Y	Public Funds
Czech Republic	NA	scattered/ urban	Y-	Y	Public Funds
Hong Kong	(E)	urban	N	N	Public Funds
India	(D) 80,000 (1959)	22; N India	Y	Y	Tibetan Organ.
Iran	(D) 450,000	NW border with Iraq	Y-	N	Public Funds
Israel (West Bank Gaza)	(D) WB 524,200 ('96) (D) G 700,790 ('96)	WB: 28% In c. G: 55% in 8 c.	N	N	UNRWA, NGO, RG, Palest. Authority
Jordan	(D) 1,140,000 (E) 240,000	10; scattered	N	Y	UNRWA
Lebanon	(E) 250,000- 400,000	15; scattered	N	N	UNRWA
Mexico	(E) 22,500 - 46,000[85] (1999)	40; Chiapas, Campeche Quintana Roo	N	Y-	UNHCR Public Funds
New Zealand	(E) NA	scattered	Y	Y	Public Funds
Pakistan	(D) 3m	244; NW frontier, 62; Balu	Y	N	UNHCR, NGO, RG, Public Funds
Papua New Guinea	(D) 8,000 ('99 (E)3,500 + 4,000 in informal camps	East Awin (Western province)	Y-	Y-	UNHCR, NGO, RG, Public Funds
Russian Federation	NA	scattered	N	Y	Public Funds
Somalia	(D) 350,000 (2000); 2m (1992)	200; Mogadishu, also Puntland, Somaliland	Y	Y	UNHCR, NGO, RG, Public Funds
South Africa	(E) NA	10; scattered	N	Y	Public Funds
Sri Lanka	(D)1.2m (E) 787,877	scattered in North	N	Y	UNHCR, NGO, RG, Public Funds
Sudan	(E)148,000 (1998); (E) 500,000 (pre-1991)	Northeast border regions	N	Y	UNHCR, NGO, RG, Public Funds
Sudan	(D)400,000 (1983) (E)150,000 (1999)	25; Eastern regions	N	Y	UNHCR, Public Funds

Table 1.3.   Demographic, Social, and Economic Characteristics of Encampments (continued)

Host country	Encampment Pop. (E) Displaced Pop. (D) Estimates	Geograph. Character. (#camps; location)	Free. of Movt.	Citizenship	Principal source of funding
Tanzania	(E) 20,000-300,000 (1999)	Pangale Ulyankulu, katumba, Mishano	Y	N	UNHCR, NGO, RG, Public Funds
Thailand	(E) 13,000[86] 110,000[87]	Northern border areas	N	N	UNHCR, NGO, RG, Public Funds
Turkey	(D) 560,000	Southeast regions	Y-	Y	NGO, Public Funds
Uganda	(E)190,000	25; Northern areas	Y	N	UNHCR, NGO, RG, Public Funds
United States	(E) 900,000	283; scattered	Y	Y	Public Funds

Note: (I) initial population, (c) current, (p) peak, (NA) not available, (Y) yes, (N) no, (Y-) qualified yes. Geographical characteristics include number of camps and location.
Source: country descriptions on www.unhcr.ch and www.refugees.org; USCR 2000, 6, 11.

Population size.   A discussion of the number of displaced persons must be prefaced by a disclaimer because of problems inherent in the enumeration and reporting process. There is no consensus pertaining to the number of people displaced in any country and often very divergent claims are made. This lack of consensus is due to the bias that underlies enumeration. Indeed, the motivations of host governments and international organizations are different, and this discrepancy shows up in their population estimates. For example, a Turkish Foreign Ministry official stated in 1999 that there are no internally displaced people in Turkey, while the Turkish Human Rights Association puts the number at 3 million.[88] The U.S. State Department uses the number 560,000. Similarly, the Mexican government claimed that there were only 10,000 Guatemalan refugees in Mexico, while UNHCR reported there were 120,000. Catholic and Protestant relief organizations report that some 100,000 Guatemalans are living in camps on the Mexican border.[89]

Another problem arises because in the course of enumeration, encampment residents self-report, and sometimes they have mysterious motivations for identifying themselves as one group rather than another. For example, according to the U.S. Census there has been a near doubling of the population size of Native Americans (in 1990, there were 1.8 million self-reported Indians).[90] Similarly, in Australia, there has been a steep increase in the indigenous population from 1971 to 1981 (from 115,953 to 228,000).[91]

There is also confusion associated with real fluctuations in encampment populations. Some camps are more subject to repatriation than others, some have higher birth and death rates than others, and some are more likely to take on new caseloads than others. Alternatively, some groups are more mobile than others, adding to difficulties in their enumeration (for example, there is no reliable estimate of the number of Romas in the Czech Republic).[92] This implies that within a short period of time, the population size of the encampment might change dramatically over its previous measurement.

Compounding the problem of enumeration is variation in the way different sources disaggregate camp populations. Some sources lump together residents of several neighboring encampments and fail to distinguish between ethnic groups and countries of origin. Such reporting practices result in inconsistency and undermine the reliability data (for example, in Ruzizi in Tanzania, the Burundians number 20,000, although, if the Congolese and Rwandans are included, the number of encampment residents rises to 285,000).[93]

In order to maximize consistency and legitimacy of encampment population data in this study, every effort is made to use sources such as the UNHCR and USCR. When that is not possible, then alternative sources are introduced, and, if they vary widely, then the highest and the lowest is presented (as in the case of the Kurds in Turkey and Guatemalans in Mexico, described earlier).

On the basis of the population statistics presented in table 1.3, it is clear that the largest encamped group under study consists of the Palestinians, numbering 3.3 million people. The smallest consists of the Irian Jayas, numbering less than 8000. The remaining cases fall in between those two extremes.

Spatial characteristics of encampment. There is variety in the geographical characteristics of encampments. Some encampments are concentrated, with several settlements close enough to enable interaction (such as the four Saharawi camps in Algeria). Others are spread out over a large territory, precluding interaction (such as the camps of the Hill Tribes of Myanmar, spread out along the 2000 km. border with Thailand).[94] Some encampments are urban, while others are rural. The former may be in the city center (as Vietnamese camps in Hong Kong) or on the outskirts (as Palestinian camps outside Beirut, and Roma settlements outside Czech cities). Sometimes, the encampment is an entire town (such as the Tibetan encampment in India, which contains the residence of the Dalai Lama and the government in exile. It is surrounded by thirteen farming settlements and nine industrial ones)[95]. The majority of encampments are rural because land is cheaper and it is easier to keep the displaced populations from dispersing.[96] Sometimes, neither urban nor rural land is an option (as among the refugees from Myanmar, whose only option was the jungle. Indeed, in Thailand, most of the 350,000 refugees live in what the USCR refers to as "refugee-like" circumstances along the jungle borders). Reservations in the New World tend to be large and spread out. In the United States, about half of the Native American population of 1.8 million live on 283 reservations spread out in most states. In Canada, there are 610,000 native peoples, but only 325,000 are the "status" Amerindians (70 percent of which live on 2,242 reserves).[97]

Permanent encampments do not necessarily remain in the same spatial location they were in at the time of their inception. Host governments may change their mind about the land they gave refugees and/or the goals they want to achieve. As a result of such a reevaluation, the refugee camps in Thailand were reduced from thirty to nineteen over some fifteen years, displacing peoples in order to achieve new government goals.[98] Also, in Beirut, there is discussion of the displacement of Palestinians from two urban camps in order to use the land for a shopping mall.

Freedom of movement. Policies pertaining to freedom of movement vary across host states. Some encampment residents, such as the Tibetans in India and the Palestinians in Jordan, are given freedom to roam throughout the country and to find housing and employment for themselves. At the other extreme, refugees are allowed no freedom of movement outside their encampments (such extreme cases of freedom restrictions exist in the Sudan, where refugees are often treated as little more than hostages by the military that commands them. Severe restrictions are also imposed on the Vietnamese in Hong Kong and the Burmese Hill Tribes in Thailand). However, the majority of encamped refugees are subject to some mobility regulations that, while stringent, are not suffocating. For example, in Papua New Guinea, refugees get freedom of movement only after they have had "permissive residency" for eight years. Such delays in mobility often result in an explosion of pent up demand for residency permission. A similar explosion was witnessed in the former Soviet Union, where displaced peoples were not allowed to move within the country until 1987. After that date, there was a burst in relocation as Chechens, Azerbaijanis, and Armenians vied to return to their original homes.

Denying freedom of movement is more difficult for populations that are internally displaced. Because they are citizens, rules limiting their mobility are harder to enforce. While that difficulty has not hampered the activities of governments in the Sudan or South Africa, it has affected policies in countries such as Cyprus, the Czech Republic, and Azerbaijan. There, while encampment residents have the right to relocate, they lack opportunity. A similar argument applies to the native peoples of North America, Australia, and New Zealand. While *de jure* they have the right of movement, *de facto* their options are restricted.[99]

Citizenship rights. The question of citizenship is relevant for refugees, especially those who are stateless, having lost their home country's citizenship when they fled and having been denied host country citizenship. It is rare that host countries, housing permanent encampments, offer citizenship to their refugees. Indeed, authorities in Mexico, Lebanon, Costa Rica, and Algeria are among the many hosts that are reluctant to grant citizenship rights. The cases of Jordan and India stand out as exceptions to the trend. In Jordan, many refugees have, in fact, become Jordanian citizens (a right that was not shared by their fellow refugees who are encamped in Lebanon, which denies them citizenship, reducing them to a stateless peoples). In India, the government extended citizenship rights to the Tibetans, who refused them (incidentally, a similar right was not extended to refugees from, for example, Myanmar or Bangladesh). In rare instances, citizenship is automatically granted to refugees as long as they are of the same ethnic group. For example, in Azerbaijan, the Law on Citizenship (1999) has permitted the automatic acquisition of citizenship by refugees from Armenia. Israel gives every Jew the right to move to Israel and become a citizen. This right is not shared by non-Jews, especially Palestinians who, under the international covenant pertaining to the right of return, seek to return and reclaim their former lands. Since the creation of the state of Israel, a series of legal measures were taken to institutionalize the blockage of such Palestinian return.[100]

The question of citizenship rights does not arise when people are internally displaced. Indeed, the Romas and the Kurds living in *de facto* encampments in the Czech Republic and Turkey, respectively, did not lose their citizenship when they were displaced. Native peoples on reservations and in homelands were given citizenship, albeit with a lag (with the exception of Maori men, who received suffrage from Britain twelve years before it was granted to the European settlers in New Zealand).[101] Some tribes in the United States even have dual citizenship (from the United States and a variety of Indian Countries).

Primary source of funding. It is rare for permanent encampments to be entirely self-sufficient. Most rely on outside sources of funding. The nature of the funding depends upon the nature of encampment residents, namely whether they are refugees or internally displaced people. Refugee encampments fall under the jurisdiction of international organizations. As such, they are primarily funded by the UNHCR (the Palestinian population dispersed in the Middle East is so large that it has a separate organization created for its needs: the United Nations Relief and Works Agency for Palestine Refugees in the Near East [UNRWA]).[102] Additional funding is provided to encampments by international agencies outside the UN body (such as the International Red Cross, American Friends Service Committee, etc). Also, bilateral agreements with host states sometimes allow donor countries to fund encampments directly (such as, for example, the USCR). In addition, NGOs and religious groups operate in a variety of contexts. The diaspora of the ethnic or national group in the encampments is another important source of funding. As is discussed in chapter 5, the Palestinian diaspora, as well as that of the Greek Cypriots, Tibetans, Saharawis, and Tamils, have been active in aiding their displaced conationals. More often than not, such diasporas have strong political motivations, ensuring that issues of repatriation and independence loom large on their agenda.

In the case of internally displaced persons, funding is more complicated because the UN body has no jurisdiction over the encampments. As there is no internationally agreed upon mechanism for transmitting aid, nor any regulations pertaining to basic needs satisfaction, displaced persons are largely at the mercy of home governments.[103] Given that those governments are often (albeit not always) the propagators of the forced movements, their generosity in supporting encampments is rarely abundant.

Working Definition of Permanent Encampments

The sources of involuntary migration, as well as its solutions, are depicted in figure 1.1. It is clear that permanent encampments are but one possible end result of population displacement. They are not the most popular and they are rarely viewed with positive enthusiasm. Indeed, residents don't want to live in them, host countries don't want to host them, and international agencies prefer to find alternate solutions. International personnel working with displaced persons might define successful encampments as those having the following life span: in the beginning, they address the immediate and basic needs of displaced peoples; in the end, encampments have achieved a durable permanent solution; in other words, integration, repatriation, and third country asylum have been so successful that encampments no longer exist.

Yet, permanent encampments continue to exist. While there are some camps in which basic needs have been successfully met, and while there are some camps that have ceased to exist because alternative solutions were found for their populations, in reality, many camps linger and linger, achieving little success in any goals the international community sets for them. For these camps, "the best conditions" described above do not exist. Instead, they are stuck in time and space, their populations unable to go back or to go forward. In these camps, temporary has become permanent, impermanence has become institutionalized, and limbo has characterized entire lifetimes. These conditions form the hazy area in the study of displaced populations that is neither here nor there; that is hard to quantify, painful to contemplate, and even harder to resolve. The reality of these encampments is one that the international community is ill equipped to deal with. Their reality is one that policy makers have no blueprints for.

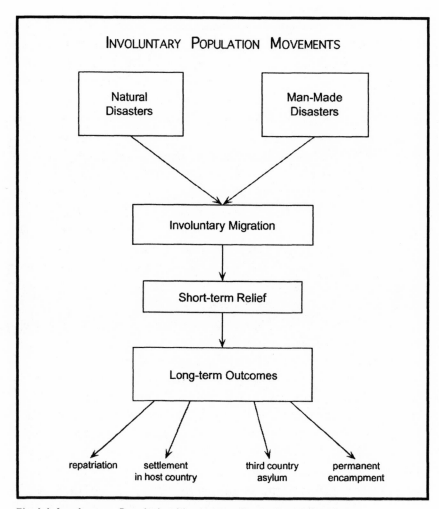

Fig. 1.1. Involuntary Population Movements: Sources and Solutions

It is precisely these limbo encampments that are the focus of this study. The goal of this research is to facilitate the understanding of encampments on the fringes and murky edges. In other words, the goal is to study the "unsuccessful" encampments, the ones that do not fit into the preconceived pattern of creation-followed-by-obliteration-as-a-result-of-solution. The goal is to study the areas of encampment existence that are imprecise, unclear, and enigmatic and their effect on long term camp solutions, or rather, nonsolutions. A similar motivation was eloquently expressed by Anne Fadiman in the preface to her book about Hmong refugees in the United States: "I have always felt that the action most worth watching is not at the center of things but where edges meet. I like shorelines, weather fronts, international borders. There are interesting frictions and incongruities in these places, and often, if you stand at the point of tangency, you can see both sides better than if you were in the middle of either one."[104] So, too, by studying permanent encampments, I hope to convey a new perspective in the other two extremes; namely the first humanitarian response and the long-term solution. While very challenging endeavors, they seem so simple by comparison with the permanent encampment that must transform itself from a short run camp to a permanent camp while resisting acceptance of the fundamental basis of its transformation, namely its permanence.

In an effort to accomplish the above goals, it is necessary to adopt a broad definition of encampments. Such a broad definition enables the comparative study of a large number of long-term "solutions" (in the form of permanent encampments) to involuntary displacement. As noted in the introductory pages, such an umbrella definition lumps together all long-term living arrangements provided as solutions for peoples forcibly removed from their homes: refugee camps, internally displaced resettlement communities, native lands, etc. In addition, it includes *de facto* encampments in which targeted ethnic groups live in "refugee-like" conditions consisting of poverty, marginalization, and the lack of opportunity for change.

Such a broad range of encampments warrants the identification of a common denominator. All encampments under study share the following characteristics: they contain people who are involuntarily displaced, who are involuntary residents, and who are of a different ethnic group from the titular majority of the host state (if they are internally displaced, host equals home). These fundamental characteristics underlie native lands in the New World, urban ghettos where Romas live, and rural settlements where Turkish Kurds are concentrated (the only exception is Cyprus, where displaced Greeks are living in the land of Greeks. However, the basis of the exception disappears if we consider that they were displaced by Turks from lands currently occupied by Turks). Thus, involuntary displacement followed by involuntary residence of a distinct ethnic group justifies this comparative study of native lands in Canada and Eritrean camps in the Sudan; Black South Africans in homelands and the Karen in Thai jungles. It is not apples and oranges that are being compared, but rather involuntarily displaced peoples who share dilemmas pertaining to their economic existence, their political lives, and their social identities.

Involuntary displacement coupled with involuntary residence of distinct ethnic groups forms the core of our working definition of encampments, as it is shared by all cases under study. On the periphery of that core, other characteristics may or may not manifest themselves in the encampments. For example, some residents have freedom of movement, others don't; some have citizenship rights, others don't. This periphery is more nebulous than the core, it has hazier boundaries and it is less predictable. The boundaries of the periphery are fluid and dynamic; those of the core are solid.

If both core and periphery characteristics are included in the working definition of permanent encampments, then does it become so generously all-inclusive that it ceases to have meaning? Also, does its large embrace imply that attention to detail is impossible? I believe the answer to these questions is negative. Any attempt to limit the types of encampments would only restrict the scope of the study and prevent the learning of lessons that might be applicable across types of encampments (for example, omitting native lands might prevent finding solutions to encampment problems in Algeria).

NOTES

1. *La Repubblica*, August 20, 1992.

2. *The State of the World's Refugees*, cited in Donna E. Arzt, *Refugees into Citizens* (New York: Council on Foreign Relations, 1997), 102.

3. UNHCR, *The State of the World's Refugees* (New York: Oxford University Press, 1995), 34-35.

4. R. Chambers, *Settlement Schemes in Tropical Africa* (New York: Praeger, 1969), 12.

5. F. Stewart, "War and Development: Can Economic Analysis Help Reduce the Costs?" *Journal of International Development* 5, no. 4 (1993); K. Tamas and C. Gleichmann, "Returned Exiles on the Namibian Labour Market" in *The Integration of Returned Exiles, Former Combatants and other War-Affected Namibians*, ed. R. Preston (Windhoek: Namibia Institute for Social and Economic Research, 1993); Patricia Daley, "From the Kipande to the Kibali: The Incorporation of Refugees and Labour Migrants in Western Tanzania, 1900-1987" in *Geography and Refugees*, ed. Richard Black and Vaughan Robinson (London: Belhaven Press, 1993).

6. John R. Rogge, *Refugees, A Third World Dilemma* (Totowa, N.J.: Rowman and Littlefield, 1987); Black and Robinson, *Geography and Refugees*.

7. See chapter 3 in Roberta Cohen and Francis M. Deng, *Masses in Flight Case Studies of the Internally Displaced* (Washington: Brookings Institution, 1998).

8. G. Loescher and L. Monahan, eds. *Refugees and International Relations* (New York: Oxford University Press, 1989); Leon Gordenker, *Refugees in International Politics* (London: Croom Helm, 1987).

9. Howard Adelman, "Modernity, Globalization, Refugees and Displacement" in *Refugees, Perspectives on the Experience of Forced Migration*, ed. Alastair Ager (London: Cassell Publishers, 1998), 83-110; E. A. Brett, "Rebuilding War Damaged Communities in Uganda" in *In Search of Cool Ground: War, Flight and Homecoming in Northeast Africa*, ed. T. Allen (London: James Currey, 1996); M. Parker, "Social Devastation and Mental Health in Northeast Africa" in *In Search of Cool Ground: War, Flight and Homecoming in Northeast Africa*, ed. T. Allen (London: James Currey, 1996).

10. Caroline Brettel and James Frank Hollifield, eds., *Migration Theory: Talking across Disciplines* (New York: Routledge, 2000). Also, an edited volume brings together economics, sociology, anthropology, and political science in the study of involuntary resettlement: Michael M. Cernea, ed., *The Economics of Involuntary Resettlement* (Washington, D.C.: World

Bank, 1999). In addition, see Rosemary Preston, "Researching Repatriation and Reconstruction: Who is Researching What and Why?" in *The End of the Refugee Cycle?* ed. Richard Black and Khalid Koser (Oxford: Berghahn, 1999).

11. Graeme Hugo, "Postwar Refugee Migration in Southeast Asia: Patterns, Problems and Policies" in Rogge, *Refugees, A Third World Dilemma*, 237.

12. World Bank, *Entering the 21st Century: World Development Report 1999/2000* (Oxford: Oxford University Press, 2000), 37-38.

13. The next largest share of migrants move across national boundaries within the less developed countries (henceforth LDCs). The remainder of migrants move from the LDCs to the more developed countries (henceforth MDCs). In the latter, population movements from the LDCs represent a major shift in immigrant origins: before the mid-1960s, most migrants tended to be from Eastern Europe and Russia, Southern Europe and the Mediterranean, and Northern Europe, all in different historical periods. Although proportionally small, migrants from LDCs to MDCs are large in absolute terms and are growing.

14. John R. Rogge, *Too Many, Too Long: Sudan's Twenty-Year Refugee Dilemma* (Totowa, N.J.: Rowman and Allanheld, 1985), 2, 4.

15. *The Economist*, Millennium Special Edition, December 31, 1999 69.

16. D. Eltis, "Free and Coerced Transatlantic Migrations: Some Comparisons," *American Historical Review* 88, 255. Eltis is quoted in Timothy J. Hatton and Jeffrey G. Williamson, *The Age of Mass Migration* (New York: Oxford University Press, 1998) 7.

17. Herman M. Schwartz, *States Versus Markets* (New York: St. Martin's Press, 1994), 117.

18. Andrew Bell-Fialkoff, who wrote the most comprehensive book to date on the practice, defined it as "a planned, deliberate removal from a certain territory of an undesirable population distinguished by one or more characteristics such as ethnicity, religion, race, class or sexual preference. These characteristics must serve as the basis for removal for it to qualify as cleansing". He goes on to describe a spectrum along which population removal ranges, with genocide on one end, emigration under pressure on the other, and, in the middle, deportation/expulsion, transfer, and exchange. Andrew Bell-Fialkoff, *Ethnic Cleansing* (New York: St. Martin's Griffin, 1999), 3.

19. Not all governments that cause population movements do so out of design or malice. Indeed, some are simply incompetent and are unable to

lead their populations or offer them adequate standards of living. For example: government incompetence led to hunger in Somalia and Ethiopia, while political instability in Lebanon in the 1970s led to chaos, and both created destabilizing population movements.

20. David Osterfeld, *Prosperity versus Planning* (New York: Oxford University Press, 1992), 208.

21. *OMRI Daily Digest* #120, June 21, 1995.

22. *U.S. News and World Report*, November 30, 1992, 36.

23. Bill Frelick, *The Wall of Denial: Internal Displacement in Turkey* (Washington, D.C.: U.S. Committee for Refugees, 1999), 13.

24. Aristide Zolberg, Astri Suhrke, and Sergio Aguayo, *Escape From Violence: Conflict and the Refugee Crisis in the Devoloping World* (New York: Oxford University Press, 1989), 3.

25. Jeff Crisp, "Who Has Counted the Refugees? UNHRC and the Politics of Numbers" *New Issues in Refugee Research* (Working Paper no. 12, UNHRC Policy Research Unit, June 1999), www.unhcr.ch/refworld/pub/wpapers/wpno12.htm (accessed November 2000).

26. Quoted in Black and Robinson, *Geography and Refugees*, 7.

27. Leon Gordenker, *Refugees in International Politics* (New York: Columbia University Press, 1987), 63.

28. Roberta Cohen and Francis M. Deng, *Masses in Flight* (Washington, D.C.: Brookings Institution Press, 1998) and Cohen and Deng, *The Forsaken People*.

29. Cohen and Deng, *Masses in Flight*, 16.

30. Frelick, *The Wall of Denial*, 1. The estimate is given by the Turkish Human Rights Association (Frelick, 6).

31. According to Luke Lee, the significance of border crossing emerged for historical reasons. The distinction really became implemented at the time of the Cold War, since border crossing became synonymous with persecution, namely, from Communism. Indeed, he provides evidence from the time of Japan's invasion of China and from the Korean War that the distinction between internally displaced persons and refugees was not made. Luke T. Lee, "Internally Displaced Persons and Refugees: Toward a Legal Synthesis?" *Journal of Refugee Studies* 9, no.1, (1996), 30-32.

32. Moreover, when boundaries are the determining point, then diplomatic recognition of those boundaries had the power to get refugees aid or not. The example of the former Yugoslavia is a case in point. During the breakup of Yugoslavia and the ensuing wars of the 1990s, some 2.5 million people were involuntarily displaced. The majority would have re-

mained internally displaced persons if it was not for the international community recognition of the new successor states of Bosnia, Croatia, and Macedonia, and, thus, would not have been eligible for international refugee aid. This means, for example, that the 800,000 refugees from Kosovo into Macedonia would have been treated as internally displaced persons if Macedonia had not been recognized as an independent country and, therefore, they would not have been eligible for international intervention and aid.

33. This does not mean that UN covenants are always heeded. While most signatory countries adhere to international laws pertaining to refugees most of the time, events do occur all to often that show disrespect for rules and norms (for example, in May, 1991, the last Sudanese refugee camp in Ethiopia was attacked and some 400,000 were forced to trek back to Sudan. Many of those who did not die during the two-week trip were then killed by the Sudan Air Force aerial bombardment (Hiram A. Fuiz, "The Sudan: Cradle of Displacement" in Roberta Cohen and Francis M. Deng, eds. *The Forsaken People* (Washington: Brookings Institution, 1998), 150) Thus, both the host and the home country broke international law pertaining to refugees.

34. Lee, "Internally Displaced Persons and Refugees," 37.

35. It is not entirely correct to say that internally displaced persons are not eligible for outside aid, since they may receive aid from organizations such as, for example, the International Committee of the Red Cross, the World Food Program, the World Health Organization, and UNICEF.

36. The term indigenous is often misused since it refers to people who originate in an area; in other words, are born there. In that way, any person born in Australia or Canada is indigenous. Yet, according to the common usage of the term, it refers to populations that are native to the region.

37. Malcolm Shaw, *Title to Territory in Africa: International Legal Issues* (Oxford: Clarendon, 1986), 31-46.

38. Ted Robert Gurr, *Minorities at Risk: A Global View of Ethnopolitical Conflicts,* (Washington, D.C: United States Institute of Peace, 1993), 162.

39. Joke Schrijvers, "Fighters, Victims and Survivors: Constructions of Ethnicity, Gender and Refugeeness among Tamils in Sri Lanka," *Journal of Refugee Studies* 12, no. 3, (1999), 309.

40. This was taken from a statement by the Ambassador to the Security Council on January 13, 2000. Cited in Guy S. Goodwin-Gill, "UNHCR and Internal Displacement: Stepping into a Legal and Political Minefield," USCR, *World Refugee Survey 2000*, 26.

41. USCR, *World Refugee Survey 2000*, 266.

42. The notorious thirteen-foot wall was erected in Usti nad Labem, and the attempt to resettle hundreds of "socially unacceptable people" (the code name for Romas) in a fenced in area outside of town took place in Plzen. See Jonathan Fox and Betty Brown, "The Roma in the Post-Communist Era" in *Peoples Versus States,* ed. Ted Robert Gurr (Washington, D.C.: United States Institute of Peace, 2000), 146. Also, see http://www.bhhrg.org/czechrepublic/czechrepublic1999/wall.htm

43. Lynn Turgeon, "Discrimination against and Affirmative Action of Gypsies in Eastern Europe" in *The Political Economy of Ethnic Discrimination and Affirmative Action,* ed. Michael Wyzan. (New York: Praeger, 1990), 161.

44. After the short-term refugee tents served their immediate purposes, those who did not find accommodations on their own were housed by the government in refugee housing estates. Fourteen thousand such housing units were made available to refugees by 1995, free of charge. http://kypros.org/PIO/cyprus/society/housing.htm (accessed January 18, 2001).

45. W. R. Smyser, "Refugees, a Never Ending Story" *Foreign Affairs* (Fall 1985), 157-59.

46. Giorgia Dona and John W. Berry, "Refugee Acculturation and Re-Education" *Refugees. Perspectives on the Experience of Forced Migration,* in ed. Alastair Ager (London: Cassell Publishers, 1999), 170.

47. The latter two are included in Anne Fadiman, *The Spirit Catches You and You Fall Down* (New York: Farrar, Strauss and Giroux, 1997), 167.

48. Rogge, "introduction to Part Two" in *Refugees, A Third World Dilemma,* 45.

49. Joffee, 136.

50. Thomas G. Weiss and Cindy Collins, *Humanitarian Challenges and Intervention,* 2nd edition (Boulder, Colo.: Westview Press 2000), 143.

51. Allen Buchanan, *Secession* (Boulder, Colo.: Westview Press, 1991).

52. Arzt, *Refugees into Citizens,* 21.

53. Edith Bowles, "From Village to Camp: Refugee Camp Life in Transition on the Thaliand-Burma Border" *Forced Migration Review,* 2, (1998), This regulation was enforced even more stringently in the late 1990s. Even after one year, refugees have not been allowed to build houses, but only bamboo platforms with a roof of plastic sheeting.

54. Frelick, *The Wall of Denial,* 4.

55. There is also a certain degree of forced idleness in camps. Those who claim that camp life weakens the motivation for incentive and mobi-

lization include J. D. Cohen, "Psychological Adaptation and Dysfunction among Refugees" *International Migration Review* 15, (1981), and J. Hammond, "War Uprooting and the Political Mobilization of Central American Refugees" *Journal of Refugee Studies* 6, no. 1, (1993). A contrary view is presented by Roman Krznaric, "Guatemalan Returnees and the Dilemma of Political Mobilization" *Journal of Refugee Studies* 10, no. 1, (1997).

56. USRC, *World Refugee Survey 1997*, 129.

57. Vilfredo Pareto, quoted in Michael Hechter, *Internal Colonialism* (Berkeley: University of California Press, 1975), 311.

58. Anthony Smith, "Chosen Peoples: Why Ethnic Groups Survive" *Ethnic and Racial Studies* 15, no. 3 July (1992), 450.

59. While the definitions provided in the text as well as in the above footnote may vary in focus, they all connote a group of people that are united (or perceive to be united) in some way. Such a lack of clarity fosters a wide range of interpretations so that the real-world applications of ethnic group boundaries result in a lack of comparable classifications. This confusion is best illustrated by the attempts to classify the various peoples inhabiting the Balkans. The unconventional official divisions of the Balkan populations have given rise to a plethora of groupings that belie the above classifications: peoples are distinguished by religion (the Bosnian Muslims, Bosnian Croats, and Bosnian Serbs, as well as the Bulgarians and the Pomaks), by levels of development (the Albanian Albanians and the Kosovo Albanians), and by language (the Albanian Tosks and Gegs). For the sake of simplicity, peoples of the Balkans will be referred to as ethnic groups throughout the text, even though they do not necessarily conform to the standard definitions of ethnicity.

60. Editorial, *Nature Genetics* 24, (February 2000), 97.

61. Susan Olzak, *The Dynamics of Ethnic Competition and Conflict* (Stanford: Stanford University Press, 1992), 8.

62. P. L. Van den Berghe, "Class, Race and Ethnicity in Africa" *Ethnic and Racial Studies* 6, (1983), 222.

63. There is an ongoing debate about how to call the country that lies between India and Thailand. In the nineteenth century, it was the Upper and Lower Burmas. Then, under colonial rule, it became Burma, and so remained after independence. In 1988, the state, under army leadership, changed the name to Myanmar. However, the democratic forces that won the election of 1990 refused to accept the new name. Some believe that since the government that introduced the name Myanmar no longer has legitimacy, the name they chose for their country is no longer valid (see for

example, a recent compendium of scholarly articles called *Burma, Prospects for a Democratic Future*, ed. by Robert I. Rotbert). However, in this study, the name used by the United Nations is used as a guide, so the country will be called Myanmar.

64. Dan Rabinowitz, "National Identity on the Frontier: Palestinians in the Israeli Educational System" in *Border Identities*, ed. Thomas M. Wilson and Hastings Donnan (Cambridge: Cambridge University Press 1998), 159.

65. Guatemalan refugees were in camps in Chiapas, Campeche, and Quintana Roo in Mexico. They came in the 1980s and while some returned in the mid-1990s, there were still 33,000 left. See Krznaric, "Guatemalan Returnees," 62.

66. The military government, as part of the counterinsurgency campaign, destroyed some 440 villages and killed some 1200 people in an attempt to eradicate the guerrilla organization Guerrilla Army of the Poor that had established itself in the area.

67. See Cohen and Deng, *The Forsaken People*.

68. Central America also has very few encampments. One million peoples were displaced during the 1970s, yet only 120,000 have benefited from UNHCR assistance. Rogge points out that no other part of the world has such low levels of encampment. Rogge, "Central America" in *Refugees, A Third World Dilemma*, 159.

69. These are Camp Pendelton, California; Fort Chaffee, Arkansas; Fort Indianton Gap, Pennsylvania; and Eglin Air Force Base, Florida.

70. Native reserves were areas left untouched by white settlers for the use of Blacks during the nineteenth and pre-World War II twentieth century. Alan Mabin, "Unemployment, Resettlement and Refugees in South Africa" in Rogge, *Refugees, A Third World Dilemma*, 82.

71. Incidentally, the Palestinians in Jordan are overall better off than anywhere else in the Middle East (USCR, *World Refugee Survey 1997*, 156).

72. There are four main ethno-linguistic groups: Nguni (including Xhosa, Zulu, Swazi, and Ndebele), Sotho, Venda, and Tsonga.

73. Native peoples in North America are generally treated as one homogeneous group, while, in fact, they differ greatly. This reflects a disservice done to them by the first white arrivals, who failed to distinguish between the Sioux, the Cherokees, and Miccosukes. A similar situation occurred in Australia, where the category Aboriginal included, at the time of contact with white man, some 500 tribes, each with its recognized territory and distinct language. Indeed, before the arrival of white settlers in Australia, there were at least 250 different aboriginal languages and several

hundred dialects. Most of these have died out unrecorded (*Economist*, September 9, 2000, Survey Australia, 12).

74. Walter Williams, *South Africa's War against Capitalism* (New York: Praeger, 1989), xi.

75. Frelick, *The Wall of Denial*, 1, 5.

76. USCR, *World Refugee Survey 1997*, 84.

77. USCR, *World Refugee Survey 1997*, 228.

78. As a result, all Chechens over forty were either born or lived in exile. See Thomas Greene, "Internal Displacement in the North Caucasus, Azerbaijan, Armenia and Georgia" in Roberta Cohen and Francis M. Deng, eds. *The Forsaken People, Case Studies of the Internally Displaced* (Washington, D.C.: Brookings Institution Press, 1998), 243-44.

79. In New Zealand, 1872 marks the end of three wars between the colonizers and the Maoris. This was the year when great tracts of Maori land were confiscated and their culture irrevocably disrupted.

80. Other areas, including West Papua (renamed Irian Jaya by the Indonesians), did not follow a pattern of direct invasion. In 1963, the departing Dutch enabled Indonesia to assume administrative responsibility under a United Nations agreement. However, it was contingent upon a referendum on self-determination to be held by 1969. A sham "Act of Free Choice" took place, which was accepted by the United Nations in 1973 (Freedom House, *Freedom in the World: The Annual Survey of Political Rights and Civil Liberties 1998-1999*, 522). An army offensive in 1984 against the guerrilla Free Papua Movement resulted in the displacement of hundreds of villagers into neighboring Papua New Guinea.

81. The nature of the displacement of Palestinians has been under dispute due to the different interpretations of the two sides. At the announcement of Israeli independence in 1948, the question of why exactly did the Arabs from Palestine flee is crucial. Did they leave because they voluntarily decided not to live under Israeli rule, or were they pushed out. Both sides substantiate their arguments, and it is likely that the reality contains a little bit of both truths. See chapter 1 of Arzt, *Refugees into Citizens*.

82. China invaded Tibet, a sovereign state, in 1949. In 1959, popular uprisings had been crushed, resulting in 87,000 dead in Lhasa alone and 80,000 fled to Dharamsala India with the Dalai Lama. In 1965, China created the Tibet Autonomous Region on less than half of the original territory.

83. See the role of numbers and population size in Milica Z. Bookman, *The Demographic Struggle for Power* (London: Frank Cass, 1997).

84. The civil war was between the (Arab) governments in Khartoum and the Southern Sudan people's Liberation Movement, focused on the pastoral and animist ethnic groups of Kinka, Shilluk, and Nuer from the districts of Bahr el-Ghazal and Upper Nile.

85. This is the number of Guatemalans who were officially registered in refugee camps in Mexico, although the number who fled to Mexico during the counterinsurgency campaign has been estimated to be closer to 150,000 (estimation by J. Dunkerely, cited in Krznaric, "Guatemalan Returnees."

86. There has been no official enumeration of the hill tribe refugees from Burma. This estimate is for 1980. Netnapis Nakawachara and John Rogge, "Thailand's Refugee Experience" in Rogge, *Refugees, A Third World Dilemma*, 271.

87. The estimate of 110,000 refers to 1998. See Bowles, "From Village to Camp."

88. USCR, *World Refugee Survey 2000*, 280.

89. Bruce Harris and Miguel Ugalde, "The Guatemalan Refugee Situation in Chiapas, Mexico" in Rogge, *Refugees, A Third World Dilemma*, 167.

90. Fergus M. Bordewich, *Killing the White Man's Indian: Reinventing Native Americans at the End of the Twentieth Century* (New York: Anchor Books, 1996), 66.

91. *Encyclopeida Britannica* (15th edition, 1992, 14), 425.

92. http://www.bhhrg.org/czechrepublic/czechrepublic1999/government.htm

93. Country profile in www.unhcr.ch

94. Some of the camps are located along the roads, but many are in remote areas in mountains and heavily forested areas. See Bowles, "From Village to Camp."

95. Dorsh Marie de Voe, "Keeping Refugee Status: A Tibetan Perspective" in Scott Morgan and Elizabeth Colson, eds. *People in Upheaval* (New York: Center for Migration Studies, 1987), 55.

96. They cannot disperse easily because camps are usually in remote locations with no easy access and no mode of transportation.

97. There are also 25,000 Inuit who live north of the tree line and more than a quarter "non-status" native peoples (mostly mixed descent) who live in urban areas. Gurr, *Minorities At Risk*, 165-66.

98. This took place from the early 1980s until the mid-to-late 1990s. See Bowles, "From Village to Camp."

99. In the United States, there is de facto immobility among native peoples since they lose access to the extensive services provided by the Federal Bureau of Indian Affairs if they move off the reservations.

100. For example, the Abandoned Areas Ordinance of 1948, the Emergency Regulations concerning the Cultivation of Waste Lands of 1949, the Absentees Property Law of 1950, and the Land Acquisitions Law of 1953, all of which legalized the expropriation of Arab land.

101. This was the result of the Native Representation Act of 1867.

102. Set up in 1948 after the UN General Assembly resolution 302 to administer and provide relief and employment in large-scale regional labor projects for the refugees of 1948.

103. Some international organizations do manage to get into some host countries and come to the aid of some encampment residents. These exceptions are discussed in chapter 5.

104. Fadiman, *The Spirit Catches You*, viii.

2

ENCAMPMENTS IN A
TWO-TIER WORLD

While permanent encampments are not new, the global environment within which they exist is. This environment is the result of numerous social, economic, and political changes that have characterized the late twentieth century. Some indicators of this change are easily discernible: electronic mail has displaced the handwritten note, television broadcasts into homes across the globe, and cellular telephones reach from Kuala Lumpur to Cape Town, Vancouver to Buenos Aires. In addition, other less clearly visible signs of change permeate most countries of the world. Capitalism has become borderless, communism has become meaningless, and socialism has become modified. A unipolar world has emerged, with the United States at the helm, in which the free market and democracy are the prevailing mantra. Liberal democracies proselytize the universal applicability of their political values (while authoritarian governments struggle to reject what they perceive to be yet one more form of imperialist intrusion). An alliance of high-income democracies, under the auspices of NATO, fights a war to protect human rights, in sharp contrast to the Great War that opened the twentieth century. Globalization, both glorified and vilified, takes many forms and spreads far and wide. Economic growth has produced both an overall increase in the standards of living, as well as a widening gap between the rich and the poor.

One aspect of this international environment is particularly useful for the study of permanent encampments and their future prospects. It is the emerging division of the world states into two distinct groups. One group consists of highly developed, liberal democracies and the other of less developed, authoritarian states. This new configuration of states emerged at the end of the Cold War and the ensuing frenzied pace of globalization. The relevance of this for encampments is that the particular group of states in which encampment occurs determines its social, political, and economic character, as well as its future prospects.

This chapter sets the groundwork for the study of encampments by looking at the forest (namely, the place of home and host states in the new configuration of states) while subsequent chapters deal with the individual trees (namely, the encampments within those states). This chapter describes the political, economic, and social nature of home and host countries; subsequent chapters apply that information to the study of permanent encampments. This chapter tells the superstory; subsequent chapters tell the individual stories.

A TWO-TIER WORLD

During the Cold War, the classification of states was easy and clear. From the Western perspective, there was the West, the Communist countries, and the undecided. The latter sometimes called themselves the nonaligned. They were either part of the Third World or not, depending on their levels of development.[1] The cold war shaped not only international economic and political relations, but also each individual country's domestic policies pertaining to trade, finance, investment, employment, migration, social policy, etc. In this way, the economic classification of states into communist and capitalist overlapped with the political classification of democratic and authoritarian, forming a clean and neat prism through which to observe the world.

The Cold War ended, and policy makers, leaders, academics, and the media scrambled to understand and describe the international environment that took its place. Amidst some Cold War nostalgia and scattered refusals to acknowledge the fundamental changes unfolding before our eyes, several bold attempts to clarify and explain were made. Francis Fukuyama was the first to make sweeping statements about the new era by proclaiming the victory of capitalism and the death of communism.[2] The end of the Cold War clearly showed the superiority of liberalism and the free market system. Political democracy and the society it created proved impermeable to internal and external pressures and therefore sustainable over the long run. Capitalism, said Fukuyama, triumphed and proved itself as the most successful economic system.

Samuel Huntington also offered an interpretation of the new world order.[3] He claimed that the post-Cold War period is characterized by a division of the world states that clash. However, this clash and schism is not based on political or economic systems but rather on civilizations. As the title of his book suggests (namely, *The Clash of Civilizations and the Remaking of the World Order*), the new order will increasingly be characterized by conflict between the worlds greatest civilizations (Western, Muslim, Hindu, Eastern Orthodox). About a decade later, Huntington, with Lawrence Harrison, continued on the theme of civilizations by claiming that culture matters in determining the pace and level of economic development, and thereby whether a country falls into the more developed or the less developed category.[4]

In explaining the post-Cold War vacuum, Robert Kaplan offers a more pessimistic view of the current reality.[5] The new world order, according to Kaplan, is characterized by tribal warfare, interethnic animosities, poverty, and unequal distribution of income, all of which will ultimately culminate in a complex form of anarchy. He says "the past is dead," and we are left with a new future with fewer of the structures we are familiar with and have come to rely upon.[6] Kaplan is not alone in his view of upcoming anarchy: Zbigniew Brzezinski also views the current period as full of turmoil that can be expected to spiral out of control.[7]

Considerably more optimistic in his outlook, Thomas Friedman identified the new international system as globalization, and touted its power to unite disparate tribes, ethnic groups, and income groups in one great quest for participation in the international economy. According to Friedman, others have "vastly underestimated how the power of states, the lure of global markets, the diffusion of technology, the rise of networks and the spread of global norms" affect societies.[8] As a result, he sees the upcoming period as one that will have both clashes and homogenization, but they will all take place within an environment of globalization.

In his study of immigration policy, Martin Heisler also presented a division of the world states. As the source of that division, he focused on political culture and political values in the changing global arena. He went on to classify countries as introverted and extroverted, depending on their political orientation.[9]

This study is built on the partial synthesis of the above research, coupled with data, media reporting, and additional scholarly discourse. It, too, is based on a division of countries. However, that division has roots in a combination of numerous factors, including economic, political, and social cleavages. While the study adopts Heisler's division of the world into tiers, it builds and expands on that division as well as on his terminology. Heisler called countries in the two tiers introverted and extroverted. In this study, those terms are used interchangeably with guarded/outgoing and hesitant/bold.

Extroverted countries are focused on the outside world. They have open markets and movements of goods, capital, and ideas across their borders. They do not define themselves by their ethnicity and their history, but rather by the economic niche they have created for themselves in the contemporary world. They have accepted the inevitability of globalization and have hopped on for the ride. These countries are integrated into the international community and are comfortable in it because they share values and policies with others like them. These include democratic practices and values pertaining to human and civil rights. Extroverted countries uphold these values and believe in their universality (thus justifying the term "universal values"). This gives them a common denominator with selected other countries, thus encouraging and enabling their willingness to compromise their sovereignty and form mutually beneficial unions. The importance of their state borders is shrinking and the importance of interdependence in the international economic arena is growing. In the words of Peter Slater, the new world that has emerged "sees the death of geography and in particular, the death of the nation-state."[10] According to Yasemin Soysal, states have become postnational, as they are now instruments for the implementation of human rights norms more than anything else.[11] Some of their sense of ethnicity is also relinquished, as they become postnational. The mobility of capital, labor, and information is crucial to them, further weakening borders. Extroverted states, thus, are post-Copernican: each state and its citizens realize that they are not the center of the world and that the world does not rotate around them. They are aware of their membership in the global community and their dependency on it. Their domestic policies reflect that awareness. Such a common denominator leads to cohesion in view and cooperation in affairs that was unthinkable during the Cold War era, hindered as it was by the clash of ideology between East and West.

Economic growth, respect for human rights, and political and economic participation; these are all characteristics of extroverted countries. In the words of Robert Kaplan, such countries are inhabited by "Hegel's and Fukuyama's Last Man, healthy, well fed and pampered by technology."[12]

By contrast, in introverted states, the Last Man does not exist and the First Man prevails. Indeed, "Hobbes's First Man, condemned to a life that is poor, nasty, brutish and short,"[13] populates the vast majority of countries in the second tier. Within this group, countries are less developed and tend to have erratic and unpredictable growth rates. Their economies are dependent on land, be it for agriculture or natural resources (such as oil). Therefore, territory is very important for them, and they are willing to go to war to protect it (and even to expand it). They do not participate fully in the global community, and the flow of capital and labor across their state boundaries is minimal. Their populations do not share a global perspective, and their exposure to the international community is limited by the lack of travel opportunities, CNN, and the internet. They are suspicious of the global economy. They are threatened by international interactions. They do not have sufficient self-confidence in their culture, their politicians, their institutions, and their borders that they can withstand the onslaught of global integration, be it in the form of trade or migration.

Governments in introverted states are authoritarian, associating democracy with foreign values. Leaders rarely have the self-confidence to test their legitimacy at the ballot box. They tend not to uphold Western values. They are especially leery of international goals and universal values, and seek to distance themselves from such ideology. Instead, they define themselves by their ethnic and state boundaries. In contrast to the developed, liberal states, introverted countries value their sovereignty very much and look with disfavor upon what they view as international meddling. They protect their state borders ferociously. Their leaders tend to be nationalist and derive their legitimacy from the confirmation of national supremacy. The leadership fosters nationalist sentiment in order to keep the citizens loyal and introverted. Their populations tend to value the boundaries of their ethnicity and their self-image is tied first and foremost to their national identity relative to others. Far from being postnational, they are entrenched in their nationality in the ethnic, not civic, sense. In this way, introverted countries and their populations are pre-Copernican: they think the universe revolves around them.

While some states are clearly introverted and others extroverted, many lie in the middle and exhibit characteristics of both. Despite its failure to encompass all the world's countries, the two-tier classification is nevertheless useful as a typology. It enables us to infer the direction of change that the "undecided" states will move in if they (governments and/or populations) opt to join the globalization and democratization bandwagon. It also enables us to infer the behavior these countries will exhibit while getting there and once they get there. (It is useful to note, however, that the process of moving from introverted to extroverted cannot realistically be compared to another process of transition that occurred in the post-Cold War era, namely the movement from Communism to Capitalism. Today's introverted states have a tougher time than yesterday's Communist states. While the former were embraced, advised, and tugged, the latter were left to their own devices. No extroverted country is rushing to transform an African economy as they did for Eastern Europe; no international lending institution is seeking to undertake risky loans in the name of freedom as they did in Poland and Hungary; no group of Western countries is willing to open its doors to those who run from a broken system, as they did to the East Europeans and former Soviet Balts.)

The principal distinguishing features of the two tiers can be classified into economic, political, and social categories. Numerous elements within these categories have already been discussed earlier, but warrant elaboration. For the purposes of the discussion later, these three categories will be treated separately, although in reality they overlap and affect each other in a mutually reinforcing causation cycle. The boundaries between them are fuzzy at best. For example, political systems and economic systems tend to go hand in hand. In other words, a liberal political system tends to coexist with a market economy; a restrictive political system tends to be associated with a command economy. This positive relationship extends also to liberal political systems and economic development. (Indeed, according to Milton Friedman, the democratic political system is conducive to economic growth because it fosters and protects personal economic freedoms such as free markets and property rights.[14] Seymour Lipset stated that there is a positive relationship between prosperity and the propensity to be democratic.[15] Finally, Robert Barro found that when the level of political rights is low, an expansion of those rights increases economic growth.[16])

Economic Features

Extroverted countries tend to have a higher income per capita than introverted states. This implies that their populations can buy more goods and services and can enjoy a higher standard of living. Despite David Morawetz's contention that the relationship between income per capita and the satisfaction of basic needs is not necessarily positive, there is little doubt that a difference in standards of living exists between countries with $20,000 and those with $200 annual income per capita.[17]

Among the many repercussions of high income is the potential for governments to use redistributive fiscal policy to provide goods and services. The funds for such expenditures are raised primarily through taxation (as consumers, producers, savers, and investors are taxed and their income is transferred into government coffers). The higher the national income, the higher the taxable income, and, therefore, the higher the tax revenue of the government. Introverted countries tend to have lower income per capita, and therefore they have lower revenue-generating capacity and a lower capacity to fund a wide range of programs for their populations.

Extroverted countries tend to have highly developed economies. In other words, the structural transformation of their economies has advanced to the point where they derive most of their national income from services and, to a lesser degree, manufacturing. The agricultural sector, while usually producing sufficient output to satisfy domestic demand, is insignificant as a contributor to national income and even less as a source of employment. In this sense, extroverted countries are mature, or even postmature, economies. In contrast, introverted countries have middle or low levels of income per capita. Their economies are based on agriculture and manufacturing, in which the production methods do not reflect state of the art technology. Economic development is a major focus and concern of their governments since their economies have yet to be propelled into sustained long-term growth.

Economic development of extroverted countries tends to be spatially diffused across their territory. A multitude of urban concentrations ensure that infrastructure is not localized solely in one city. As a result, differences in economic performance and potential between the capital and the countryside are not as marked as they are in introverted states where a single urban concentration usually houses the economic, administrative, political, and social elite. Rural areas and smaller cities lack the infrastructure to participate in the urban economy. In these countries, the "urban bias" described by Michael Lipton some three decades ago has yet to be reversed.[18]

Extroverted countries are market economies. While they may resort to minor government intervention in the form of pricing, regulation, management and ownership, on the whole, the role of the state in the economy tends to be limited. Unlike introverted countries, the economies of extroverted states are not characterized by central planning and price fixing. Instead, their product, labor, and money markets overwhelmingly reflect freely fluctuating prices in response to supply and demand. In introverted countries, on the other hand, the state tends to play a major role in the economy. Not only does it own and administer a larger segment of the economy, but its bureaucracy tends to be more pervasive in the economic activities of lower level, small producers. Both consumers and producers tend to have limited sovereignty.

Possibly the clearest economic difference between extroverted and introverted countries lies in the extent of their participation in the global economy. The former participate vigorously, since they derive benefit from such participation. They strive to maximize their role in the international economic community and to place themselves at the forefront of the globalization wave. They are enthusiastic proponents of trade, financial, and resource flows across boundaries. Introverted countries, on the other hand, approach the global economy with apprehension.[19] As participants with limited resources, they do not exert as much economic clout as their extroverted competitors. As less advantaged participants, they bear costs that, in the short term at least, seem to outweigh the benefits. As a result, they do not take the "international bull by the horns," so to speak, but attempt to control the extent and nature of their international transactions.

Political Features

Extroverted countries are politically mature democracies. They have multiparty political systems and they hold regular elections to ensure adequate representation of the population. Leaders cater to the electorate and are sensitive to the demands and needs of the population. The constitution and legislation reflect those demands and needs. All of these characteristics of democracies have led Alex Inkeles to say that in democratic systems, people have more freedom "to influence the course of public events, express themselves and realize their individual human potential."[20] By contrast, introverted countries tend to have fledgling democracies at best, and usually authoritarian regimes. They may hold elections, but these are rarely sufficiently regular that the electorate can count on them to displace undesirable leaders. All too often, these elections are rigged, unfair, and underrepresentative of the population at large. Introverted countries may have multiparty systems in theory, but they often have one dominant party that enjoys the favors of the media, effectively ensuring its monopoly in the political arena. Leaders are often personality figures, creating cults in their wake. They enjoy vast powers, they demand unquestioning allegiance from their bureaucracy, and they generously compensate loyalty. In the political culture, democratic institutions and practices are underrepresented. The description of authoritarian and repressive regimes by Uruguayan writer Eduardo Galeano applies to introverted states worldwide: "democracy is afraid of remembering and language is afraid of speaking."[21]

The political institutions described above are based on political values that dominate in society. In extroverted countries, political values and political culture are said to be liberal, emanating from the Western tradition. These liberal values include respect for freedom of individuals and human rights. The Western governments' secular tradition of toleration, moderation, and compromise is reflected in the dominant culture. Constitutions reflect respect for individuals, and subsequent laws reinforce it. In most democracies, the rights of individuals are protected, irrespective of gender, race, religion, and the like. Democracies tend to extend this right outside their borders, as exemplified by the rights given to immigrants and asylum seekers. The political values that democracies advocate (such as human rights, minority rights, and personal freedom) are said to be universally valid. All Western democracies have accepted the prescribed international norms of human rights, and adherence to these universal values is ensured by signatures on international covenants of rights. Moreover, noncompliance with respect to those norms of behavior leads to punitive measures (for example, China's violation of human rights led its delayed acceptance into the WTO). By contrast, introverted countries do not share what they have come to call Western values. Their leaders claim that they and their populations march to a different drummer. They claim that concepts of freedom, equal representation, and participation are foreign to their cultures and outside of their traditions. This rejection of Western ideals and goals led to the promulgation of Asian values, the resurgence of Confucian thinking, and other efforts to differentiate oneself from Western values (Singapore, under the rule of Lee Kuan Yu, has led in this effort).

While extroverted countries may well be multi-ethnic, they are also integrationist, and the role of the nation is reduced to a minimum in the political arena. Indeed, the importance of ethnicity (race, religion or language) and the nationalist sentiment in political affairs that it engenders is not overt in extroverted countries. This is clearly visible by the rare existence and low popularity of ethnic parties. What are these parties? Party systems, according to Donald Horowitz, may be ethnic (such as in the Sudan, Sri Lanka, Kenya and Nigeria), multiethnic (such as in the United States, Italy, Philippines, etc.), or nonethnic (the vast majority of countries fall in this range).[22] In extroverted states, parties tend to be multiethnic or nonethnic. However, in introverted countries, ethnic parties reflect the countries' vertical split of the population along rigid tribal, religious, or ethnic lines. In such a system, members of ethnic groups vote for leaders from their own ethnic group; thus ethnic loyalties take precedence over economic, regional, and social considerations.[23] As a result of the importance of ethnicity and the way in which the political system allows nationalism to flourish, introverted countries have significantly more interethnic conflict than extroverted countries. Indeed, in many introverted countries, interethnic conflict is the natural, equilibrium state.

While most countries in the twenty-first century have universal suffrage, it is the extroverted states that have had it for longer and applied it more seriously. Universal suffrage enables participation in the electoral system to all and grants power to minorities of all kinds to pursue their interests in the political arena. When minority groups can vote and mobilize to express their demands as a cohesive electoral block, the benefits of direct democracy are clearly visible to them. Their political power is underscored by their participation in mainstream politics since they often get courted by competing politicians. In Israel, for example, after the Israeli Arab community began to shift its vote from the Rakah (the pro-Arab communist party) to the mainstream, then all parties, including Labor and Likud, began competing for their votes.[24] Similarly, in the United States, the courting of minorities was evident in the presidential campaign of 2000, as commentators proclaimed "Whoever wins the votes of the new immigrants will win political power in America."[25] Such empowerment of minorities in societies with universal suffrage is not possible in countries that lack regular elections and voter representation, as is often the case in introverted countries. There, even when rules of universal suffrage are respected in theory, in practice, large segments of the population are prevented from exerting their political rights.

Extroverted states are sufficiently mature and self-confident to relax about their sovereignty. Their institutions are strong enough to ensure their longevity, the threats they face are unlikely to topple them, and they can operate without a constant show of support. While institutions are strong, the role of the state as a provider of financial, economic, and legal infrastructure increases.[26] Many liberal democracies are willing to give up some of their sovereignty in exchange for benefits that accrue with suprastate unions. Such unions indicate that state boundaries are no longer deemed as important as they once were.[27] Indeed, monetary unions, common employment policies, and shared political goals undermine independence in domestic monetary and fiscal policies. Such integration and union is accomplished more easily among liberal democracies because they share a political culture.[28] As a result, we can call extroverted states post-Westphalian states. Indeed, while the Peace of Westphalia (1648) set the precedent for international law insofar as it established the rights of states to sovereignty over a defined territory; some states today are willing to compromise those rights.[29] They are, in the words of Walter Mattli, trading soverignty for prosperity.[30] This has led Camilleri and Falk to claim "the end of soverignty."[31] Their view is shared by numerous scholars in the late twentieth century, as indicated by the titles of their books: Sassen's *Losing Control? Sovereignty in an Age of Globalization* and "Beyond Sovereignty: De Facto Transnationalism in Immigration Policy," Ruggie's *Multilaterism Matters*, Rosenau and Czempiel's *Governance Without Government*, and Smith, Solinger and Topik's *States and Sovereignty in the Global Economy* are a case in point.[32] However, introverted countries have a different view on this subject. There, issues of state territory, boundary, and sovereignty are very important. As many are relatively new states with new institutions, they lack confidence in their ability to ensure longevity. As a result, they turn to ideologies, such as nationalism, to sustain themselves. They fear the loss of sovereignty over their territories and they take steps to protect it. They are suspicious of unions or collaborations that give up decision making and control to outside political and economic bodies.

Social features. In the post-World War II period, development economists viewed modernization as the panacea for Third World problems. "Becoming Modern" was more than the title of a book by Inkeles and Smith, it was the prevailing mantra.[33] By the turn of the new millennium, becoming modern, with its emphasis on industrialization, was no longer sufficient to achieve and maintain a leading place in the global economy. It was now necessary to move beyond mere modern; it was now necessary to become postmodern, or global. Extroverted states have made that leap, they have moved into the post-modern or global mindset. Introverted states are still pursuing modernity in the old fashioned sense of the word.

Postmodern, extroverted states are integrated into the world economy, and, therefore, their populations tend to be more global in their outlook, more appreciative of diversity, and more tolerant in their interactions with others. They are aware of the world around them, and they eagerly participate in it. Individuals across extroverted societies tend to share consumer preferences and recognize the same incentives. While it has become cliché to say that they listen to the same music, watch the same films, and eat the same fast food, it is nevertheless true, especially among the youth. Robert Holton reviewed the literature on the social and cultural effects of globalization and found that one of the effects is homogenization, referred to also as Coca-colonization or McDonaldization.[34] Extroverted countries have experienced partial cultural homogenization, despite continued resistance (such as by French leaders). While tendencies for cultural homogenization are also witnessed in introverted states, there is significantly more domestic resistance to them (such as the ban on cell phones in Morocco). There, allegiance and loyalty to universal goals and internationalism does not exist. Rather, small-minded ideals are more common, the radius of trust is limited to ethnic kin, and, often, even religious leaders warn against the cultural penetration of foreign ways.

Openness and awareness follow from education and literacy. Extroverted states have more educated and literate populations than introverted ones. Such education not only contributes directly to the capital stock of the economy, but also indirectly to the overall modernization of the population and society. Education has also been positively associated with democratization, as a more aware population has the capacity and the incentive to participate in the political process. Generally, extroverted societies will tolerate, encourage, and subsidize greater literacy and education among their populations than introverted states. As a result, their populations are more likely to adopt new ideas, be open to change, and be predisposed to new ideas.

Like education, health also contributes to society's human capital. The healthier a population, the more likely it is that its basic needs have been satisfied. Liberated from daily concerns about basic health, a population is more likely to participate in the economy and the political system. On the whole, extroverted states have healthier populations. Progress in science and technology has brought numerous diseases under control, and death from simple illnesses and unsanitary conditions has been steadily decreasing over time.

When people no longer worry about basic health issues, they can move on to other loftier concerns. So too, when people no longer worry about daily subsistence, they can specialize, exchange, and participate in wage employment. Working outside the home and outside a subsistence plot increases the range of exposure. Working for wages also increases power and control, no matter how minimal the earnings (clearly, by comparison to sharecropping or subsistence farming, any nonzero wage reflects earning power). In extroverted societies, a greater proportion of the labor force is employed in the formal sector, and more workers receive wages than in introverted states.

INDICATORS OF TIERS

The economic, political, and social characteristics of extroverted and introverted states described above are operationalized with appropriate indicators. This enables encampment host and home states, presented in chapter 1, to be classified by tier.

Economic indicators of tiers are presented in tables 2.1 and 2.2. GNP and GNP per capita, indicators of the size of economies, are presented together with their ranking among countries. For the former, the World Bank ranking was adopted, while, for the latter, the following categories were used: low income ($760 or less), lower middle income ($761-$3,030), upper middle income ($3,031-$9,360) and high income ($9,361 and more). The indicator used to assess the level of development is the percent of national income derived from agriculture (the lower that percentage, the greater the structural transformation of the economy and, therefore, the higher the level of development). Diffusion of that development across the country is measured by the ratio of the biggest urban concentration (usually the capital) to the next largest (the lower the ratio, the greater the diffusion). Two indicators of the diffusion of infrastructure throughout the country are presented: the extent of paved roads throughout the country and the consumption of electricity. The more diffused the infrastructure, the greater the development. Two indicators of government involvement in the economy are presented: the burden of regulation and the protection of property

Table 2.1.   Economic Characteristics of Host States

Host State	E1 GNP (ranking)	E2 GNP/P (ranking)	E3 Devel. (% GNP agri.)	E4 Diffu- sion cities	E5 Infras. roads	E6 Infras. Elect. cons.	E7 Regu- lation	E8 Pro. Rights	E9 Global Links X as % GNP
Algeria	46.5 (50)	1,550 LM	12	3.6	69	692	NA	NA	20-29
Australia	380.6 (14)	20,300 H	3	1.2	39	9,706	3.9	6.4	10-19
Azerbaijan	3.9 (125)	490 L	19	5.9	94	2,284	NA	NA	<10
Burundi	0.9 (173)	140 L	49	2.9	7	25	NA	NA	20-29
Canada	612.2 (9)	20,020 H	3	1.6	35	17,047	3.6	6.1	20-29
Congo	5.3 (108)	110 L	58	5.5	NA	108	NA	NA	20-29
Costa Rica	9.8 (85)	2,780 LM	14	1	17	1,422	2.7	4.8	10-19
Cyprus		6,828 (1990) NA	4	1.3	57	3,319	NA	NA	20-29
Czech Rep.	51.8 (48)	5,040 UM	5	3.1	13	5,656	3.5	3.8	>50
Hong Kong	158.3 (24)	23,670 H	0	1	100	5,549	5.2	6.4	>50
India	421.3 (11)	430 L	25	1.3	50	448	2.8	4.7	10-19
Iran	109.6 (33)	1,770 LM	18	3.4	59	1,190	NA	NA	10-19
Israel	95.2 (36)	15,940 H	2	1.6 (g 1.8)	100	5,211	3.3	6.2	30-39
Jordan	6.9 (100)	1,520 LM	3	2.8	100	1,045	3.8	5.2	30-39
Lebanon	15.0 77)	3,560 UM	12	7.9	95	1,852	NA	NA	30-39
Mexico	380.9 (13)	3,970 UM	5	6.1	36	1,646	3.2	4.2	10-19
New Zealand	55.8 (46)	14,700 H	8	1.1	73	9,653	4.3	6.4	30-39
Pakistan	63.2 (44)	480 L	25	1.8	55	441	NA	NA	10-19
Papua N.G.	4.1 (120)	890 LM	28	1	6	416	NA	NA	30-39
Russian Fed.	337.9 (16)	2,300 LM	9	2.0	79	5,661	3.5	2.6	10-19
Somalia	.1 (1990)	210 (1990) L	65	12	NA	29	NA	NA	10-19
South Africa	119.0 (32)	2,880 LM	4	1.2	33	3,992	3.5	5.6	20-29

Table 2.1. Economic Characteristics of Host States (continued)

Host State	E1 GNP (ranking)	E2 GNP/P (ranking)	E3 Devel. (% GNP agri.)	E4 Diffusion cities	E5 Infras. roads	E6 Infras. Elect. cons.	E7 Regulation	E8 Prop. Rights	E9 Global Links X as % GNP
Sri Lanka	15.2 (76)	810 L	22	3.4	11	268	NA	NA	30-39
Sudan	Na	891 (1990) L	42	1.3	36	50	NA	NA	<10
Tanzania	6.7 (101)	210 L	46	6.5	4	58	NA	NA	20-29
Thailand	134.4 (29)	2,200 LM	11	21.3	NA	1,447	3.5	4.7	30-39
Turkey	200.5 (22)	3,160 UM	15	2.6	23	1,332	3.4	4.9	20-29
Uganda	6.7 (102)	320 L	43	1	8	34	NA	NA	20-29
United States	7921.3 (1)	29,340 H	2	2.1	91	12,663	3.6	6.4	20-29

Note: GNP refers to billions of 1998 U.S. dollars; GNP per capita refers to 1998; WB refers to the World Bank classification of states into low income (L), low middle income (LM), upper middle income (UM), and high income (H); composition of output refers to 1998; diffusion-cities refers to the ratio of capital city to next largest city; electricity consumption refers to 1995 per capita consumption in kilowats per hour; paved roads refers to the percent of roads that are paved; global trade links refers to 1991.
Source: World Bank, *World Bank Development Report 1999/2000*, tables 1, 12; Encyclopedia Britannica, *Book of the Year 1999*, Nations of the World (various country pages), Comparative Statistics (762, 820, and 826); UNDP, *Human Development Report 1999*, tables 6, 11, 30; World Economic Forum, *The Global Competitiveness Report 2000*, tables 3.01 and 3.11; John Allen, *Student Atlas of World Politics*, 4th edition, no city: Dushkin/McGraw Hill, 2000, 58.

rights. These values are presented in the form of scores (from one to seven) developed by the World Economic Forum. The higher the score, the less pervasive burdensome administrative regulations are and the more property rights are clearly delineated and protected by law. Both regulation and property rights are indicators of a competitive economic environment. Finally, the degree of participation in the global economy is assessed by the percent of GNP that is derived from exports. The greater this number, the more integrated a country is in the global economy.

Political indicators of tiers are presented in tables 2.3 and 2.4. Evidence of democracy is assessed by regular elections and a multiparty system.[35] Further evidence of democratic institutions as well as democratic values is indicated by political rights and civil

Table 2.2. Economic Characteristics of Home States

Host State	E1 GNP (ranking)	E2 GNP/P (ranking)	E3 Devel. (%Y agri.)	E4 Diffusion cities	E5 Infras. roads	E6 Infras. Elect. consumption	E7 Regulation	E8 Prop. Rights	E9 Global Links
Afghanistan	0.4 (1981) NA	250 (1981) L	49	2.9	13	38	NA	NA	10-19
Armenia	1.8 (156)	480 L	41	10.4	97	1,535	NA	NA	<10
China (Tibet)	928.9 (7)	750 LM	18	1.1	90	839	2.5	3.7	10-19
Eritrea	0.8 (176)	200 L	9	1	21	Na	NA	NA	10-19
Guatemala	17.7 (72)	1,640 LM	21	2.7	28	304	NA	NA	10-19
Indonesia	138.5 (28)	680 L	16	3.3	47	348	3.2	3.7	20-29
Iraq	NA	NA	35	6.6	86	1,443	NA	NA	10-19
Morocco	34.8 (56)	1,250 LM	16	1.0	50	480	NA	NA	20-29
Myanmar	NA	NA	59	8.0	12	84	NA	NA	<10
Nicaragua	1.9 (1997) NA	410 L	34	7.0	10	412	NA	NA	20-29
Rwanda	1.9 (155)	NA	6	1	10	34	NA	NA	20-29
Vietnam	25.6 (60)	330 L	26	2.0	26	201	3.1	3.8	10-19

Note: See table 2.1.
Source: See table 2.1

liberties. The values for these were taken from the Freedom House, which ranks political rights and civil liberties in countries across the globe by 1 through 7 (where 1 represents the greatest degree of freedom). In tables 2.3 and 2.4, these values of democratic freedoms were presented as Yes (1, 2), No (6, 7) or Middle (3, 4, 5). In the international arena, the extension of democratic rights is assessed by the willingness to extend rights to those from outside of one's territorial jurisdiction (an indicator of the acceptance and adherence to the protection of universal human rights is indicated by a country's acceptance of, for example, the United Nations 1951 Convention on Refugees and the 1967 Protocol Re-

Table 2.3. Political Characteristics of Host States

Host State	P1 Reg. elect.	P2 Multi- party	P3 Politic. rights	P4 Civil Libert.	P5 Uni. valu.	P6 Ethn. part.	P7 Eth. conf.	P8 Imp. Bord.
Algeria	N	Y	N	M	Y	Y	Y	24
Australia	Y	Y	Y	Y	Y	N	N	23
Azerbaijan	N	Y-	N	M	Y	Y	Y	19
Burundi	N	N	N	N	Y	Y	Y	19
Canada	Y	Y	Y	Y	Y	N	N	23
Congo	N	Y	N	N	Y	Y	Y	20
Costa Rica	Y	Y	Y	Y	Y	N	N	21
Cyprus	Y	Y	Y	Y	Y	Y	Y	22
Cz. Rep.	Y	Y	Y	Y	Y	N	N	19
Ho. Ko.	N	Y-	M	M	Y	N	N	7
India	Y	Y	Y	M	N	Y	Y	21
Iran	Y	Y	N	N	N	Y	N	19
Israel	Y	Y	Y	M	Y	Y	Y	20
Jordan	Y-	Y-	M	M	N	N	N	21
Lebanon	N	Y-	N	M	N	Y	Y	20
Mexico	Y-	Y	M	M	N	N	N	23
N. Zealand	Y	Y	Y	Y	Y	N	N	23
Pakistan	Y	Y	M	M	N	Y	N	22
Pap. N.G.	Y	Y	Y	M	Y	Y	Y	23
Rus. Fed.	Y	Y	M	M	Y	Y	Y	20
Somalia	N	Y	N	N	N	Y	Y	22
S. Africa	Y	Y	Y	Y	Y	Y	N	20
Sri Lanka	Y	Y	M	M	N	Y	Y	22
Sudan	N	N	N	N	Y	Y	N	23
Tanzania	Y-	Y-	M	M	Y	Y	N	22
Thailand	Y	Y	Y	M	N	Y	N	21
Turkey	Y	Y	M	M	Y	Y	Y	22
Uganda	Y-	Y-	M	M	Y	Y	Y	22
United States	Y	Y	Y	Y	Y	N	N	24

Note: Y- refers to political rights and civil liberties that exist in theory but in reality there is a crackdown on the opposition or rigged elections or cancelled elections or unfair elections or an elected parliament but not monarchy (as in Jordan) or single dominant party (as in Tanzania and Uganda).
Source: Freedom House, Freedom in the World 1998-1999, 554-55; U.S. Committee for Refugees, World Refugee Survey 2000, 9; Encyclopedia Britannica, Book of the year 1999, 750-55,

lating to the Status of Refugees).[36] The importance of ethnicity and the existence of nationalism is assessed by ethnic parties within the political array of electoral choices. The degree to which this nationalism is divisive in multiethnic states is assessed by interethnic conflict and measured by an excess of 1000 casualties to violence (this can include interreligious conflict also, in order to

Table 2.4.   Political Characteristics of Home States

Home Country	P1 Reg. elect.	P2 Multi- party	P3 Politic. rights	P4 Civil Libert.	P5 Uni. valu.	P6 Ethn. part.	P7 Eth. conf.	P8 Imp. Bord.
Afghanistan	N	N	N	N	N	Y	Y	18
Armenia	Y	Y	M	M	Y	Y	Y	18
China (Tibet)	N	N	N	N	Y	N	Y	23
Eritrea	N	Y-	N	M	N	N	Y	19
Guatemala	Y-	Y	M	M	Y	N	Y	21
Indonesia	N	Y-	N	M	N	Y	Y	23
Iraq	N	N	N	N	N	N	Y	21
Morocco	N	Y-	M	M	Y	N	Y	21
Myanmar	N	N	N	N	N	N	Y	20
Nicaragua	Y	Y	Y	M	N	Y	Y	21
Rwanda	N	N	N	N	Y	Y	Y	19
Vietnam	N	Y-	N	N	N	N	N	21

Note: See table 2.3
Source: See table 2.3

accommodate countries, such as India and Algeria, in which religion is the chief distinguishing feature). The importance of sovereignty, as well as the degree to which leaders are willing to compromise it, is indicated by membership in international unions and regional economic alliances that necessitate cooperation in policies and goals. The associations include UN organs and affiliated intergovernmental organizations, Commonwealth of Nations, regional multipurposes (such as OAS) and economics (including OPEC and EEC).[37]

Social indicators of tiers are presented in tables 2.5 and 2.6. Literacy rates indicate the level of education, while life expectancy indicates the overall health conditions. The higher the literacy and the better the overall health of the population, the greater the modernization of the state. Two additional indicators of modernization are presented: television viewing and the use of cellular telephones (both positively associated with integration into the domestic and possibly even international society).[38] Finally, activity rates are an indicator of the extent to which people interact with formal institutions outside the home.

None of the above indicators, on their own, provide the necessary or sufficient conditions to place a country in one tier rather than an-

Table 2.5.   Social Characteristics of Host States

Host State	S1 Literacy	S2 Life Expect.	S3 TV[39]	S4 Cell Phones	S5 Activity Rates
Algeria	61.6	67	67	0.2	23.6
Australia	99.5	78	638	128	49.9
Azerbaijan	97.3	70	211	0.8	36.2
Burundi	87.8	46	10	0.1	52.2
Canada	99.6	78	708	88	50.4
Congo	77.3	49	43	Ins.	36.1
Costa Rica	94.8	76	403	5.6	36.9
Cyprus	95.2	75	143	61	47.0
Czech Republic	100	74	447	4.7	51.5
H.K. Chin	92.2	76	412	129	50.8
India	52.0	59	69	0.1	37.5
Iran	72.1	66	148	0.2	26.4
Israel	95.6	78	321	54	37.9
Jordan	86.6	68	43	2.6	22.2
Lebanon	92.4	70	354	30	26.5
Mexico	89.6	72	251	7.0	39.4
New Zealand	100	72	501	108	48.7
Pakistan	37.8	58	65	0.3	27.9
Papua N. G.	72.2	56	24	Ins.	24.6
Russian Fed.	98.0	67	390	0.6	49.8
Somalia	24.0	47	13	Ins.	40.9
South Africa	81.8	58	125	13	37.5
Sri Lanka	90.2	72	91	3.0	40.5
Sudan	46.1	51	76	Ins.	35.1
Tanzania	67.6	47	21	0.1	46.0
Thailand	93.8	67	234	18	55.5
Turkey	82.3	68	286	7.1	37.1
Uganda	61.8	40	26	0.1	43.6
United States	95.5	76	847	128	50.1

Note: Life expectancy refers to males; TV refers to television sets per 1000 people; cell phones refers to subscriptions per 1000 persons in 1995; Ins. refers to insignificant number.
Source: World Bank, *Development Report 1999/2000*, table 19; Encyclopedia Britannica, *Book of the Year 1999*, 778, 790, 832, 880; Freedom House, *Freedom in the World 1998–1999*, various country reports.

other. Nor do all manifestations of extroversion and introversion occur simultaneously. It is only when a large number of the indicators consistently point to a given tier that placement of that country is justified. Given this imprecision inherent in the process of selection, the lines of demarcation between tier one and tier two are murky.

Moreover, countries are dynamic, and their economic, political, and social characteristics are constantly in flux. As a result, their

Table 2.6.   Social Characteristics of Home States

Host State	S1 Literacy	S2 Life Expect.	S3 TV	S4 Cell Phones	S5 Activity Rates
Afghanistan	31.5	46	10	Ins.	30.3
Armenia	98.8	73	218	Ins.	43.1
China (Tibet)	81.5	71	270	3.0	57.9
Eritrea	20.0	54	11	Ins.	NA
Guatemala	55.6	65	126	2.8	33.5
Indonesia	83.8	62	134	1.1	42.9
Iraq	58.0	59	74	Ins.	24.7
Morocco	43.7	72	160	0.1	29.3
Myanmar	83.1	61	7	0.04	40.2
Nicaragua	65.7	63	190	1.1	35.2
Rwanda	60.5	43	2	Ins.	50.2
Vietnam	93.7	67	180	0.3	47.4

Note: See table 2.5.
Source: See table 2.5.

placement within a given tier is neither fixed nor immutable (as illustrated by formerly low income countries such as Brazil, Gabon, Malaysia, Mexico, and South Korea that are presently in the upper middle income group, as well as Singapore and Hong Kong that have moved into the high income category [surpassing Australia, Italy, Canada, and the United Kingdom].

HOME AND HOST STATES BY TIERS

The data provided in the tables above enable a comparative view of home and host states, their economies, their political systems, and their societies. In order to operationalize the data in those tables, a score (ranging from 0 to 3) is assigned to each variable. The sum of these scores by country enables its classification by tier. In other words, by assigning a score to each economic, political, and social indicator, adding each country's score, and ranking countries by their scores, we can group countries into tiers. Table 2.7 explains the scores assigned to various indicators while table 2.8 shows the scores assigned to each country.

Table 2.7. Scores Assigned to Economic, Political, and Social Indicators

	Indicator	Score=0	Score=1	Score=2	Score=3
E1	GNP	>90	51-90	21-50	<20
E2	GNP/P	L	LM	UM	H
E3	% GNP in Agri.	>40	39-25	24-6	<5
E4	Cities	>7.6	5.1-7.5	2.6-5	<2.5
E5	Roads	<40	41-60	61-80	>80
E6	Electricity	<1000	1001-5000	5001-8000	>8000
E7	Regulation	<2	2.1-4	4.1-6	>6.1
E8	Property Rights	<2	2.1-4	4.1-6	>6.1
E9	Global Links	<10; 10-19	20-29	30-39	40-49; >50
P1	Elections	N	Y-	Y	
P2	Multiparty	N	Y-	Y	
P3	Political Rights	N	M	Y	
P4	Civil Liberties	N	M	Y	
P5	Values	N	Y-	Y	
P6	Ethnic Parties	Y			N
P7	Conflict	Y			N
P8	Borders	<10	11-20	>21	
S1	Literacy	<50	51-70	71-90	91-100
S2	Life expectancy	<50	51-60	61-70	>71
S3	TV	<100	101-200	201-300	>301
S4	Cell Phones	<1	1.1-5.0	5.1-15	>16
S5	Activity Rates	<30	31-38	39-45	>46

The total score attained in table 2.8 enables the placement of countries under study into tiers (see table 2.9). Countries with a score of 20 or below are clearly introverted; countries with a score of 45 or above are clearly extroverted. Together, those groups account for 20 of the 41 countries under study. The scores of the remaining states fall between 21 and 44. They contain fragments of both tiers; they straddle both worlds. They do not lend themselves to facile classification. However, even within that group, there is a differentiation among countries. Those that have scores between 21 and 32 are classified as lower middle while scores between 33 and 43 define the upper middle tier.

Tiers and Encampments

It is proposed that the tiers of the home and host countries determine numerous aspects of the political economy of permanent encampments. Furthermore, it is proposed that encampments hosted

Table 2.8. Values of Economic, Political, and Social Indicators in Host and Home States

	E1	E2	E3	E4	E5	E6	E7	E8	E9	P1	P2	P3	P4	P5	P6	P7	P8	S1	S2	S3	S4	S5	Tot
Afghanistan	0	0	(0)	2	0	0	(0)	(0)	0	0	0	0	0	0	0	0	0	0	0	0	0	0	2
Algeria	2	1	2	2	2	0	(0)	(0)	1	0	2	0	1	2	0	0	2	—	2	0	0	0	20
Armenia	0	0	0	0	3	1	(0)	(0)	0	2	2	1	1	2	0	0	0	3	3	2	0	2	22
Australia	3	3	3	3	0	3	—	3	0	2	2	2	1	2	3	3	2	3	3	3	3	3	52
Azerbaijan	0	0	2	—	3	0	(0)	(0)	0	0	—	0	0	2	0	0	—	3	2	2	0	—	20
Burundi	0	0	0	2	0	0	(0)	(0)	0	0	0	0	2	2	0	0	—	2	0	0	0	3	11
Canada	3	3	3	3	0	3	—	3	—	2	2	2	0	2	3	3	1	3	3	3	3	3	53
China	3	—	2	3	3	0	—	—	—	0	0	0	2	2	3	0	2	3	3	2	3	3	32
Congo	0	0	0	0	(0)	0	(0)	(0)	0	0	2	0	0	2	0	0	2	2	0	0	—	—	10
Costa Rica	—	0	2	0	0	—	—	2	—	2	2	2	0	2	3	3	—	3	3	3	0	—	37
Cyprus	(2)	2	3	3	0	—	(1)	(1)	0	2	2	2	2	2	0	0	—	3	3	2	2	3	41
Czech Rep.	2	2	(2)	0	0	2	—	—	2	2	2	2	2	2	3	3	2	3	3	3	3	3	44
Eritrea	0	0	2	2	0	0	(0)	(0)	0	—	—	—	—	0	0	0	—	3	—	0	—	0	9
Guatemala	—	—	2	2	0	0	(0)	(0)	0	0	2	—	—	2	3	0	—	0	2	—	0	—	24
Hong Kong	2	3	3	(3)	3	2	2	3	3	2	2	2	—	2	3	3	2	—	(3)	3	—	3	51
India	3	0	—	3	—	0	—	2	0	0	—	0	—	0	3	3	(1)	3	—	0	3	—	23
Indonesia	2	0	2	2	—	0	—	—	0	2	2	2	—	0	0	0	2	2	2	—	0	2	22
Iran	2	—	2	2	—	—	(0)	(0)	0	0	0	0	0	0	0	0	2	—	2	0	—	—	24
Iraq	(2)	(1)	(1)	—	3	—	(0)	(0)	2	2	2	2	—	0	0	0	2	—	—	—	—	0	16
Israel	2	3	(2)	3	3	2	—	3	2	0	—	—	—	2	3	0	—	3	3	3	0	—	44
Jordan	0	—	3	3	3	—	—	2	2	2	—	0	—	0	0	3	2	2	2	3	3	0	33
Lebanon	—	2	2	0	0	—	(0)	(1)	0	—	2	—	—	0	3	0	—	3	2	0	3	2	26
Mexico	3	2	3	—	—	—	—	2	—	0	—	—	0	0	0	3	2	2	3	3	2	2	37
Morocco	—	—	2	3	0	0	(0)	(0)	0	—	2	0	—	2	3	0	2	0	3	2	2	0	23
Myanmar	0	0	0	0	0	0	(0)	(0)	—	0	2	2	—	0	3	0	—	2	2	—	0	2	10
Nicaragua	(1)	0	—	—	2	0	(0)	(1)	2	2	2	2	2	0	0	0	2	—	2	—	—	—	20
New Zeal.	2	3	(2)	3	2	3	2	3	2	2	2	2	2	2	3	3	2	3	3	3	3	3	52

Table 2.8. (continued)

Pakistan	2	0	1	3	—	(0)	(0)	0	2	2	—	—	0	0	3	2	0	1	0	0	19
Papua N.G.	0	1	—	0	0	(0)	(0)	2	2	2	—	2	2	0	0	2	2	—	0	0	18
Russia	3	1	2	3	2	—	—	0	2	2	—	2	2	0	0	—	3	2	3	3	35
Rwanda	0	0	2	0	0	(0)	(0)	0	0	0	—	0	0	0	0	—	0	0	0	0	8
Somalia	(0)	0	0	0	(0)	(0)	(0)	0	0	0	0	0	0	0	0	0	0	0	(0)	2	6
S. Africa	2	1	3	3	—	—	2	—	2	2	2	2	0	3	0	2	—	2	2	—	35
Sri Lanka	1	0	—	0	0	(0)	(1)	2	0	2	—	0	0	0	2	3	0	3	—	2	23
Sudan	0	0	0	0	0	(0)	(0)	0	0	0	0	0	0	0	0	0	0	0	0	0	7
Tanzania	0	0	—	0	—	(0)	(0)	0	0	—	0	0	0	3	—	—	0	0	0	0	18
Thailand	2	1	2	—	—	—	—	2	—	2	2	2	3	0	2	3	2	2	3	3	37
Turkey	2	2	2	2	2	—	2	2	2	—	2	0	0	2	—	2	2	—	2	—	31
Uganda	0	0	0	0	0	(0)	(0)	0	—	—	0	2	0	0	0	—	0	0	2	2	12
United States	3	3	3	3	3	—	3	2	2	2	2	3	3	3	3	3	3	3	3	3	55
Vietnam	1	0	—	3	0	—	3	1	—	0	0	2	0	2	3	2	3	2	3	3	19

Note: E1, E2, etc., stands for economic indicators presented in tables 2.1 and 2.2 in the order presented there; P1, etc., represents political indicators in the order presented in tables 2.3 and 2.4; S1, etc., stands for social indicators as presented in tables 2.5 and 2.6. Also, numbers in parentheses represent values assigned on the basis of qualitative information rather than statistics, because those are not available.

Table 2.9.   Host and Home Countries by Tier

	Host	Home
U Tier (>45)	Australia, Canada, Hong Kong, New Zealand, United States	Australia, Canada, New Zealand, United States
UM Tier (33-44)	Costa Rica, Cyprus, Czech Republic, Israel, Jordan, Mexico, Russia, South Africa, Thailand	Cyprus, Czech Republic, South Africa
LM Tier (21-32)	India, Iran, Lebanon, Sri Lanka, Turkey	Armenia, China, Guatemala, Indonesia, Morocco, Sri Lanka, Turkey
L Tier (<20)	Algeria, Azerbaijan, Burundi, Pakistan, Papua New Guinea, Somalia, Sudan, Tanzania, Uganda	Afghanistan, Congo, Eritrea, Iraq, Myanmar, Nicaragua, Rwanda, Somalia, Sudan, Vietnam

Note: States that are both home and host to encampments appear in both columns.

in democratic, market economies are better off than those hosted in authoritarian, command economies. In other words, extroverted host countries are better "hosts" than introverted host countries. In order to explore this proposal, the following three chapters focus on the formulation and elaboration of several propositions pertaining to three levels of the economy: the micro, the macrodomestic and the macrointernational levels. An additional chapter addresses the importance of nationalism in encampments.

Proposition #1: Permanent encampments located in extroverted states are better off than those in introverted states. They have more potential for developing self-reliance as well as fostering economic growth (chapter 3).

Proposition #2: Permanent encampments located in extroverted states are more integrated into the local economy than those in introverted states (chapter 4).

Proposition #3: Permanent encampments located in extroverted states have stronger links to the global economy than introverted states. This occurs through connections with international organizations and diasporas (chapter 5).

Proposition #4: Permanent encampments located in extroverted states are less prone to nationalism (both inside and outside the camps) than those in introverted states (chapter 6).

This book strives to provide theoretical and empirical evidence in support of the above proposals. An effort is made to operationalize the proposals: variables are chosen, their indicators are identified, and the nature of the hypothesized relationships is observed. However, in order to be convincing, evidence must be provided to show that encampments really are different in introverted and extroverted countries. Empirical evidence must clearly show causality. Alas, this was not possible due to the lack of comprehensive and comparable data on encampments. As a result, these propositions cannot be developed into full-fledged hypotheses to be scientifically proven. While an effort is made to address encampment issues in a systematic way, sometimes only anecdotal evidence is available. While an effort is made to challenge existing views and to offer alternative explanations, at times there is a gap between the theoretical and empirical parts of the book. Nonetheless, every effort is made to offset the data limitations by raising relevant questions that frame a general discussion, by offering commentary of historical processes, and by providing overall depth of detail. The broad nature of the material under study sometimes necessitates a reliance on possible effects and causes, rather than the actual.

Moreover, the relationships described in the above propositions are so complex and dynamic that the choice of variables to prove causality relationships is very dicey. While the complexity of the relationships precludes a monocausal explanation, an effort is nevertheless made to identify the conditions under which economic processes play themselves out in encampments, ethnic groups in camps articulate their demands, and different host country policies follow different logics. Every effort is made to approach these interlocked phenomena from an interdisciplinary standpoint.

NOTES

1. Even from the Chinese perspective, the Cold War period lent itself to an easy three-way classification: one group contained the two dominating imperialist superpower states (the United States and the Soviet Union), ringed by their smaller puppet states (another group). and, separate from them, China and its friends (yet another group).

2. Francis Fukuyama, *The End of History and the Last Man* (New York: Free Press, 1992).

3. Samuel P. Huntington, *The Clash of Civilizations and the Remaking of the World Order* (New York: Touchstone, 1997).

4. Lawrence E. Harrison and Samuel P. Huntington, eds. *Culture Matters: How Values Shape Human Progress* (New York: Basic Books, 2000).

5. Robert Kaplan, *The Coming Anarchy* (New York: Random House, 2000).

6. Kaplan, *The Coming Anarchy*, 30.

7. Zbigniew Brzezinski, *Out of Control: Global Turmoil on the Eve of the 21st Century* (New York: Scribner, 1993).

8. Thomas L. Friedman, *The Lexus and the Olive Tree* (New York: Anchor Books, 1999), xx.

9. Speech by Martin Heisler at a roundtable discussion at the annual meetings of the International Studies Association (Los Angeles, March 16, 2000).

10. Peter Slater, *Workers without Frontiers. The Impact of Globalization on International Migration* (Boulder, Colo.: Lynne Reinner, 2000), 2.

11. Yasemin Soysal, *Limits of Citizenship* (Chicago: University of Chicago Press), 1994.

12. Kaplan, *The Coming Anarchy*, 24.

13. Kaplan, *The Coming Anarchy*, 24.

14. Milton Friedman claimed that political and economic freedoms were interrelated. See Milton Friedman, *Capitalism and Freedom* (Chicago: University of Chicago Press, 1962).

15. Seymour Martin Lipset, "Some Social Requisites of Democracy: Economic Development and Political Legitimacy" *American Political Science Review* 53, (1959).

16. Robert J. Barro, *The Determinants of Economic Growth* (Cambridge, Mass.: MIT Press, 1998), xi.

17. David Morawetz's study found that the relationship between economic growth and the satisfaction of basic needs is positive only in the case of 5 out of 16 indicators of basic needs. David Morawetz, *Twenty-Five Years of Economic Development* (Washington: World Bank, 1977).

18. Michael Lipton, *Why Poor People Stay Poor* (Cambridge: Harvard University Press, 1977).

19. One example of an introverted country is Sudan, in which a military Islamic government has so isolated itself from (and, as a result of its behavior, has been isolated by) the international community to such a degree that

it gets no international aid while being one of the world's poorest countries. The IMF suspended its membership in 1993. The *Economist*, August 19, (2000) 37.

20. Alex Inkeles, ed. *On Measuring Democracy: Its Consequences and Concomitants* (New Brunswick, N.J.: Transaction, 1991), x.

21. Eduardo Galeano, *Upside Down*, cited in the *New Yorker*, January 8, 2001, 85.

22. Donald Horowitz, *Ethnic Groups in Conflict* (Berkeley: University of California Press, 1985), 302.

23. When ethnic parties exist, the size of an ethnic group is crucial in the determination of who rules. This view of the importance of size is also voiced by Olugbemi, who claims that ethnic groups believe might is right. Stephen O. Olugbemi, "The Ethnic Numbers Game in Inter-Elite Competition for Political Hegemony in Nigeria" in *Ethnicity, Culture and Identity*, ed. William C. McCready (New York: Academic Press, 1983), 266.

24. Daniel Byman, "Immoral Majorities: A First Look at a Neglected Source of Communal Conflict" paper presented at the annual meetings of the International Studies Association (Los Angeles, 2000), 25.

25. *New York Times* (March 5, 2000).

26. Friedman, *The Lexus and the Olive Tree*, 157, 163.

27. Wilson and Donnan countered the modern view that borders have become increasingly obsolete. Their research highlighted the importance of strong identities at international frontiers. Thomas M. Wilson and Hastings Donnan, "Nation, State and Identity at International Borders" in *Border Identities*, eds. Thomas M. Wilson and Hastings Donnan (Cambridge: Cambridge University Press 1998), 1.

28. Moreover, membership in suprastate unions is another way in which domestic policies toward minorities are kept in check and interethnic conflict is contained.

29. See Malcolm Shaw, *Title to Territory in Africa: International Legal Issues* (Oxford: Clarendon, 1986), 2. For a recent analysis of current changes in the Westphalian order, see James Caporaso, "Changes in the Westphalian Order: Territory, Public Authority, and Sovereignty" *International Studies Review* (Special Issue), 2, no. 2, (2000).

30. Walter Mattli, "Sovereignty Bargains in Regional Integration" *International Studies Review* (Special Issue), 2, no. 2, (2000), 162.

31. J. A. Camilleri and J. Falk, *The End of Sovereignty? The Politics of a Shrinking and Fragmenting World* (Aldershot: Edward Elgar, 1992).

32. Saskia Sassen, *Losing Control? Sovereignty in an Age of Globalization* (New York: Columbia University Press, 1996) and "Beyond Sovereignty: De Facto Transnationalism in Immigration Policy" *European Journal of Law and Immigration*, 1, (1999); John Gerard Ruggie, *Multilateralism Matters: The Theory and Praxis of an Insititutional Form* (New York: Columbia University Press, 1993); J. N. Rosenau, "Governance, Order and Change in World Politics" in *Governance Without Government: Order and Change in World Politics*, eds. J. N. Rosenau and E. O. Czempiel (New York: Cambridge University Press, 1992); and David Smith, Dorothy J. S. Solinger, and Steven C. Topik, eds., *States and Sovereignty in the Global Economy* (London: Routledge, 1999).

33. Alex Inkeles and David Horton Smith, *Becoming Modern: Individual Change in Six Developing Countries* (Cambridge, Mass.: Harvard University Press, 1974).

34. *New York Times*, November 25, 2000.

35. The others are polarization and hybridization. Robert Holton, "Globalization's Cultural Consequences" in *Dimensions of Globalization*, eds. Louis Ferleger and Jay R. Mandle (The Annals of the American Academy of Political and Social Science, 570, July 2000), 140-152.

36. In his study of the spread of democratic institutions across the globe, Richard Easterlin used two measures, one relating to the executive branch of the government and the other to the legislative (Richard A. Easterlin, "The Globalization of Human Development" cited in Ferleger and Mandle *Dimensions in Globalization*, 42). The former has to do with procedures for executive recruitment and the limits on power, while the latter relates to the effectiveness and role played by the legislature. Measurement for the former has been developed by Jaggers and Gurr (and called the measure for institutional democracy), while for the latter by Banks (and called legislative effectiveness). See Keith Jaggers and Ted Robert Gurr, "Polity III: Regime Change and Political Authority, 1800-1994" [computer file], 1995; Arthur S. Banks, *Cross-Polity Time Series Data* (Cambridge, Mass.: MIT Press, 1971) both cited in Easterlin, op. cit., 42. Only the former is reflected in the choice of indicators used for this study (insofar as regular elections, multiparty systems, and political and civil rights all reflect recruitment and limits to power).

37. These two international documents establish the legal standards for refugee protection by prohibiting signatory states from expelling or returning refugees to countries where their lives would be threatened. A country's

signature of these documents indicates willingness to conform to the international obligations.

38. The complete set of possibilities is reviewed in the Encyclopedia Britannica, *Book of the Year 1999*, 751.

39. Ownership of television sets is an underestimate of television viewing since numerous people can watch one television set.

3

THE MICROECONOMY
OF ENCAMPMENTS

As a result of media exposure, many television viewers have a vague idea of what refugee camps look like. They have seen agonizing photographs of desperate people too weak to shoo the flies off their faces, malnourished children with protruding bellies, temporary shelters inadequate for existing weather conditions, and long lines for relief handouts. Since these scenes make "great TV," they are readily broadcast.[1]

However, few people can envision an encampment that has endured years, or decades, in which only the strong have survived and the shelters are sturdy enough to endure climactic vacillations. It is useful to envision those encampments as a prelude to the study of their microeconomies.

Most permanent encampments are located on inferior land with few resources and far from adequate infrastructure. Many persist for decades on the brink of poverty and change little over time. Malnutrition and disease are rampant. Camp residents live in crowded quarters with few amenities. Yughi's description of Palestinian refugee camps could apply to many other encampments worldwide: "Housing units in the camps are crowded together in compact lines with no more than one meter separating one from the other. Some of them are enclosed by a crudely constructed wall of tin sheeting, sack cloth, brick or cement blocks to ensure a minimum of privacy. The roads leading to these houses are muddy in winter with streams of dirty water running down the middle due to lack of a proper underground sewage system . . . since most of the roads are not paved and because there is much rain in winter, the streets in the camps become mud fields. . . . Drains are mostly inadequate . . . many camps have no proper electricity networks."[2]

The fact that permanent encampments have been in existence over the long run leads to the conclusion that some minimal threshold of basic need satisfaction has been achieved. However, that is an erroneous conclusion, as illustrated by the internally displaced southerners in Sudan. They sought refuge in Khartoum, where they survived for years by making themselves cardboard and plastic shelters on wastelands or garbage dumps. They lived with no water or sewage, let alone health or educational services. What money they had they spent on the purchase of water from donkey cart vendors. The welcome they received from the government included measures such as cutting off water supplies, destroying shacks, and preventing non-Muslim relief groups from providing assistance.[3]

While the conditions illustrated by the Palestinian and Sudanese encampments are common, they are by no means universal. Economic conditions in encampments vary, and, even at the micro level, it is impossible to provide a single description. What does seem to be true is that displaced persons can and often do fight back their conditions. They make the most of their conditions and they change their conditions. Evidence of efforts at self-sufficiency among Eritrean refugees in Sudan, Tibetans in India, and Saharawis in Algeria underscore the resilience and determination people have while making the most of their situation. This human trait was described by Thomas and Wilson, who pointed out that "societies build capacities in even the most unpromising of circumstances. Indeed, part of the process of capacity-building may be driven by the necessity that arises from an adverse environment. . . . Societies make conscious efforts to build capacity in spite of their circumstances."[4]

In this chapter, attention is turned to how encampment residents build an economy under adverse conditions. The fundamental economic questions that are answered in every economic system, namely, "who gets what, when and how?" and "what is produced, how and for whom?" are addressed in this chapter. In the process, the mechanism of internal coordination within encampments is explored. The nature of the product and labor markets is observed, and the requirements for growth are assessed. Given the proposition suggested in chapter 2, namely, that encampments in extroverted countries are better off than those in extroverted states, this chapter identifies the rationale and provides support for that proposition.

AUTARKY AND DEPENDENCY; SELF-SUFFICIENCY AND SELF-RELIANCE

When displaced persons first reach shelters, there is no question of their dependency on goods and services provided by others. Indeed, they are completely dependent on logistical and financial support from home and host governments, international organizations, and their conationals in the diaspora. However, once encampments become permanent, *de facto* or by intent, the extent of their dependency on inflows of aid and the degree to which they can provide for themselves become relevant.

Permanent encampments are economic entities in which people produce, exchange, consume, and otherwise interact with each other in order to improve the quality of their lives. In the course of such interactions, the encampment economy develops a relationship with other economies. That relationship ranges from total dependency at one extreme to total autarky at the other (and includes other possibilities that lie in between). A discussion of these follows.

Encampment dependency refers to complete reliance on outside organizations, governments, or persons, with no spontaneous or organized efforts on the part of displaced persons to organize economic activity. In other words, it describes a one-way economy in which money, products, and know-how, flow only in one direction, namely, into the camp. By contrast, autarky refers to a closed economy in which camp residents have attained complete self-sufficiency in the satisfaction of all their economic needs, in the absence of outside interaction. In reality, total dependency is only a short-term phenomenon, and total autarky, to the extent that it is even feasible, is not sustainable over the long run.

However, partial dependency and partial autarky can be maintained, and, therefore, are worth exploring. While it seems meaningless to modify terms that, by definition, convey absoluteness (in other words, either one is dependent or not; either one is autarkic or not), doing so reveals a dimension that enriches the discussion.

Dependency may be separated into two categories: international dependency (namely, dependency on international organizations and the diaspora) and host dependency (namely, dependency on the host country economy and authorities). It is also useful to distinguish between primary dependency (when the encampment necessitates infusion of the most basic goods, such as food) and secondary dependency (when there is reliance on markets, infrastructure, and capital investment of the host economy). Partial dependency occurs when one or more (but not all) of the above is present.

A similar reasoning is applied to autarky. Encampments may have autarky relative to the neighboring host economy (such as those in Thailand and Hong Kong) or autarky relative to international agencies (such as Kurdish encampments in Turkey). In the short run, all refugee encampments have international dependency (camps for internally displaced persons may or may not, depending on the host government's inclination). This changes over time: the greater the camp longevity, the lower their dependency on international agencies. More often than not, while the encampment can function without infusions of aid, it cannot function in the absence of interaction with the local community. Such interaction includes jobs outside the camp, trade and exchange in the local markets, and use of neighboring infrastructure and facilities. Therefore, in the long run, international dependency is replaced by host dependency. It follows that autarky is only partial, since interaction with the local economy indicates the lack of autarky relative to the host community. There may or may not be autarky relative to the international community.

As evident from figure 3.1, partial autarky lies to the right of partial dependency, thus connoting a lower level of dependency. How does it differ from partial dependency, given that by definition both contain a mix of dependency and autarky? The answer lies in degree rather than in fundamental characteristics: partial autarky entails self-sufficiency, while partial dependency entails self-reliance. These terms are discussed below.

What does self-sufficiency mean in the context of encampments?[5] Haines formulated this question, asking whether self-sufficiency means only a reduction in aid dependency or something else, something much broader.[6] In its narrowest sense, self-sufficiency may be defined merely as the ability to satisfy encampment food needs without recourse to aid from the host government or international organizations. In a broader sense, self-sufficiency extends to non-food goods. In either sense, self-sufficiency does not mean that the encampment has no recourse to the local community, with whom it often trades and with whom it participates in a mutually beneficial exchange relationship. Indeed, it is neither feasible nor desirable to seek self-sufficiency without participation and integration into the local community. Striving for that goal predisposes the encampment

	Dependency	Partial Dependency	Partial Autarky	Autarky
Type	Primary And Secondary	Primary Or Secondary	Primary Or Secondary	Neither Primary Nor Secondary
Target	Host And International	Host Or International	Host Or International	Neither Host Nor International
Outcome	Neither Self-Reliance Nor Self-Sufficiency	Self-Reliance	Self-Sufficiency	Complete Autarky

Figure 3.1. Encampment Dependency and Autarky

for failure. (For example, the Ukwimi Mozambican Refugee Settlement, cited by international agencies as the hope for African refugees for its ability to achieve food security, was found to have failed to achieve self-sufficiency.[7])

How does a camp become self-sufficient? It must first become self-reliant. Rogge has pointed out that self-reliance must precede self-sufficiency, after self-help and self-support have been achieved.[8] Self-reliance is also described by Rolfe, Rolfe, and Harper. They define it as the phase in encampment life when "all refugee services, such as health, education and so on, become more dependent on the refugees themselves. Many of the relief agencies have gone, or the relief period has finished, leaving only a few trained workers."[9] In the effort to become self-reliant, the primary focus shifts to income generating activities that enable consumption, stimulate production and create further employment. Such activities include relief substitution (in other words, residents must begin to produce relief goods, such as blankets, previously provided by outside donors), followed by development investment, including building and maintenance of infrastructure (making roads, buildings, water supply systems), and environment (growing trees, building dams, setting up erosion walls). Rolfe, Rofle, and Harper also highlight the importance of income-adding starters (small grants or loans to start enterprises to bring in some income—not necessarily to grow later—such as chickens and small gardens). Ultimately, self-reliance includes some basic skill utilization (village crafts schemes and agricultural schemes) as well as vocational training and production.[10]

Self-reliance and ultimate self-sufficiency have become the goals of choice among policy makers and politicians. In formulating their goal for permanent encampments, international organizations chose neither dependency nor autarky; rather, they chose to create conditions for encampment self-sufficiency. This is, according to the UNHRC, one of the possible durable solutions to refugee problems.[11] John Rogge says that "once it is apparent that the refugees' sojourn will be of medium to long term duration, priority is placed upon reducing the burden upon host governments by fostering in the migrant population as high a level of self-sufficiency as is possible, in as short a time-frame as is practical."[12] Simmance also focuses on the local burden of encampments when he describes the efforts of international organizations to develop refugee self-sufficiency.[13] However, not all efforts at self-reliance and self-sufficiency are made at the donor level. There is plenty of evidence of spontaneous development efforts by refugees themselves. Hanne Christensen described such efforts by displaced persons in Somali and Pakistani camps, in which "the refugees were not solely and passively relying on support from the outside world; they were actively and energetically supplementing it with efforts to obtain more secure sources of livelihood and to achieve satisfactory living conditions."[14] Similarly, among the Saharawi encampments in Algeria, a clear effort to decrease dependency both of the encampments themselves as well as of the future state of Western Sahara to which the residents hope to return. When the Guerrilla Liberation Front, Polisario, declared, from their camps, the birth of its state (the Saharawi Arab Democratic Republic), it listed as its primary goal the decrease of its dependency on foreign agencies and aid through a focus on production, technology, and the building of human capital.[15]

It is noted that, while encampments may have the capacity to strive for self-reliance and self-sufficiency, they may chose not to. Their incentive for achieving that goal may be hampered by their assessment of the consequences. Indeed, as Rolfe, Rolfe, and Harper pointed out, "the real problems [of refugees] are political and it may be that alleviating the immediate problems makes the long-term political ones less urgent."[16] This is clearly visible in the ambivalence associated with the goal of self-sufficiency on the part of West Saharan Polisario. If their encampment economies are too successful, then international visitors will assume that the problem is settled, that they are well ensconced in their new host states, and will forget them and their cause.

In conclusion, between total dependency and total autarky lie other possibilities. Encampment economies are a melting pot of characteristics, often contradictory, sometimes seemingly mutually exclusive. Nevertheless, it is possible to identify some crucial microeconomic activities and processes, as discussed later.

THE NATURE OF THE ENCAMPMENT MICROECONOMY

Permanent encampments have transcended the focus on mere survival. Their longevity speaks for itself and conveys successful survival. They have graduated into a new phase in which the dominant question is how to sustain themselves over the long run, and even how to grow and prosper. In order to sustain themselves, encampment populations must be able to consume; in order to consume, encampment residents must have income. Assuming that international aid has largely dried up, residents must work in order to earn the income that enables consumption. Moreover, in order to consume, residents must have access to a supply of goods and services. They can either produce these or they can buy them in other markets. Therefore, consumption and production, or demand and supply, are the elementary building blocks of the encampment microeconomy. They are the basis of the product market and the labor market. They are also fundamental components of the circular flow of economic activity within the encampment.

Internal Coordination Mechanism

The internal coordination mechanism is among the most important distinguishing characteristics of economic systems. It refers to the way in which activities of households, businesses, and governments are coordinated. Dahl and Lindblom distinguish four processes for such coordination: market system, hierarchy, polyarchy, and bargaining.[17] For the purposes of this study, this list is reduced to the first two, simply called market and command systems. The former is a social process for controlling economic actions in the absence of any central direction. It is a system in which prices guide plans and an invisible hand balances the plans and desires of economic participants. A command system is one in which hierarchically structured bureaucracies make decisions and power is passed from top down. Decisions are made on the basis of budget rather than market. In discussing internal coordination mechanisms across systems, it is difficult to divorce the economics from the politics. Indeed, political methods of control and coordination often permeate into the economic sphere, and vice versa. This overflow of one into the other, or the cross-bleeding of economics and politics, is even more evident in small, isolated communities such as permanent encampments.

A permanent encampment is an economic system, albeit one that does not adhere to the definitions and rules set by comparative economic discourse, because it cuts the established boundaries of systems, borrowing, liberally, characteristics of one and another. By their nature, encampments are microcosms of artificial economic relations. They have features that are too contradictory to survive in less artificial settings (for example, the nature and degree of monopolistic behavior that is condoned in encampments would be prohibited by rules and regulations in most Western states).

In describing the internal systems of coordination that have emerged in the encampments under study,[18] it is useful once again to observe the extreme cases in order to understand the less extreme ones. If we view coordination mechanisms as lying along a spectrum, at one end there are camps in which economic coordination is entirely centralized, with a central body that decides what is to be produced and how it is to be distributed. It also decides who will work to produce the output and how much they will receive in compensation. In other words, product and labor market decisions are reached centrally, and there is no role for the price mechanism. Supply and demand play a role insofar as they are considered by the decision-making body rather than as instruments that convey information and incentives. Among the command-type encampments, the vertical flow of decision making may be headed by the host government (such as some Vietnamese camps in Hong Kong, in which economic decision making is entirely withheld from the residents. It is the Correctional Services Department that is responsible for all the coordination and management of the camps, together with an adjacent prison). Alternatively, command economies have encampment residents at the helm (for example, the Saharawi camps in Algeria are run as a single party state and a collective society.[19] They have a centrally planned economy with its own Ministry of Development that oversees production and distribution).[20] Similarly, in the Palestinian camps in Gaza and the West Bank, the mechanism of internal coordination is a vertical combination of Israeli occupation influence, coupled with Palestinian Authority economic control, finally decentralized at the local level. Given the upper level directives, local initiative for the development and exploitation of markets failed to develop.

At the other end of the spectrum are encampments with viable market economies. They have functioning product and labor markets in which prices are determined by demand and supply. They support a healthy exchange of goods and services. Such market economies are witnessed in native lands and reserves across Canada, the United States, and New Zealand. Among the Guatemalan refugees in Mexico, evidence of spontaneous efforts to establish markets was found. Residents were forced to create opportunities for land and work themselves since no one else did it for them (they also had to organize in order to secure emergency aid, negotiate their stay in Mexico, provide education, and have a dialogue about their return with the Guatemalan government).[21] In the process, some kind of coordinating structure of necessity had to emerge.[22] A similar experience was noted in Tamil encampments in Sri Lanka. Joke Schrijvers reported that the existence of the labor market enabled displaced women to work in small trade, small industries, and the informal service sector.

Irrespective of whether economic coordination is centralized or decentralized, an informal system of barter tends to emerge within encampments. In this system, exchange and trade takes place in the absence of money, as prices of goods and services are denominated in terms of other goods and services. Barter arrangements are especially popular and useful in encampments that do not use money (such as the Saharawi camps in Algeria).

The Product Market

Francis Deng et al. identified six long-term economic considerations that are relevant in managing conflict among ethnic groups.[23] To the extent that encampments are ethnic entities that require management, at least one of those considerations is relevant, namely, the individual freedom in exercising economic decisions concerning production and consumption.[24] Applied to encampments, this condition implies that residents must be able to participate in demand and supply of goods and services in their economies. Do they in reality participate, and if so, how does this participation take place?

(i) *Demand (Consumption).* In order to exercise their consumer rights, encampment residents are subject to two constraints: their purchasing capacity and the availability of consumption goods. The variety and quantity of consumer goods is directly proportional to the availability of goods in the camps or neighboring markets as well as the spending capacity of the residents.[25]

Some examples illustrate how camp residents have consumed within these constraints. In Uganda's Gulu region, permanent encampment residents go to the village market to purchase a large variety of goods. How do they have the money to do this? They sell their agricultural products at the village market and then spend their earnings on consumer goods.[26] A similar process takes place outside of agriculture. In Sri Lanka's Tamil camps, women consume in local markets the money they earned by working in neighboring small trade, small industries, and informal sector.[27] In Lebanon, Palestinian men and women encamped on the outskirts of Beirut often spend their earnings in the city, where they have earned them. By contrast, residents in Saharawi encampments find their consumptive choices limited because their labor is not compensated in currency. As their economy is not monetized, workers are not paid in money and their consumption is limited to what is available to camp residents, also not for money.

What goods do encampment residents purchase? Food continues to account for the biggest share of the consumption budget. While many rural encampments have allowances for subsistence plots and gardens that produce basic foodstuffs, these are insufficient and households are compelled to incur out-of-pocket expenditures on additional food items. Despite the purchase of supplementary food, food requirements are often not met in encampments (even in those that have highly complex economies or that produce for export. Indeed, according to the USCR, 30 percent of the Saharawi children in Algerian camps are undernourished, and 70 percent of children have anemia).[28]

To the extent that food demand is satisfied and income is left over for additional consumption, then taste factors into the consumer equation. While few studies have addressed consumption patterns among camp residents, some have offered interesting data. Bousquet found that one of the first items that Vietnamese refugees purchased from their earnings in a Hong Kong camp were suitcases.[29] Not only did they serve as storage facilities, they also had great symbolic value. Hitchcox found a high level of consumption of fish tanks (and televisions) among the Vietnamese in open camps (namely those who could work outside the camps and had potential for income generation).[30] No explanation was offered for such choices.

(ii) Supply (Production). According to the UNHCR, the first aim of long-term encampments is to produce those goods that the residents had previously received from donors. Borrowing from the concept of "import substitution," this type of production might be called relief substitution, as it's goal is to decrease dependency on outside markets and increase self-reliance. Clearly, food is the first priority, although relief substitution also includes bedding, clothing, tents, utensils, school items.

In addition to producing those priority goods, encampment residents also engage in informal activities that generate goods for sale. These include: gathering (mushrooms, honey, beeswax, wild fruits), small scale production (basket weaving, clay pots, production of mats, chairs, sewing, shoe mending), hunting (game and fish), construction (houses, granaries, schools), agro-industries (beer brewing and distilling, baking of bread), and extracting (timber, charcoal). While some of these products are produced for camp consumption, many require markets in the local communities (such interaction is discussed in chapter 4).

While such petty production may be the norm, encampments are by no means limited to it. There is also evidence of great creativity and enterpreneurship. Some camp residents have managed to exploit their positions and their conditions. They have engaged in highly sophisticated and complex economic activities that are productive as well as lucrative. The clearest example of this is the so-called "tribal gaming" associated with the United States Native population. This legalized gambling activity began first with Bingo games on Seminole land in Florida in 1979 and then spread. It was abetted by the Indian Gaming Regulatory Act of 1988, designed to promote tribal self-sufficiency and remove them from the federal dole. By 1994, more than 160 tribes were operating some form of gambling activity, with forty full-fledged casinos in twenty states.[31]

In all production activities, be they hunting/gathering or gambling, camp residents are limited by scarce resources. These include both their own capacities as well as supporting inputs. With respect to the former, their education and skills need to be considered. However, it is not just the quantity of skills that residents have, it is their appropriateness to the encampment conditions. Most encampments are rural and require familiarity with agricultural production. A French language teacher with no agricultural experience will not fare well, while those who were farmers before their displacement have a comparative advantage. With respect to the lack of supporting inputs, encampment residents are worse off than they were in their home environments. Displaced peoples lost the supporting inputs that previously contributed to their productivity. Rural residents lost their land and their livestock; urban residents lost their equipment. In addition, both rural and urban residents lost or sold their movable assets and used up all their savings in order to get to where they were going. These losses were not offset by new inputs in the encampment environment. To the contrary, production is restricted by lack of availability of supporting materials. For example, workers skilled in carpentry or tailoring often cannot use their skills because they have no equipment with which to work, they have no raw materials, and no capital. Thus, they are stripped bare and their contribution to the production process in encampments is hampered, at least in the short run. Moreover, in their study of production in Saharawi camps, Thomas and Wilson describe the disruption of textile production as a result of scarce (or unreliable) inputs.[32] Some textile workshops in Saharawi camps have no electricity, therefore they are limited to old fashioned, mechanical sewing machines.

At other times, "work was held up three to four months a year because of lack of fabric, threat and needles and for a further month
because of lack of oil for the diesel generator to power the electric
sewing machines."[33]

Clearly, constraints on production necessitate adjustments to the
production function. In encampment situations, this means more
labor-intensive production since capital is scarce and opportunity and
cost of labor is low (as discussed later).

The Labor Market

Employment did not factor into traditional views of encampments. Camps were conceived as temporary holding stations useful
only until a permanent solution could be found. Camp residents
were expected to be dependent on handouts to satisfy their basic
needs. Employment was viewed as a long-term concern while encampments, by definition, were expected to be short-term. However, persistent reality succeeded in changing those traditional
views. Indeed, since holding stations became permanent camps, and
permanent settlements for displaced peoples were set up, employment increasingly attracted attention. Camp residents want jobs because that generates income for the consumption of goods and services; host countries want encampment jobs because they decrease
their financial obligations and contributions; and international organizations want residents to work so they can withdraw their participation.

Employment in encampments is divided into formal and informal
sectors. The former includes regular work in camp enterprises or in international agencies and non-governmental organizations (NGOs). The
latter includes irregular and petty economic activities such as crafts, services, gathering, and occasional agricultural work. Both formal and informal sectors are characterized by the same labor market conditions.

The demand for camp labor tends to be low. This results from the
depressed economic activity in encampments and the subsequent
low rates of job creation. At the same time, the supply of labor is
high. Camp residents want jobs in order to earn incomes and sup-

plement their handouts. This labor market disequilibrium is further exacerbated by demographic factors that make the supply of labor grow faster than demand. New workers enter the labor force faster than jobs are created through growth and development. This occurs both because new caseloads of displaced persons are added to the old and because of the high rate of natural population growth (in Gaza, it is 5.2 percent, making it among the highest known rates of natural increase in the world).[34] Given the laggard increase in labor demand, such a birth rate puts additional pressure on the encampment labor market.

Given the above labor market conditions, most camp residents are unemployed, underemployed, or irregularly employed (this reality is reflected in unemployment statistics across host states. In Indian Country reservations across the United States, unemployment reaches up to 80 percent, despite the increase in economic activities such as motels, college, radio stations, shops and gambling.[35] Among Palestinian camp residents in Lebanon, only 6.4 percent are regularly employed).[36] The enforced idleness of unemployed camp residents is further reinforced by the nature of encampment life that entails wasted time and a lot of waiting time. Smythe notes that "time hangs heavy in many camps: one waits for food distribution, one waits for the water truck, one waits at the clinic."[37] Not only do unemployed workers lack income with which to participate in the economy but they may also become restive and, as discussed in chapter 6, become prone to criminal and destructive nationalist activity.

Since work opportunities within encampments are limited, residents turn to labor markets in neighboring communities (see chapter 4). This overflow into the host economy is most prominent in urban areas, where camp residents cannot fall back on subsistence agricultural production.

CONDITIONS FOR ENCAMPMENT GROWTH

Since permanent encampments are more than holding stations, questions pertaining to their economic future have to be addressed.

International organizations, host authorities, and camp leaders are all seeking to identify conditions conducive to growth and development. The following prerequisites for encampment economic expansion have been selected for study: appropriate human capital, technology, capital accumulation, and access to markets.

Human Capital

When involuntarily displaced peoples are forced to flee, they take little baggage. They leave behind most of their assets, including livestock, furniture, and bank accounts. As a result, their most valuable asset is the most portable one, namely their human capital (such capital is embodied in the skills, training, and education that they have accumulated in the course of their schooling and employment). In regions where the risk of displacement is historically high, investment in human capital has the highest return. As a result, the accumulation of human capital has been a goal throughout history among people who tended to be displaced often (indeed, the Jewish cultural emphasis on education can be traced to the risk associated with investment in land and other immovable property).

Economic studies have consistently shown the positive relationship between human capital and economic growth. While this relationship holds across economic systems and levels of development, the particular conditions of encampment economies (such as extreme poverty, dysfunctional markets, lack of consistent policy, and very limited resources under conditions of semiautarky and dependency) necessitate a qualification of the human capital prerequisite to economic growth. For example, it is not merely any kind of human capital that is conducive to growth of encampments. Rather, the human capital must be *appropriate* for local conditions, otherwise its productivity-enhancing properties cannot be fully exploited. In fact, not all economies, at all times, require a highly qualified labor force. As education economist Mark Blaug pointed out, countries at low levels of development derive greater economic benefits from primary education than from university education.[38] Similarly, encampment economies do not need (and cannot use) highly specialized skills.[39] While in highly developed economies, brainpower is currently more important than manpower, horsepower, and material power; in encampments, sheer physical manpower remains quintessential. To the extent that encampments seek competitive advantage in their production, it will come from things, not ideas.

In reality, the accumulation of human capital among encampment residents tends to be low. Most long-term residents were at the low end of the educational and income spectrum to begin with. Once they arrived to the camps, survival of the fittest came into play. Accordingly, displaced peoples who had skills managed to leave after a short time (or managed never even to enter). Indeed, those with education, wealth, property, friends, and family (especially abroad) rarely became permanent residents.

To the extent that educated displaced persons remain in encampments over the long run, they rarely use their skills Those with professional skills have little occasion to use them. Those who are in a new host country have obstacles to overcome before they can put their human capital to use: for example, their qualifications may not be recognized or they may not be allowed to practice their occupation without further recertification. Moreover, they have to learn the local language, customs, and laws. Those who were previously skilled in nonagricultural activities and who find themselves in rural encampments are forced to acquire new skills, such as cultivation, that they never previously needed. Those who were previously nomadic, such as the Saharawis and the Aborigines, could not use their hunting and gathering skills in settled camps. Similarly, Kurds who lived in rugged mountain terrain were resettled by the authorities in centralized villages on state lands near major population centers where their agricultural skills were wasted.[40]

Over time, displaced persons that stop using their skills experience de-skilling. In his study of de-skilling, Schrijvers focused on the process of displacement. He noted that human capital in encampments is eroded because displaced persons lost everything all of a sudden, including supporting inputs.[41] Cohen and Deng focused the de-skilling process that follows disuse.[42] They report how craftspersons often lose their tools during displacement and, upon encampment, find no use for their skills without their tools. Also, farmers who have lost their land have no use for their farming skills and do not have the ability to pass them on to their children. Evidence of de-skilling has been associated with the increasing passivity that has been identified among some encampment residents. It was found that the Vietnamese in Hong Kong had become increasingly despondent and suffered loss of initiative, in part due to the long period of time in which they were unable to work.[43] Those same reasons have been attributed by others who found an infantilization of the populations, given the loss of control of their own lives.[44]

De-skilling and the erosion of human capital represent an economic loss in terms of individual future opportunities, as well as overall economic potential of the encampment. The loss extends to the home country, should displaced people ever be repatriated; it extends to future generations who will have less to inherit; and it extends to the host country that might one day absorb them. As a result of such economic loss, the following questions must be asked: Can something be done to prevent de-skilling and to encourage appropriate skill formation? How can international organizations help encampments by enhancing the level and appropriateness of human capital in order to stimulate growth?

The following successful examples of skill-enhancing projects show that international organizations and local leaders have been addressing these questions. Among the Afghani refugees in Pakistan, a special program of assistance to skilled refugees began in 1985 by paying special attention to the skills available in the encampments (namely, the *Action International Contre la Faim*). Residents applied for and were awarded assistance for a vareity of income generating activities (in 1985, 795 people were given assistance and 1129 jobs were created that were skill specific and with the aim of maintaining those skills).[45] The Austrian Relief Committee also helped out with skill enhancement in Pakistan by training community health workers and traditional birth attendants. The Quakers went to Somalia and began a program in 1982 for the one million refugees from Ethiopia who entered Somalia in 1979–1980 alone. Their focus was on imparting skills and then enabling a few income-adding starters (especially with chickens and gardens).[46] In Saharawi camps, the Polisario leadership has made education a priority and has made great strides in primary education and adult literacy campaigns to offset the deficiency associated with illiteracy (in 1975, when Morocco invaded Western Sahara and the Saharawi population became encamped, the illiteracy rate was 99 percent).[47] The Tibetans in India have provided their encampment residents with libraries, archives, residential schools, and medical training schools,[48] and selected reservations of American Indians have created universities to offset their people's lack of skills.

While programs that emphasize skill creation and maintenance are crucial, other components of human capital should not be overlooked. These include adaptability to new conditions, the willingness to think creatively, the courage to take risks, the ability to follow instructions, and the personal freedom to respond to incentives. While the ability to adapt to new conditions and to recognize new opportunities may be important for development, in encampment conditions, it is crucial for survival. The encampment residents who have the above attributes tend to be the ones who are better able to cope with displacement.

Coping is a crucial skill in the encampment environment. Not all residents are equally endowed with it, just like not all people outside encampments are equally resourceful. The importance of coping has been underscored by the numerous examples UNHCR personnel use to motivate encampment residents. They tell success stories of residents who have used whatever means they could to procure goods for themselves and their families, to use the resources at their disposal and to make the best of a bad situation. According to the UNHCR, "to realize their basic needs and aspirations, exiled and displaced populations are usually obliged to develop a whole range of practical coping strategies. . . . When refugees buy and sell ration cards, register children several times over, split their families between a relief camp and external economic activities and set up markets around camps to trade in relief grain and other commodities, they are demonstrating qualities of resourcefulness and ingenuity."[49] There is also plenty of evidence of coping skills resulting in positive transformations of camps and residents. Krznaric reports how the experience of the Guatemalan refugees in Mexico empowered the residents, especially women.[50] Joke Sjiviers notes that the adaptability of displaced Tamil persons enabled some of them to drastically change their economic reality.[51]

Technology

Simon Kuznets has highlighted the crucial role of technological change in long-term economic growth.[52] Such technological change entails new and improved, cost-saving ways of producing old products, as well as the production of entirely new products. Sometimes, technological change results in higher output using the same quantity of inputs. More often than not, it entails labor-saving progress in which higher levels of output can be achieved with less labor (computers, mechanical threshers, automated looms, and high speed electric drills are all examples of products that are more productive than manpower).[53] Societies with abundant entrepreneurs and inventors are most likely to develop, introduce, and profit from such productive technological innovation.[54]

Is a discussion of technological change, labor saving production, and enterpreneurship relevant for encampments? Is it relevant for impoverished and de-skilled displaced peoples concentrated in remote lands amidst what are often hostile hosts? Microlevel studies of encampments repeatedly indicate that questions of technology and enterpreneurship are of the essence. In his study of technological capacity of small-scale enterprises in Zimbabwe, Wilson identified the following essential components of technological capacity building: institutional support, education and training, scope for learning by doing, and scope for enterpreneurship.[55] All of these are present in varying degrees in most permanent encampments.

Technology is relevant for encampments for several reasons. First, technological change does not necessarily entail new capital inputs and production processes. It may merely entail the adaptation of old technologies to new conditions. Encampments neither need nor can use state-of-the-art technology. The adoption and adaptation of old technology is not only adequate enough for camps, it is even prefer-able. Second, the principal input provided by international agencies and NGOs consists of improved technology and know how. As a result, attention is given to technology on a daily basis. Third, risk-taking activity is associated with technological change, and there is plenty of evidence that encampment residents take risks. Indeed, studies have shown that the loss of assets is sometimes associated with the loss of inhibitions, leading displaced people to take risks in production and exhibit creativity and entrepreneurial skills that might not have come to the surface in their home environments. In her study of Afghani refugees in Pakistan, Christensen reports "The refugees appeared to possess outstanding skills, a flair for appropri-ate technology, and training potential for handicrafts and trades. They showed a remarkable willingness to use their skills and re-sources to earn a livelihood."[56] (This observation is not universal, as indicated by an alternative assessment made of Nicaraguan refugees in Costa Rica's encampments. Pacheco describes the encampment environment as one that "discourages initiative and independent thought and action—the very same qualities that the nonrefugee immigrants must depend on to survive and prosper in their adopted lands.")[57]

Capital Accumulation

Capital accumulation includes new investments in land, machin-ery, and physical equipment. While investment in these is directly re-lated to output, investment in infrastructure (such as roads, sanita-tion, and communications) indirectly facilitates economic activity. Capital accumulation occurs when some portion of present income is saved and invested in order to augment future output and income.[58]

Like any other economic unit, encampments need capital accumu-lation. Unlike many other economic units, encampments cannot rely on savings as a source of such accumulation since their residents have no excess income. This deficiency of private savings is compensated for in two ways. Public savings and debt enable host governments to siphon funds to encampments for capital investment purposes. Also, international multilateral and bilateral flows of capital have compensated for local and domestic deficiencies and fueled the economy of numerous encampments. Most often, the external inflow of capital originates with international agencies that extend low interest loans or outright grants to selected encampments. Numerous NGOs and religious groups provide seed money for capital projects. To the extent that capital investment comes from individuals, it is from members of the diaspora that have emotional ties to encampment residents and have sympathy for their political cause (see chapter 5). Encampments are not viewed as potentially lucrative investments that might attract profit maximizers with no motivation save financial gain.

Access to Markets

In order to ensure sustained economic growth, an encampment must have access to markets both for the sale of its output and for the purchase of its inputs. In theory, encampments with sufficient domestic demand for output and domestic supply of inputs need not actively search for outside markets. In practice, no encampment can sustain long-run growth without access to external markets. To the extent that there is a "natural" market for encampments, it is the neighboring host community. Buying and selling on its markets is natural insofar as the logistical hurdles associated with exchange (such as transportation) are lowest. However, access to local host markets depends on host country policy toward encampments, as will be discussed in chapter 4.

THE MICROECONOMY OF ENCAMPMENTS IN EXTROVERTED AND INTROVERTED STATES

In chapter 2, it was proposed that encampments in extroverted states are better off than in introverted states. The above discussion of encampment microeconomies provides three reasons why that might be true. First, encampments in extroverted states can more easily achieve self-reliance and self-sufficiency. They can minimize their international dependency sooner and more effectively than in introverted states. Second, encampments in extroverted states tend to have an internal system of coordination that is based on the market. They tend to have functioning product and labor markets, and they tend to have monetized economies. Third, encampments in extroverted states are more likely to meet the requirements for growth and development. They are more likely to foster and maintain appropriate skills, adopt technological change, accumulate capital, and seek access to outside markets.

The above follow from characteristics of extroverted countries as described in chapter 2. Among these, high levels of income and development are quintessential. Indeed, a high GDP per capita tends to be accompanied by greater forward and backward linkages that affect numerous sectors and regions of the economy. Growth is diffused across towns and rural areas. Infrastructure, such as roads and electricity, is not limited to the capital and its environs. The benefits of these economic characteristics tend to spill over into the encampments. Indeed, the geographical setting of encampments in extroverted states, be it rural, suburban, or urban, tends to be more developed and, therefore, more conducive to generating income and propelling growth than in introverted states. In the latter, income levels are low and development levels are also low. Income and growth tend to be concentrated in urban areas, while the countryside, where the majority of encampments are located, tend to have little infrastructure, fewer services, and even less opportunity. Encampment residents in poor countries partake in their host country's poverty and plight.

Moreover, countries with high incomes are more likely to have fiscal policies that can sustain a transfer of money and assets to encampments via public coffers. Indeed, taxation supports numerous programs that bring education, health care, medicines, income-generating projects, and start-up grants to encampments. Countries with lower incomes have less scope for generous public programs that benefit encampments.

Also, high-income states are more likely to have surplus and redundant inputs to transfer to encampments. Technological change is so fast that outdated technology is rapidly recycled to encampments.

It would be erroneous to overlook the role played by the tier of the *home* country in assessing the potential for encampment self-reliance and economic growth. Indeed, it is in the home state, from where the displaced persons came, that determined the "baggage" that accompanied refugees. In other words, to the extent that camp residents have human capital, coping skills, initiative, and entrepreneurship abilities, these skills were formed in the home states. Extroverted home states are more likely to have invested in human capital, which turned out to be advantageous in unexpected ways (for example, highly educated refugees from the former Yugoslavia, where socialist ideology emphasized education, were at an advantage due to the skills they took in their baggage when fleeing).

Dependency Revisited

Clearly, long-run autarky is not feasible because camps are simply too small with respect to their resources and their markets to sustain themselves over time. Similarly, long-run international dependency is not feasible since international agency fatigue sets in and assistance dries up. After economic sustenance through autarky and/or international dependency have been exhausted, the logical next step is interaction with the neighboring host economy.

The nature of this interaction is discussed in chapter 4. Suffice it to say here that such interaction can lead to a new kind of dependency. When encampments pursue economic growth by participating in the outside economy, they are opening their economy and forsaking autarky goals. In production, they seek external markets for the purchase of inputs and the sale of their outputs; in consumption, they seek external markets for greater supply and variety. In the process of economic interaction in the labor, product, and money markets, encampment dependency on external economic interactions grows while its self-sufficiency decreases. Thus, a new type of dependency develops. This dependency is not for aid and handouts, but, rather, for trade and exchange. It is the secondary dependency described above, namely, the one that develops when the encampment economy becomes dependent on the local economy for its markets and its economic activities (such as in the West Bank and Gaza, where some 80 percent of trade is with Israel).[59] In this way, the development mantra of the 1960s, namely trade-not-aid, rings very true for encampments.

Over time, such dependency may develop in both directions. Local communities may come to depend on the labor resources of encampments, as well as the demand generated by camp consumers. Such a two-way dependency, based on mutually beneficial economic ties, is the foundation of a small-scale circular flow of economic activity between camps and neighboring host communities that generates economic growth and development for the entire region. A few examples illustrate this point. Mexican landlords have come to depend on the cheap source of abundant labor provided by Guatemalan refugees so much that the leaders of the Soconusco commercial agricultural empire pressure the government to retain the *status quo* when it comes to the refugees. The Ugandan population in the Gula region has come to depend on the consumptive activities of camp residents. The extent to which these successful examples can serve as universal models for camp economies is explored in chapter 4.

NOTES

1. The Goma refugee camp in the Democratic Republic of Congo across the border from Rwanda, where the Hutus fled after they exterminated some 1 million Tutsis, became a center for human suffering which, according to some cameramen, made "great TV." Philip Gourevitch, *We Wish to Inform You that Tomorrow We Will Be Killed with Our Families* (New York: Picador USA, 1999), 163. It is because the cameras were at the camp that the world saw the suffering and was prompted to do something about it. Never mind that they did nothing when those same Hutus were committing genocide against the Tutsis just some years earlier. Even humanitarian organizations felt awkward, given that these were not refugees in the traditional sense of the word, but rather fugitives since the camp leaders were war criminals. (Gourevitch, *We Wish to Inform You,* 167).

2. H. Yughi, unpublished Masters Thesis (1973), cited in Musa Samha "Camp Refugees in Jordan's East Bank: Distribution and Problems" in

Refugees A Third World Dilemma ed. John R. Rogge (Totowa, N.J.: Rowman & Littlefield, 1987), 189.

3. Millard Burr, *Khartoum's Displaced Persons: A Decade of Despair* (Issue Brief, Washington, D.C.: U.S. Committee for Refugees, 1990).

4. Angharad Thomas and Gordon Wilson, "Technological Capabilities in Textile Production in Saharawi Refugee Camps" *Journal of Refugee Studies* 9, no. 2, (1996), 182.

5. This also raises the question of how do we recognize self-sufficiency when we see it? Armstrong suggested that no encampment can be assessed for self-sufficiency until the second generation has taken over. Allen M. Armstrong, "Planned Refugee Settlements: The Case of the Misharno Rural Settlement, Western Tanzania" *Land Reform, Land Settlement and Cooperatives* 1–2, (1986), 49, cited in Richard Black and Thomas Mabwe, "Planning for Refugees in Zambia, the Settlement Approach to Food Self-Sufficiency" in *Third World Planning Review* 14, no.1 (1992), 7.

6. C. W. Haines, "The Pursuit of English and Self-sufficiency: Dilemmas in Assessing Refugee Programme Effects" *Journal of Refugee Studies* 1, nos. 3/4, (1988).

7. Richard Black and Thomas Mabwe, "Planning for Refugees in Zambia, The Settlement Approach to Food Self-Sufficiency" *Third World Planning Review*, no. 1 14, (1992), 7–12.

8. Self-help refers to encampment residents taking over much of their own needs, such as the building of huts, the clearing of land, and the development of their own services. Self-support entails a minimum level of food production. Self-reliance refers to fully supporting food production and possibly generation of income from sale of surplus food, thus requiring little need for external assistance for day to day expenses. John Rogge, "When is Self-Sufficiency Achieved? The Case of Rural Settlements in Sudan" in *Refugees, A Third World Dilemma*, 88–89.

9. They describe an option called flexible development, which includes several types of encampments: camps that are free to trade, camps that are free to trade and whose residents have freedom of movement, camps that have separate status but equal opportunities with locals (it also includes two others that are at the extreme), camps that have a totally separate existence from the host state (such as in Thailand and Hong Kong), and settlements that are completely integrated (such as in Tanzania). It is the three middle ones that have arisen in recent decades. Chris Rolfe, Clare Rolfe, and Malcolm Harper, *Refugee Enterprise, It Can Be Done* (London: Intermediate Technology Publications, 1987), 8–9.

10. Incidentally, a report by the U.S. Refugee Policy Group suggested that out of the 116 refugee settlements established during 1960 to 1980, only 9 achieved self-reliance. Twelve were closed due to repatriation. Refugee Policy Group, *Older Refugee Settlements in Africa* (Washington, D.C.: Refugee Policy Group, 1986) cited in Richard Black and Thomas Mabwe, "Planning for Refugees," 2.

11. Black and Mabwe, "Planning for Refugees."

12. John R. Rogge, "When is Self-Sufficiency Achieved?"

13. In order to reduce the burden on local communities Alan J. F. Simmance, "The Impact of Large-Scale Refugee Movement and the Role of UNHCR" in *Refugees, A Third World Dilemma*, 10.

14. Hanne Christensen, "Spontaneous Development Efforts by Rural Refugees in Somalia and Pakistan" in *Refugees, A Third World Dilemma*, 204.

15. Thomas and Wilson, "Technological Capabilities in Textile Production, 183.

16. Rolfe, Rolfe, and Harper, *Refugee Enterprise:* 125.

17. Robert A. Dahl and Charles E. Lindblom, *Politics, Economies and Welfare* (New York: Harper & Row, 1953) described in John Elliot, *Comparative Economic Systems*, 2nd edition (Belmont, Calif.: Wadsworth, 1985), 21.

18. The prevailing system of internal coordination in encampments results from both external and internal factors. In other words, it can be imposed from the outside (by host authorities or international organizations) or it can emerge from within the camp (either from the authorities or spontaneously from the population).

19. Thomas and Wilson, "Technological Capabilities in Textile Production, 195.

20. The fact that it is collective is not unusual, given the particular circumstances as well as the fact that it is at war with Morocco. Many countries in wartime have such economies.

21. Roman Krznaric, "Guatemalan Returnees and the Dilemma of Political Mobilization" *Journal of Refugee Studies* 10, no. 1, (1997), 69.

22. Indeed, while they were in exile, they formed two organizations—the Mama Maquin and the human rights organization, Opodedhgua. This is in contrast to encampments that are internally displaced and rely on their governments for aid, and, thus, are less self-sufficient.

23. Francis M. Deng, Sadikiel Kimaro, Terrence Lyons, Donald Rothchild, and I. William Zartman, *Sovereignty as Responsibility* (Washington, D.C.: Brookings Institution, 1996), 94.

24. They also include satisfying basic needs; equitable access to economic opportunities; "fair" distribution of wealth and income, domestically, regionally, and globally; protecting individual rights to property and income; and, finally, financial stability.

25. There is a contradiction with respect to aid. If aid includes clothes that come fit to be worn, then there will be little demand for local production. This problem was faced with textile production in camps in Algeria.

26. Gulu is a town in Northwest Uganda, north of Kampala. It has large number of refugee camps where Sudanese, Rwandanese, and Congolese refugees, who entered Uganda in early 1960s, are permanently settled. It is a thriving marketing center for the entire agricultural northern region.

27. It is women, rather than men, who work and make consumptive decisions in Tamil camps since most husbands and sons and fathers are engaged in the war effort. It has been very conducive to the empowerment of women in the area.

28. U.S. Committee for Refugees, *World Refugee Survey* (Washington, D.C.: Immigration and Refugee Services of America, 2000), 64

29. Gisele Bousquet, "Living in a State of Limbo: A Case Study of Vietnamese Refugees in Hong Kong Camps" in *People in Upheaval*, eds. Scott Morgan and Elizabeth Colson (New York: Center for Migration Studies, 1987), 45.

30. Linda Hitchcox, *Vietnamese Refugees in Southeast Asian Camps* (New York: St. Martin's Press, 1990), 100.

31. Not surprisingly, such activities brought the Indians in conflict with state governments that did not approve of economic activity they could not tax (and that was in competition to their own lotteries). Fergus M. Bordewich, *Killing the White Man's Indian: Reinventing Native Americans at the End of the Twentieth Century* (New York: Anchor, 1996), 107–8.

32. The others are lack of incentive (in part because of centralized control of production, design, and distribution) and lack of encouragement for experimentation in design (there are few materials with which to experiment). Thomas and Wilson, "Technological Capabilities in Textile Production," 191.

33. Thomas and Wilson, "Technological Capabilities in Textile Production, 186.

34. Donna E. Arzt, *Refugees into Citizens* (New York: Council on Foreign Relations, 1997), 41.

35. Indian Country refers to the sum total of reservations and their residents throughout the United States. Some 800,000 people live on such

reservations, at least one third of which live below the poverty line. Per capita income is often below $3500 per year. Fifty five percent of Indian children drop out of high school while only 7 percent graduate from college (less than half the rate for other Americans). While this is the overall picture, there are some reservations in which progress has unequivocally occurred. For example, Bordewich describes Pine Ridge Reservation as one in which there now is a supermarket, public housing, tribal college, and a tribal radio station. Bordewich, *Killing the White Man's Indian*, 15–16.

36. The majority of women are employed in irregular service activities in camps. Men, on the other hand, tend to be in the construction sector and small industries. Some 64 percent of total wage earners of both sexes work inside or near the encampments. Some 28 percent work outside the camp in seasonal jobs. What kind of jobs do they do? Of the 38 percent that work in institutions, 10 are with international agencies (mostly UNRWA), 14 in the private sector, and 14 with NGOs. Services absorb most workers, followed by agriculture. Leila F. Zakharia and Samia Tabari, "Health, Work Opportunities and Attitudes: A Review of Palestinian Women's Situation in Lebanon" *Journal of Refugee Studies* 10, no. 3, (1997), 419, 421–22.

37. Mabel M. Smythe, "Refugees: A Problem and Opportunity for African Economic Development" in *Refugees, A Third World Dilemma*, 62.

38. Mark Blaug, *Education and the Employment Problem in Developing Countries* (Geneva: International labor Office, 1974).

39. Even the high-growth economies such as Canada, Australia, and the United States need a wide variety of skills to satisfy the wide range of manpower demands. They often have to import low-skilled workers because the domestic economy fails to produce enough of them.

40. Bill Frelick, *The Wall of Denial: Internal Displacement in Turkey* (Washington: U.S. Committee for Refugees, 1999), 20–21.

41. Joke Schrijvers, "Fighters, Victims and Survivors: Constructions of Ethnicity, Gender and Refugeeness among Tamils in Sri Lanka" *Journal of Refugee Studies* 12, no. 3, (1999), 322–23.

42. Roberta Cohen and Francis M. Deng, *Masses in Flight* (Washington, D.C.: Brookings Institution, 1998), 25.

43. Bousquet, "Living in a State of Limbo," 35.

44. B. E. Harrell-Bond, *Imposing Aid: Emergency Assistance to Refugees* (Oxford: Oxford University Press, 1986).

45. Rolfe, Rolfe, and Harper, *Refugee Enterprise*, 17.

46. These focused on chickens and gardens, but took the entire community into account.

47. Thomas and Wilson, "Technological Capabilities in Textile Production," 187.

48. Dorsh Marie de Voe, "Keeping Refugee Status: A Tibetan Perspective" in *People in Upheaval*, eds. Scott Morgan and Elizabeth Colson (New York: Center for Migration Studies, 1987), 55.

49. UNHCR, *The State of the World's Refugees* (New York: Oxford University Press, 1995), 235.

50. Encampment entails the loss of social pressures to fulfill traditional roles. It also entails the loss of social cohesion. Encampments mix people from different communities, backgrounds, and occupations. It is thus a broadening experience. It raises levels of toleration. It comes to rely on individuals in different ways and forces them to accept roles that they did not have before. Krznaric, "Guatemalan Returnees and the Dilemma of Political Mobilization," 70.

51. Schrijvers, "Fighters, Victims and Survivors."

52. Simon Kuznets, *Economic Growth of Nations* (Cambridge, Mass.: Harvard University Press, 1971), chapter 1.

53. Indeed, labor saving technology has drastically increased worker productivity, as the average Western European today is some twenty times more productive than in 1800. The *Wall Street Journal*, December 28, 1999.

54. What conditions give rise to entrepreneurs? See Benjamin Higgins, *Economic Development* (New York:) 88–105.

55. G. A. Wilson, "Help or Hindrance: The Role of UK-Based NGOs in Building Technological Capacity in Small-Scale Development Projects" *Development in Practice* 5, no. 2, (1995) discussed in Thomas and Wilson, "Technological Capabilities in Textile Production," 183.

56. Christensen, "Spontaneous Development Efforts by Rural Refugees," 204.

57. Gilda Pacheco, *Nicaraguan Refugees in Costa Rica* (Washington: Center for Immigration Policy and Refugee Assistance, Georgetown University, 1989), 1.

58. Economists since the early 1900s have focused on the important role of capital accumulation for economic growth. The Harrod-Domar model of the 1950s formally linked economic growth to the accumulation of capital, and subsequent scholarly research has expanded and strengthened this link. According to the original model, the savings rate is crucial since it is positively related to capital accumulation, which in turn is positively related to

output (indeed, evidence from countries with high savings rates, such as Japan, show unequivocal benefit from this source of capital). (The Harrod-Domar model is named after two economists, Roy Harrod and Evesey Domar who concurrently but separately developed the theory in the 1950s).

59. The next country of importance is Jordan with a mere 2.4 percent of trade. *The New York Times* November 5, 2000.

4

ENCAMPMENTS IN THE DOMESTIC PECKING ORDER

Over time, most encampments develop economic relations with neighboring host communities. While these range from total integration (such as in Tanzania) to minor, sporadic trade activity (such as in Hong Kong), external economic interaction tends to be the norm rather than the exception among encampments. This chapter describes the nature of such interaction. It contains an analysis of host country attitudes and policies that enable or restrict economic interaction. It contains a discussion of host country institutions and regulations that determine whether displaced peoples are allowed to work, trade, own property, and make use of host social services. The political status of encampment residents is also addressed, with special focus on citizenship rights, the right of movement, and discriminatory practices.

THE ROOTS OF HOST COUNTRY ENCAMPMENT POLICIES

When faced with hoards of refugees at their borders, host governments have to make choices. Should the refugees be turned away? Should they be permitted entry, only to be resented and barely tolerated?

Should they be welcomed, possibly even absorbed and integrated into host society? The choice made by the host authorities reflects their country's immigration, manpower, and social policies (which in turn are based on the projected economic, political, and social impact of the population inflows). The choice also follows from the host country's international commitments and obligations (which are based on its adherence to international guidelines pertaining to treatment of refugees). Finally, the choice also reflects the host country's position within the community of nations. This includes its geopolitical relations with its refugees' home countries and/or its religious ties to the refugees.

The above considerations determine if refugees will be permitted to stay or will be turned away. If permitted entry, they determine whether refugees will be dispersed or concentrated within compact geographical areas. They also determine whether refugees will be integrated or quarantined. This does not imply that involuntary migrants are passive in their relationship with the host states. To the contrary, they often have strong sentiments, but given their precarious position as disempowered guests, their views are subservient to those of their hosts. Indeed, they cannot "vote with their feet" and chose the location of their residence.

The existence of encampments implies that host authorities have accepted displaced populations and have chosen to concentrate them in a single geographical location. The existence of encampments implies nothing more. It conveys no information about host country policies vis à vis involuntary migrants nor the attitude that underlies those policies. To the contrary, there is a wide range of possible attitudes toward encampments and their residents. Four of these are discussed later, including intolerance, reluctant hospitality, laissez-faire hospitality, and unconditional welcome. These four types of host sentiments may be viewed as markers along a spectrum. Active intolerance and unconditional welcome represent the least common extremes. Most encampments are met with reluctant or laissez-faire hospitality. By placing all four categories along a spectrum, the continuity is highlighted and the inability to clearly delineate boundaries of categories is underscored. It is also important to note that host country sentiments towards encampments are dynamic, changing over time in response to changing conditions and stimuli. As a result, the classification of host policies is not set in stone and countries float across categories over time (for example, when Nicaraguan refugees first began coming to Costa Rica in 1981, they were greeted with the urgency that the situation demanded: housing, food, and shelter were promptly provided. However, a decade later, after new refugees arrived and the old ones lingered, no new welcoming actions were undertaken by the authorities.[1] Saturation led to inaction. Unconditional welcome was replaced by laissez-faire hospitality, and finally by reluctant hospitality).

Intolerance

When Vietnamese boat people arrived in Singapore, they were not allowed to disembark. With little regard for international outrage, Singapore's leaders cited the precedence of domestic policies over international obligations. Such outright defiance of international norms is rare. More often, host states succumb to international pressure, accept refugees, provide them with basics, and take active steps to rapidly find other solutions (such as repatriation or third country asylum). Their underlying sentiment towards refugees is intolerance. Whether due to antipathy towards the displaced ethnic group, apprehension about the drain on their resources, or fear of political consequences, host states actively seek to close encampments and remove their populations.

Reluctant Hospitality

In contrast to Singapore's unwavering position with respect to Vietnamese refugees, authorities in Hong Kong showed greater compassion. They informed the refugees that they were not welcome and offered to replenish their supplies before they reembarked on a new journey. Those who refused were subsequently permitted entry. Such reluctant hospitality occurs when host countries accept refugees with less than enthusiasm. They provide them with basic infrastructure, condone minor economic activity, and then create such unpalatable conditions that refugees initiate their exodus. In other words, reluctant hosts attempt to place the onus (and responsibility) for "solving the encampment problem" on the camp residents. Their reluctance towards refugees translates into policy aimed at pushing (or prodding or shoving) refugees and inducing them to repatriate or to move on. Thus, when host states are reluctant in their acceptance of encampments, the displaced persons are managed, but their future is not solved.

Numerous examples illustrate reluctant hospitality. Mexico has never shown enthusiasm for its refugees from Guatemala.[2] While it allows them to remain on Mexican territory, its government authorities intentionally keep living conditions precarious. They provide only limited services in the encampments so that hunger, disease, and infant mortality rates remain high.[3] Mexico has often been criticized for this behavior and the UNHCR has cited its unaccommodating stance towards refugees as one of the main reasons why large numbers of Guatemalans returned home from Mexico.[4] In Lebanon, reluctant hospitality underlies policies pertaining to Palestinians. The goal of the government, as described by a Palestinian refugee, is to produce a voluntary exodus: "They [the Lebanese] are strangling us. All these restrictions on jobs and rebuilding the camps. *They think we will leave if our lives become unbearable* [italics mine]."[5] Lebanese officials have, in fact, often expressed the intention to expel all Palestinians; but if they left of their own volition, it would cause less international backlash.[6] Authorities in Hong Kong also took steps to make camp life unbearable and, thereby, decrease their refugee population.[7] In this respect, their policy of housing refugees in prisons was highly successful, since there was a 57 percent reduction in the number of Vietnamese arrivals within a period of less than one year.[8] Also, in the Congo, a reluctant government was seeking ways to be rid of the refugees it reluctantly accepted. A Congolese official, speaking about the hundreds of thousands of Rwandans that converged on Goma in 1994, said, "The refugee population has overwhelmed Zairian [Congolese] resources, destroyed our environment, introduced uncontrolled inflation into our market and abused our hospitality. *We want them out of here soon* [italics mine]."[9] Similarly, a Tanzanian official, upon meeting with Burundi authorities, said in 1999, "*Tanzania is now tired of living with refugees* [Emphasis added]."[10] Steps are planned for their repatriation or third country asylum.

Laissez-Faire Hospitality

In the absence of prohibitive host country policies, economic ties develop spontaneously between camps and their neighboring communities. These ties range from the minimal to the complex and develop in the labor and product markets. Left to their own devices, people inside and outside camps pursue their self-interest by producing, trading, exchanging, negotiating, managing, and otherwise interacting in a variety of economic activities. While numerous examples of such spontaneous activity can be found across the world, the Gula region in Uganda stands out as an illustration of successful establishment of complex economic ties between displaced peoples and neighboring communities.

In order for such ties to develop, host authorities must take a laissez-faire approach to the encampment's microlevel economic activities. They need not actively support such interaction with programs and financial infusions, they merely need to condone it. Laissez-faire hospitality is found in host states that recognize the positive contributions of encampments to their own economies. Such contributions include labor and skills (according to Patricia Daley, "host government policy on the incorporation of refugees may be closely associated with the demands of the labor market").[11] Sometimes, displaced persons are expected to satisfy manpower demands of the neighboring community (for example, Afghani refugees in Pakistan work as seasonal labor for local farmers, while children with small fingers are hired to weave rugs. In the Sudan, rural encampments were set up with the expectation that they would provide seasonal labor to the adjoining communities).[12] Sometimes encampments are built on land that the host authorities want to bring under cultivation. This is land that would otherwise have remained untouched. In this respect, the benefits of refugee settlements to countries such as Tanzania and Botswana have been indisputable.[13] Sometimes it is expected that cooperation between displaced persons in camps and local communities will become a conduit to economic growth. Contemporary illustrations of how economic opportunism transcends interethnic hostility are evident in Israel (where Jewish and Palestinian collaboration led to the economic revival of Ramallah,[14] and where the discovery of gas deposits off of Gaza raise the possibility of joint ventures)[15] and in the Sandzak area of Serbia (where a thriving economy resulted from cooperative production and trade among displaced Slavic Muslims, Serbs, and Muslim Kosovars).[16] Finally, sometimes host governments expect local communities to reap trickle-down benefits from international programs designed for refugees. Tristan Betts noted that such benefits lead to calls for "zonal development" of refugees together with local populations.[17]

Laissez-faire hospitality is also found in host states that recognize a political purpose is served by encampments and their residents. By embracing selected refugees, a host country supports a favored political movement (this explains Sudan's openness to refugees from Eritrea and Pakistan's towards Afghani refugees)[18] or repays a debt (this explains Uganda's reception to refugees from Rwanda; their conationals fought in President Amin's army).

Unconditional Welcome

When host governments extend an unconditional welcome to involuntary migrant groups, their support is by no means passive. To the contrary, it includes active steps in the provision of economic and political opportunities. Authorities provide resources in the form of land for encampments, goods for distribution, seed money for income generating projects, and so forth. They also provide political conditions that enable refugees to participate in the host society. These include the right to reside, work, and move about; the right to own property, borrow money in credit markets, and partake of social services; the possibility of applying for citizenship; and institutionalized protection from discrimination.

By extending such active support to incoming migrants, host authorities indicate their willingness to bear the social, political, and demographic costs of integrating displaced peoples over the long run. These are high costs indeed, and, therefore, it is rare that host governments offer unconditional welcome to displaced peoples. Indeed, they are selective, not universal, in their accommodating welcome. Sometimes selection is based on ethnicity, such as when incoming migrants are of the same ethnicity as the host majority (this was the case of the Greek Cypriots displaced by the invading Turkish army and accommodated in the Greek part of Cyprus. It was not the case of Bosnian Serb refugees who were accepted into Yugoslavia but were not extended citizenship rights). Alternatively, selection is based on political reasons. In India, Tibetan refugees have enjoyed economic and political advantages that were not extended to the Bangladeshis or Royihatans. Similarly, the Jordanian authorities have unconditionally welcomed Palestinians but not Kurdish refugees, and the Sudanese government has shown financial and political support for refugees from Eritrea, in sharp contrast to the treatment it provided to its own internally displaced populations from the south.[19]

ON THE ECONOMIC INTERACTION OF UNEQUAL ENTITIES

Economic interaction between encampments and host communities occurs when host governments offer reluctant hospitality, laissez-faire hospitality, or unconditional welcome. Whichever of these attitudes prevails, interaction takes place in the labor, product, and money markets. While the nature of these interactions is discussed later, it must be noted that they all occur within the context of inequality (as measured by wealth embodied in physical and human capital). Neighboring host communities tend to have more resources, be more developed, and have more potential for growth than encampments. Camps have a lower stock of wealth than their host communities, as well as lower inflows of resources that might offset that imbalance.

Scholars of international economics have studied the implications of regional inequality for economic interaction among spatial entities. While different terms have been given to such interaction (including uneven economic development,[20] discontinuous development,[21] relative deprivation,[22] internal colonialism,[23] and differential modernization),[24] there is overall agreement that under conditions of regional inequality, the nature of economic competition for resources is affected, as is the nature of cooperative economic interaction. In his study of uneven development across regions, Michael Hechter differentiated between relatively advanced and less advanced groups and highlighted the cleavages of interest that arise between them.[25] It is exactly such cleavages that underlie encampment-host relations in the areas of employment, trade, and finance.

Employment

In order to supplement their meager rations and subsistence production, displaced persons seek wage employment outside their encampments. The demand for such work is high, despite the obstacles faced by camp residents (including restrictive local laws, logistical constraints such as transportation, and language barriers). As a result, displaced persons usually work in temporary and irregular jobs in which they perform difficult menial tasks for long hours at low pay. There tends to be inequality between camp residents and host communities with respect to the labor market. The former experience more short-term unemployment, long-term unemployment, underemployment, and involuntary part-time employment than host populations. The incidence of discouraged workers is also higher among encampment residents. Needless to say, the slightest economic downturn affects the employment of encampment residents, as host workers hold on to jobs longer and their occupations are less susceptible to business cycle fluctuations. Numerous examples support these contentions, ranging from the Roma in the Czech Republic to the Palestinians in the Middle East (who were the first to lose their jobs during the downturn of the early 1990s and the late 1980s, respectively).

The host country labor market is a buyers market, enabling employers to set wages, dictate terms, and exercise choices. Such a buyers market developed for several reasons. First, displaced people are an abundant and a cheap source of labor. Given few alternative options and low opportunity cost of time, displaced persons are willing to accept low wages. When they flood the local labor market, overall wages tend to fall. Employers tend to opt for cheaper labor, thus favoring displaced persons over local residents. As a result, local labor is displaced when employers opt to cut costs by hiring encampment residents. The experience of the Guatemalan refugees in Mexico provides an apt illustration. When they entered the labor force in Chipas, they reduced the wages of agricultural workers, thereby increasing the profits of producers.[26] As a result, they were favored by the large landowners and the demand for their labor increased relative to that for local workers.

Second, displaced peoples have no rights and, therefore, no job tenure and no recourse in the event of disputes. Their position is precarious and their employment can be terminated at will, both by their direct superior as well as by the host government. The experience of Tutsi refugees in Uganda is a poignant example of such precarious employment. While they lived in encampments for thirty years, in the early 1980s President Obote led a xenophobic campaign against them (not all refugees, just those from Rwanda). There were mass firings of Rwandans from their jobs and some 50,000 were expelled and forcibly repatriated.[27]

Third, displaced persons rarely have adequate or appropriate skills to offer for any but the most menial jobs. As a result, they tend to be channeled into distasteful, unreliable, and dangerous occupations that no one else wants, and they perform jobs that no one else will perform (for example, Kurdish refugees in Iran are used for high-risk smuggling activities). Highly qualified displaced persons tend not to remain in camps anyway, and, even if they do, their services are rarely in demand since they are provided by outsiders (i.e., doctors, engineers, and planners tend to come from international organizations). The predominance of low-skilled work is evident among the Maoris in New Zealand, where the four fifths of the population that is urbanized works in low status occupations with low pay. Menial labor is also the norm for the Palestinian labor force. Arzt reports that "urban refugee camps, . . . which are described as 'urban slum areas,' lack an economic base independent of Israel."[28] As a result, workers from encampments in the West Bank and the Gaza strip travel to Israel for work, where they perform low-skilled jobs under poor conditions.[29]

There are exceptions to the labor market conditions described above. In rare cases, reverse employment opportunities develop so that local populations seek work from the encampments (for example, Tibetan cultivators often hire local Indian seasonal farm labor).[30] Also, camp residents sometimes provide scarce services that the local population demands. Enterpreneurship may flourish among camp residents, and business efforts may be successful. The example of Vietnamese refugees in open camps in Hong Kong is a case in point: they set up beauty shops, tailor shops, small eating establishments, a day care center, and schools.[31] In addition, some Native American reservations introduced lucrative gambling that serves the local community. Finally, Mozambiquans that settled in the Ukwimi encampment in Zambia gave more to the community than they took;[32] with international assistance, built roads, schools, health centers, training workshops, and agricultural extension services that also benefited the local community.

These exceptions indicate that the fortunes of displaced persons have changed relative to the host community. When that occurs, a new set of problems arises, not dissimilar to those that follow the consequences described earlier: the local host population begins to resent the encampments and their residents. Whether due to depressed wages, displacement, or a reversal of inequality, the competitive relationship between host and guest may become explosive. This potentially explosive nature of direct competition between newcomers and host residents is discussed by Jeannette Money in her study of immigrants.[33] Susan Olzak also recognized this problem, which in her view emerges when displaced persons penetrate into occupations previously held by the host population.[34] In his wisdom, the Dalai Lama avoided such direct competition and its consequences by restricting Tibetan bazaar activity in India so that it did not interfere with economic endeavors traditionally done by Indians.[35] Other host states introduced restrictive policies to prevent refugee incursion into host activities: before autonomy was declared in the State of Palestine, manufacturers from the Gaza strip were prevented from marketing their products outside of the strip or Israel.[36] The goal of this measure was to decrease competition with higher priced Israeli products (which would have threatened Israeli jobs).

Trade

Economic theory suggests that trade among unequal entities follows a distinct pattern. An application of this theory to camps and host communities results in the following pattern of trade: camps provide agricultural products while the more developed host communities provide manufactured goods. While such a pattern may, in fact, exist in some encampment situations, it is the exception rather than the rule. Rural encampments in Third World host countries are not significantly different from their neighboring communities with respect to the goods that they produce and the technology they use to produce them. In other words, agricultural communities produce agricultural goods, whether inside or outside the camps. Similarly, urban camps tend to produce petty goods and services, just like the neighborhoods where they are located. The difference between camp and communities lies in labor market conditions rather than the composition of their outputs.

There is ample evidence that camps and neighboring communities can have mutually beneficial trade relationships. The Vietnamese refugees in Hong Kong, who set up beauty parlors and tailors shops, and the Afghanis in Pakistan, who set up bazaars and tea shops, have all survived competition because they produce goods that people want to buy.[37] By producing goods that are demanded by both the encampment residents and host communities, these refugees are establishing patterns of specialization and exchange. They are setting up markets and participating in trade. In the process, they are earning income and reaping benefits. They are also contributing to their host country's national product (this contribution was highlighted by Black and Mabwe in their study of food exports from encampment areas).[38]

Financial Flows

Two types of financial flows take place across encampment borders: the flow of money as payment for goods and services and the one-way infusion of capital from donors.

The inflow of money that follows labor and product market transactions tends to consist of petty cash. With minor exceptions, such an inflow is insufficient in magnitude to improve individual or camp conditions in any meaningful way (exceptions include an Indian reservation in the United States where the Pequots have created the world's largest gambling complex, taking in some $1 million per day).[39] By contrast, host governments, international organizations, and other interest groups make infusions of capital and goods into some encampments. These tend to be large enough to make a difference in camp conditions (for example, the Pakistani government spent $1.2 million per day on the needs of the Afghani refugees,[40] and the United States commitment to Indians was costing taxpayers about $3 billion each year in federal appropriations).[41]

Given overall scarcity, large infusions into encampments provoke resentment among local populations. In rural regions of poor Third World countries, local communities often live in conditions no better than the displaced populations. The mere creation of the encampment is unsettling because it represents a change in "who gets what" at the micro level. Subsequent inflows of capital into encampments only add insult to injury. Sensitivity to such local sentiment has been cited by several host governments as a valid reason to withhold expenditures on encampments.[42] Indeed, the Mexican government has claimed that it cannot provide additional assistance to Guatemalan refugees because it would cause too much local resentment in Chiapas, where there is so much poverty.[43] Cleverly, the Pakistani government avoided local resentment by framing the support of Afghani refugees in a context that local communities will support, namely the jihad. Local populations tolerated infusions of capital into encampments when they were viewed as being used to fight a holy war.[44]

THE ROLE OF INSTITUTIONS

Numerous host country institutions affect encampment populations. Property rights and the social welfare system are discussed next since they are particularly relevant for camp residents.

Property Rights

Impoverishment follows the loss of property rights. This is true universally, inside and outside encampments. When Estonia denied property rights on land to Russian farmers on its newly sovereign territory (in 1991), the result was an economic marginalization of Russians; when the Indians in Fiji lost their rights to own land, they lost their only ability to generate income.[45] Under conditions of encampment, the effect of property rights loss on impoverishment is magnified. Camp residents have few options and opportunities, and the loss or denial of property rights in land, real estate, business, and any other income-generating asset affects displaced persons by reducing their present and potential future income.

For encampment residents, property rights are a lingering issue from their past and, simultaneously, a crucial issue for their future. In the displacement process, involuntary migrants lost their land, homes, and businesses. In the aftermath of their evictions, their remaining property was confiscated by the authorities, taken over by others, or simply destroyed. Compensation for losses was rarely forthcoming. Usually home countries refused to discuss it and, more often, refused to give it. The example of the displaced native populations of the New World is a clear example of how compensation questions often remain unresolved. Native peoples lost enormous tracts of land to the colonizers.[46] To this day, the expropriated land remains a point of contention, despite the creation of reservations. It remains contentious because the loss of rights to their land has necessitated a change in how the native populations define themselves (for example, to most Maoris, being Maori means being "of the land." Their identity is tied to having claims to their land)[47], as well as how they make their living (namely, hunting and gathering and roaming). Displacement without compensation is not limited to the New World. Questions pertaining to vacated property, deeds, and compensation are major points of contention between displaced populations and their home governments across the globe. Palestinians are still negotiating with Israel for the return of property and homes taken over by the Jewish settlers. Guatemalan refugees in Mexican camps wanted to return to their own homes and land and engaged in much negotiation with the Guatemalan government.[48] Saharawi refugees are demanding the Moroccan government honor their property rights in Western Sahara.

Displaced persons also view property rights as crucial to their future. In the absence of clearly defined rights to income generating property, the potential for self-sufficiency and economic growth is limited for two reasons. First, without clearly defined rights to land, displaced persons are unlikely to invest and take risks (Rogge notes that in the Sudan, the refugees resented not having any land to cultivate, and, instead, they had to work as seasonal labor on other people's land.[49] Also, during the period in United States' history when attempts were made to get Indians to become farmers (and thereby civilized), it was believed that private ownership of land would do the trick. Deloria and Lytle describe how the leadership during the 1887–1928 period, especially with the General Allotment Act of 1887, believed that "private property had mystical magical qualities about it that led people directly to a 'civilized' state."[50] Second, without clearly defined property rights, it is unlikely that external investments will flow (this explains the lack of investment on reservation lands that are legally federal trust land, so it cannot be sold or repossessed by creditors. An attorney for the reservations found this to be an impediment to outside investment, since "no one wants to do business with you unless you can be sued").[51]

With respect to host communities, property rights may become a concern if land allocated to displaced persons is coveted or owned by local residents. To the extent that encampment land belonged to the government or was purchased by it, then the theatre of dispute shifts from the neighboring communities to the level of the government. Do encampments have permanent rights on that land or do the authorities retain the right to put the land to better use whenever they choose? This question of underlying rights on permanent encampment land, who it belongs to, and how its tenure is regulated, was raised in Lebanon recently. The postwar reconstruction of Beirut included plans for the razing of two large urban camps, Chatila and Bourj al-Barajneh, and the construction of shopping malls and a sports arena on their territory. Julie Peteet describes how, before 1982, these two camps blended with the slums of Beirut and interactions were common at the social, political, and economic levels.[52] Then the Lebanese government reassumed authority over the camps and delineated their boundaries, even marking them with soldiers and checkpoints at entry sites. That resumption of authority was assumed to include the right to determine the future of camp land. By contrast, the Indian government was careful to avoid confrontation with the local population and allotted to the Tibetan refugees land that was viewed by the local Indians as worthless, malaria-infested, or jungle areas).[53]

Social Services

Howard Adelman highlights the different types of obligations host governments have toward their refugees.[54] One of these pertains to social services. According to international law, refugees have the right to host country health and educational services. Yet, if they exercise that right, host resources become strained and drained. The provision of services, therefore, tests host country magnanimity.

Authorities are torn between their international obligations and their domestic budget constraints. They resolve their dilemma in one of three ways.

First, host governments may offer generous social services to its displaced populations by ignoring the costs and designating the expenditure a priority. Most often, such policy applies to internally displaced populations (such as health and educational services for the native populations of the United States, New Zealand, and Australia). Less often, it applies to refugees. Generous programs for refugees tend to be found in resource rich areas, such as Western Europe, North America, and Australia, as well as selected Gulf states. In less developed countries, the motivation to provide social services may be present, but the outcome is restrained by the lack of resources (for example, in Uganda, social services are available to the refugees concentrated in the Gulu district. However, encampment health care centers were strained when Ebola broke out in 2000, limiting its ability to provide health care to all who needed it).[55]

Second, host governments may offer social services in theory while granting microlevel authorities leeway to determine the practice. Such policy pays lip service to international norms of host behavior while endorsing a decentralized execution of law. By allowing the quality and quantity of social services available to displaced persons to be determined locally, the host government abdicates its responsibility and relinquishes its control. As a result, the provision of services is unequal and unreliable. Costa Rica provides a good example. A single formal policy towards refugees had different effects on different encampments due to variations in policy interpretation at the micro level. In Limon, an overall deterioration in housing and education occurred while in Tilaran there was improvement.[56] With respect to health care, evidence is the opposite, with the Limon camp providing better care than in Tilaran.

When host governments merely pay lip service to international regulations pertaining to refugees, they also allow discrimination to take place at the micro level. Refugees and internally displaced persons are often of a different ethnic group, and ethnicity becomes the basis for bias. On grounds of their ethnicity, displaced peoples become shortchanged in social services. Open discrimination in health and education is facilitated when target groups are concentrated, such as in encampments. Even in countries with universal health care, displaced ethnic groups receive care that is quantitatively and qualitatively different from what the dominant groups receive. A study of the Czech Republic, conducted by Helsinki Watch, indicates that Roma women are segregated and placed in overcrowded maternity wards and Roma schoolchildren are forced to sit in separate rows in the back or simply sent to mental institutions.[57] Similarly, Israel has a fully segregated educational system in which Palestinians get a different education from Israeli children.[58]

Third, host governments may simply disregard international norms and prohibit encampment residents from using public services. The reason most often cited for such behavior is cost, as authorities claim that state resources are limited and priority must be given to domestic populations (such policy exists in Lebanon, where Palestinians are prohibited by law from using government hospitals and the secondary school system.[59] It also currently exists in Iran, where all Afghani refugees who arrived after 1992 are denied access to social services).[60] When displaced persons are thus denied basic state benefits, they have several options. They can rely on international organizations (although these are rarely willing to continue funding medical and educational services over the long run). Alternatively, they can strive for self-sufficiency in social services by fostering the provision of education and health care within the camps. Such services can be developed with few resources and can be very basic, as the Saharawi camps in Algeria show. They can also be quite complex, as the Tibetan hospitals in India are (there, refugees educated their doctors, built and manned their hospitals, and even opened their doors to Indians from neighboring communities).[61] Finally, displaced people can rely on their meager income to pay for services in the private sector, outside the camps, and the host public sector. More often than not, none of these options is exercised, and displaced persons simply forgo services.

THE POLITICAL INTEGRATION OF ENCAMPMENT RESIDENTS

The nature of interaction between encampments and host communities is determined by the political rights granted to displaced persons (including the right of movement, the right of employment, and the right to citizenship). It is also determined by institutionalized discrimination and the extent to which ethnic groups are treated differently under law. Rights and discrimination, as supported by host institutions and policies, indicate whether displaced persons are politically acknowledged and legally protected within host states. They also lubricate and define the interaction between encampment residents and host economies. Clearly, if camp residents have the right to move within the host state, they will have greater employment options because they can search across a broader territory. To the extent that they have the right to work outside the camp, residents' choices are increased and their legal status provides some protection from exploitation. Displaced persons who can apply for citizenship are more likely to feel permanently ensconced in a host state, and therefore more likely to take steps towards economic integration (such as investment and risk taking). Finally, camp residents who do not suffer from legalized discrimination against their particular ethnic group are more likely to feel welcome and, therefore, to seek integration.

The Right of Movement

For decades, the Berlin Wall has been a potent symbol of the containment of people. While the emigration policy of East Germany was clearly embodied in stone, other states with pent up demand for out-migration had equally effective policies. Indeed, the Soviet Union, the East European countries of the Soviet Bloc, Cuba, and China all had precisely enunciated rules and regulations that dictated who can leave the country and under what conditions.[62] Given such controls on population movements of citizens, it should come as no surprise that host countries control movements of refugees. They do so for a variety of reasons. If encampment residents were allowed freedom of movement, they might overwhelm the labor markets and trigger a downward movement of wages. They might put pressure on the housing market, services, and infrastructure. They might also resort to a life of crime in order to satisfy their basic needs. If encampment residents are free to move away, the camp itself ceases to be under the control of the host governments. Finally, freely moving camp residents might mingle with the host ethnic group, intermarry, and thereby dilute the pre-existing ethnic composition of the population.

In order to avoid such scenarios, authorities use a variety of measures to control the movement of encampment residents. Some are explicit, such as the Israeli prohibition of movement of Palestinians from Gaza and the West Bank without specific permission. In the apartheid-era South Africa, the pass system prevented Blacks from traveling and working outside their homelands without appropriate permission. Similarly, in Sri Lanka, the pass system controls the movement of encampment residents and allows them to go off camp grounds for work or approved visits. Displaced Tamils from the North of Sri Lanka, who have crossed the war border and placed themselves at the mercy of the government, have been housed in encampments where they are kept under strict control. According to Schrijvers, 'in practice, these camps function as detention centres as the *internal refugees here are either imprisoned altogether or allowed exit only for a few hours to one day*" [emphasis added].[63] In Hong Kong, until 1982, the authorities ran two types of camps. Closed camps housed refugees for about two to three weeks while waiting for their allocation to one of the eleven open camps or third country asylum. Closed camps by definition did not allow any movement of refugees. By contrast, open camps encouraged movement, urging their residents to get jobs in the community. However, given that the inflow of refugees kept increasing, in 1982 the government got tough and implemented a policy whereby all new arrivals would be detained in closed camps, from where they would be repatriated.[64] In these closed camps, refugees lived with other prisoners and shared their meals. They could not be visited by other refugees, they could not leave the camps without special authorization, and they could not seek work. These closed camps, located on the island of Lan Tau, were run by the Correctional Service Department and the UNHCR was not given jurisdiction.

Not all camp residents are subject to such strict movement restrictions. Some have complete freedom to move about, travel, and live anywhere they choose. The Tibetan and Palestinian refugee populations in India and Jordan have benefited from lenient host policies that granted them the right to move at will. Alternatively, some camp residents enjoy the *de jure* right of movement but *de facto* cannot enjoy it because the repercussions are prohibitive. In other words, even without explicit prohibitions, camp residents cannot move away because they cannot afford to do so. For example, if American Indians move off the reservations, they lose their federal government benefits. A similar problem is faced by indigenous populations of New Zealand and Australia, as well as Afghani refugees in Iran.[65]

Right of Employment

Closely related to the right of movement is the right to work, legally, outside the encampment. International conventions pertaining to refugees do not specify that host communities must open their labor markets to newcomers, so the decision rests entirely with host authorities. To the extent that they deem their local markets can benefit from an increase in the supply of labor, their employment policies will be more generous towards the displaced populations. Alternatively, if they deem that an increase in the supply of refugee labor will overwhelm domestic labor markets, depress wages, and displace local workers, then laws are put into effect prohibiting refugee employment.

According to Sudan's Regulation of Asylum Act of 1974, Sudan guarantees refugees the right to employment outside their camps.[66] This blanket law covers all refugees in all jobs. By contrast, Lebanon has stringent prohibitions pertaining to Palestinian workers. In 1964, a decree was passed that no foreigner may work, for pay or not, without specific permits from the Ministries of Labor and Social Affairs.

Priority was given to Lebanese, then foreign workers from Syria and Asia, and finally, at the bottom of the pecking order, the Palestinians.[67] In 1982, the Ministry of Labor and Social Affairs set out categories of employment closed to foreigners (including banking and barbering!). Work permits could be given only for the following tasks: construction, electrical installation, sanitation facilities, glass mounting, agriculture, tanning and leather works, excavation, smelting, nannies, servants, cooks, car wash and so on.[68] Lawyers and engineers were not allowed to practice their professions, and doctors and pharmacists could only work in the Palestine Red Crescent Society clinics.[69] As a result, a lot of Palestinian refugees, especially women, work in black market activities (such as housecleaning) for wages significantly below minimum wage and without any benefits.

In Costa Rica, there are both formal and *de facto* work restrictions that limit the ability of refugees to seek employment outside their camps.[70] Among the former is the regulation that when a refugee becomes employed, government assistance is terminated.[71] However meager, this assistance nevertheless represents a consistent and reliable source of sustenance. Among the *de facto* impediments is the reality that the wage earner must move off the camp and leave his/her family because there are no sources of employment near the camp and no housing where the jobs are.

Citizenship for Encampment Residents

After decades in permanent encampments, do refugees become eligible for host country citizenship? In the absence of international regulations to answer that question, host authorities enact laws that reflect their inclinations. Sometimes they apply one of the two universally used criteria: *jus sanguinis*, (according to which citizenship is contingent on that of one's parents) or *jus soli* (which entitles anyone born in a country to become a citizen). While the former is more common in the Old World, the latter is often found in the New World.[72]

An application of the principle of *jus soli* to encampments implies that children born in camps can become citizens of their host states. That is an outcome many host authorities and populations find unpalatable due to its multiplier effect. In other words, giving citizenship to refugees means giving a series of civil, political, and social rights that in turn lead to other broader and more expensive rights. When people acquire citizenship, their sense of belonging to the state increases, as does their capacity and incentive to participate in its culture. They also want to exert their power, express their opinion, and influence policy. The electoral system, newly opened to naturalized immigrants, allows them to do this. Citizenship is also about what Gwenn Okruhlik called "material exclusion."[73] In other words, those who become citizens cannot be excluded from economic participation. In short, refugees become empowered.

However, host states are leery of empowering newcomers. To the extent that they can postpone giving rights to refugees, they will often do so. Lebanon provides an extreme example of such policy, refusing to grant Palestinians citizenship except under special circumstances (indeed, only 28,000–30,000 have been naturalized).[74] At the other end of the spectrum, host states welcome refugees with offers of citizenship. Jordan has given citizenship rights to its Palestinian population and India has offered them to the Tibetans (who, in contrast to other refugees who wish to shed their "stateless state," have chosen to hold on to their refugee status and keep their stateless "yellow" identity papers).[75] Some countries, such as Tanzania and Botswana, reward encampment residents who have become self-sufficient with citizenship.[76] Others, such as Israel, discriminate with respect to their refugees, granting some immediate citizenship (Jews) while refusing others (numerous Palestinians with claims).

The question of citizenship is complicated in countries where host and home states are one and the same. While authorities might be tempted to deny citizenship to some citizens (i.e., to denaturalize them), they are prevented from doing so by international regulations. Despite its illegality, revoking citizenship of targeted ethnic groups continues to be a temptation for some governments. The Czech Republic provides a contemporary example: it has introduced laws that effectively deny citizenship to some 20,000 Romas (10 percent of their total population).[77] Given that Romas are more nomadic than other populations, their coming and going is harder to control, enabling authorities to claim they are not citizens but rather new arrivals (who can therefore be denied citizenship papers).

In the New World, debates took place over a period of decades about the desirability of granting citizenship to native populations. In Australia, the constitution of 1901 specifies that Aborigines do not have citizenship rights.[78] It was only in 1964, when the Social Welfare Act was extended to include them, that the Aborigines became *de facto* citizens. Furthermore, it was only in 1967 that the census began to enumerate them along with other peoples. In the United States, the Indian Citizenship Act, passed in 1924, gave citizenship to all those Indians who had served in the armed forces during World War I. This was later amended to include all Indians born within the continental United States. Those Indians were also granted voting rights. Some states, including Minnesota and North Dakota, required that Indians prove they have assumed a "civilized" way of life before they were allowed to participate in the electoral process.[79] Today, American Indians are citizens of the United States as well as of Indian Country. While not a homogeneous country, it consists of a variety of federally recognized nations that enjoy semi-autonomy, as well as the right to grant citizenship.[80]

Discrimination

It is not uncommon for host and home countries to discriminate on the basis of ethnicity. Discrimination (often institutionalized, explicit, and legalized) determines the nature of interaction between host populations and encampment residents because it condones different treatment and different rules (in employment, consumption, production, exchange, etc.) for different people. It justifies treating some ethnic groups better than others. How is discrimination institutionalized and how does it affect encampments?

Some host countries have constitutions that explicitly indicate equality or inequality among its ethnic groups. For example, the current Israeli constitution, as well as the apartheid-era South African constitution, both promoted the dominance of a select group. In Sri Lanka, the constitution overtly promotes the supremacy of the Sinhalese people and their language. Such explicit ranking of ethnic groups translates into differences in the way displaced peoples are treated. It gives meaning to the statement that not all refugees are the same. For example, when Sinhalese are displaced by the war, they are housed in buildings with solid walls and cement floor. Tamils, on the other hand, tend to be housed in huts covered with coconut thatch for temporary roofing. In a Tamil camp in Trincomalee, the huts were built right on the sand, near or on the beach. During monsoons, they flooded; since firewood was used for cooking, the huts often burned.[81]

Some host countries have policies that explicitly discriminate against target ethnic groups.[82] These policies extend to taxes, property rights, labor conditions and economic development, and, thus, shape the economic reality of target populations.[83]

Discriminatory policies affect encampment residents in several ways. With respect to housing, restrictions prevent target ethnic groups from participating in the housing market (for example, various cities in the Czech Republic passed legislation granting local authorities "the right to evict troublesome Romas from their apartments [on grounds such as overcrowding, lack of hygiene, etc.] and expel them from the cities without court orders."[84] Such rules effectively reinforce the *de facto* encampment of Romas). Targeted encampment residents are discriminated against in consumption (such as in the Czech Republic, where encamped Romas are denied entry into cafes used by ethnic Czechs). Discrimination policies are also evident in land matters. The most blatant and large-scale case is that of South Africa, where Blacks relocated to reserves and townships were prevented from owning land outside designated areas (the Land Act of 1913 restricted Black land ownership to a few arid, worthless parcels, thereby allotting

90 percent of the territory to Whites. The Land Act resulted in the segregation and forced resettlement of blacks on ten ethnic reserves, where, since 1960, 3.5 million Blacks have been resettled because they constituted a "surplus population").[85] Discrimination is also evident in the credit markets, making it impossible for targeted camp residents to get loans. The Palestinians in Lebanon were often denied permits to rehabilitate the housing and the infrastructure in their camps, forcing them to remain in the squalor of camps built as temporary quarters some fifty years ago.[86] Discrimination policies are also evident in education. In Burundi, the Tutsi have maintained their superiority over the Hutus in part by restricting Hutu admittance to higher and technical education, thereby ensuring an exclusive Tutsi pool of talent.[87] This policy of discrimination has been extended to the encampments.

ENCAMPMENTS IN THE DOMESTIC PECKING ORDER

The Sudanese term for refugee is *Laji*, which, literally translated, means downtrodden.[88] In virtually all host states, displaced populations are indeed downtrodden. They are poor and powerless people brought together by extraordinary circumstances. The encampments in which they live, work, marry, bear children, and die are social units at the bottom of the host pecking order. They tend to get the short end of the stick when they compete for scarce resources with host neighbors.[89] In questions pertaining to land use, water access, and resettlement, they also lose out to local communities. When they seek political legitimacy, a channel through which to make themselves heard, and, access to the legal system, again displaced people are at the bottom of the pecking order. Their position is no different in social interaction with host communities. While they seek tolerance, acceptance, and understanding from host societies, they are usually met with intolerance of encampment culture.[90] There is rarely an effort to accommodate their language, and their religion is often ridiculed. Displaced people encounter discrimination against their minority language and religion in the workplace, the housing market, and trade relations.

Thus, residents of encampments enjoy few privileges, control few resources, and have little power. They are marginalized economically, politically, and socially. They are the "kick-me" group, often subservient, fearful, and hesitant. It is as though they carry a sign that says, "kick me in the behind, kick me around, kick me out, kick me into prison." By comparison, host populations have economic and political power, control lucrative positions, enjoy numerous privileges, and have access to the best opportunities. In other words, they are empowered relative to displaced persons. They have little regard for minority groups in general, and displaced persons in particular, while making use of them in various economic capacities. Encampment residents and their neighbors on the outside live by two different sets of economic rules and regulations. These rules are formal and informal, spontaneous and institutionalized. They dictate the terms of employment, the nature of schooling, the quality of livelihood, and the cultural life of their populations.

There are exceptions to this pecking order. The experience of the Tibetans once again provides a useful example insofar as it shows that displaced persons do sometimes have power that translates into higher rank. Other examples show that pecking orders are not set in stone and do in fact change over time. Such reversal of fortunes is found in the United States.[91] On the traditional lands of the Seneca Indians is a town called Salamanca. In 1892, an agreement was extracted from the headmen of the reservation to rent land for the establishment of the town for $17,000.[92] This lease agreement resulted in rents of $1 in 1991, at the time the 99-year lease expired. The Senecas made it clear in the preceding years that the city's 6,600 (predominantly White) inhabitants were to become inhabitants of a reservation. The discomfort experienced by the population was embodied in their fear that they would go from being at the top of the pecking order to the bottom.

ENCAMPMENT/HOST INTERACTIONS IN EXTROVERTED AND INTROVERTED STATES

Encampments in extroverted states tend to interact with neighboring communities more because their economies are stronger and can support more exchange in the labor, product, and money markets. Moreover, regional imbalance is lower in extroverted states because they have more resources to implement policies that rectify inequalities. Fiscal policy is effective in redistributing resources and is fueled by the high-income base of the population. Policy reflects overall liberal intolerance for gaping pockets of poverty, and the welfare state, despite its modifications, survives to trickle benefits to encampments. Included is a spillover into social policies that reflects an inclination toward public support for public sector social services, such as education and health care.

Also, in extroverted countries, the political rights of displaced persons are more protected. Discrimination in constitutions or in policy runs counter to the professed values and ethics that predominate among Western populations. From the perspective of the liberal, democratic tradition, in which individual rights are respected and ethnic origin is considered largely irrelevant in the eyes of the law, it may seem unlikely that leaders would or could sponsor or induce discrimination by ethnicity (or race or religion). Examples of legalized discrimination in the "non-democratic" parts of the world are considered, in the words of Saffran, "oppressive and inelegant" and are viewed with concern by human rights activists.[93] Indeed, examples, such as the prohibition of Russians to own land in Latvia, the Iraqi draining of Shiite marshes, and employment restrictions against Blacks in South Africa, are but some of the cases in which peoples are judged by ethnicity. In most liberal democracies, the constitution does not distinguish between peoples, nor does it condone discrimination among peoples.[94]

NOTES

1. Gilda Pacheco, *Nicaraguan Refugees in Costa Rica,* (Washington, D.C.: Center for Immigration Policy and Refugee Assistance, Georgetown University, 1989), 1.

2. Incidentally, Mexico is not a signatory to the UN conventions on refugees, nor does it recognize refugee status within its immigration laws.

3. Elizabeth G. Ferris, "Dilemmas of Third World Refugee Policies: Mexico and the Central American Refugees" in *Refugees, A Third World Dilemma,* ed. John R. Rogge (Totowa, N.J.: Rowman & Littlefield, 1987), 163.

4. UNHCR, *The State of the World's Refugees* (New York: Oxford University Press, 1995), 41.

5. Julie Peteet, "Identity Crisis: Palestinians in Post-War Lebanon," U.S. Committee for Refugees, *World Refugee Survey* (1997), 34.

6. The Lebanese government has claimed that the Palestinian refugees upset the country's delicate sectarian balance (in which Shiite Muslims have a majority over the Maronite Christians, and the Palestinians, who are Sunni Muslims, complicate the situation). Donna E. Arzt, *Refugees into Citizens* (New York: Council on Foreign Relations, 1997), 47.

7. Gisele Bousquet, "Living in a State of Limbo: A Case Study of Vietnamese Refugees in Hong Kong Camps" in *People in Upheaval,* ed. Scott Morgan and Elizabeth Colson (New York: Center for Migration Studies, 1987).

8. Bousquet, "Living in a State of Limbo," 1987), 40.

9. Cited in UNHCR, *The State of the World's Refugees*, 37.

10. UNHCR, *The State of the World's Refugees* (Geneva 1995), 124.

11. She discusses the case of Tanzania's refugees from Burundi and Rwanda. Patricia Daley, "From the Kipande to the Kibali: the Incorporation of Refugees and Labor Migrants in Western Tanzania, 1900–87" in *Geography and Refugees,* ed. Richard Black and Vaughan Robinson (London: Belhaven, 1993), 17.

12. John R. Rogge, *Too Many, Too Long, Sudan's Twenty-Year Refugee Dilemma* (Totowa, N.J.: Rowman and Allenhed, 1985), 119.

13. John Rogge, "When is Self-Sufficiency Achieved? The Case of Rural Settlements in Sudan" in Rogge, *Refugees, A Third World Dilemma,* 86.

14. The *Wall Street Journal,* June 1, 2000.

15. The *New York Times,* September 15, 2000.

16. In the town of Novi Pazar, there are now some 600 factories producing counterfeit Levi's, Calvin Klein, and other labels worth some $100 million annually. These producers and traders, who are busting sanctions and international copyright laws, have found a way of turning Serbia's pariah status to their advantage. In the process, they have served to create an oasis of interethnic harmony as cooperation thrives. The *Wall Street Journal* February 18, 2000.

17. Tristan Betts, "Zonal Rural Development in Africa" *Journal of Modern African Studies* 7, no. 1 (1969) 149–53, cited in Richard Black and Thomas Mabwe, "Planning for Refugees in Zambia, The Settlement Approach to Food Self-Sufficiency" *Third World Planning Review* 14, no 1, (1992), 2.

18. Shifts in political winds also explain why Pakistani aid to the Afghans ceased once the Soviet Union withdrew. See Alan Findlay, "End of the Cold War, End of Afghan Relief Aid?" in Black and Robinson, *Geography and Refugees*, 185.

19. Sudan is notorious for its mistreatment of the southern involuntary migrants. By contrast, its attitude towards refugees has been remarkable. According to John Rogge, "since the arrival of the first refugees in Sudan, the reception by Sudanese has always been characterized by understanding and sympathy. Few asylum countries in Africa have made available a greater level of resources to their refugee populations." John R. Rogge, *Too Many, Too Long*, 55.

20. Tom Nairn, *The Break-Up of Britain* (London: NLB, 1977).

21. Milica Zarkovic Bookman, *The Political Economy of Discontinuous Development* (New York: Praeger 1991).

22. William Beer, *The Unexpected Rebellion: Ethnic Activism in Contemporary France* (New York: New York University Press, 1980).

23. Micheal Hechter, *Internal Colonialism: The Celtic Fringe in British National Development 1536–1966* (Berkeley: University of California Press, 1975).

24. Peter Alexis Gourevitch "The Emergence of Peripheral Nationalisms: Some Comparative Speculations on the Spatial Distribution of Political Leadership and Economic Growth" *The Comparative Study of Society and History*, 21 July 1979, 303–22.

25. Michael Hechter, *Internal Colonialism*, 39.

26. Aristide R. Zolberg, Astri Suhrke, and Sergio Aguayo, *Escape From Violence, Conflict and the Refugee Crisis in the Developing World* (New York: Oxford University Press, 1989), 217.

27. Philip Gourevitch, *We Wish To Inform You that Tomorrow We Will Be Killed with Our Families* (New York: Picador, 1999), 215.

28. Arzt, *Refugees into Citizens,* 39.

29. Even in 1991, while the Intifada was raging, 31.1% of West Bank workers and 38.8 percent of Gaza workers commuted to Israel for work. Arzt, *Refugees into Citizens,* 38.

30. Dorsh Marie de Voe, "Keeping Refugee Status: A Tibetan Perspective" in *People in Upheaval*, ed. Scott Morgan and Elizabeth Colson (New York: Center for Migration Studies, 1987), 57.

31. When they arrived at the camp, they were given one month's ration of food. Then they were expected to find factory work to support themselves and their families. They were housed in two open camps, the Jubilee Center and the Kai Tak Transit Center. They worked in the local factories to earn money for their needs. Bousquet, "Living in a State of Limbo," 44.

32. Further injections of cash had a positive effect on the local economy. Since the land was sparsely populated, each refugee family was allocated some land to farm, thereby granting productive capacity to the residents and enabling them to produce something for sale. Despite this success, when peace came to Mozambique, the residents repatriated in 1994, relinquishing the encampment site to the government. UNHCR, *The State of the World's Refugees,* 168.

33. She claims that it accentuates interethnic competition: "The native and immigrant labor forces compete more directly in times of economic recession than in periods of prosperity because workers are often willing to take otherwise unacceptable employment during periods of economic downturn." Jeannette Money, *Fences and Neighbors: The Political Geography of Immigration Control* (Ithaca: Cornell University Press, 1999), 57.

34. Olzak calls this niche overlap. Susan Olzak, *The Dynamics of Ethnic Competition and Conflict* (Stanford: Stanford University Press, 1997).

35. Cited in Marie de Voe, "Keeping Refugee Status, 157.

36. Arzt, *Refugees into Citizens,* 39.

37. Christensen reports that this was the way in which refugees could buy food and essentials (at the same time, it provided recreation facilities for men). Hanne Christensen, "Spontaneous Development Efforts by Rural Refugees in Somalia and Pakistan" in Rogge, *Refugees, A Third World Dilemma,* 203.

38. Black and Mabwe, "Planning for Refugees in Zambia," 2.

39. Jeff Benedict, *Without Reservation: The Making of America's Most Powerful Indian Tribe and Foxwoods, the World's Largest Casino* (New York: HarperCollins, 2000).

40. Dan Greenway, "Prospects for the Resettlment of Afghan Refugees in Pakistan" in Rogge, *Refugees, A Third World Dilemma*, 193.

41. Fergus M. Bordewich, *Killing the White Man's Indian: Reinventing Native Americans at the End of the Twentieth Century* (New York: Anchor, 1996), 13.

42. It has also provided a convenient excuse for them.

43. Elizabeth G. Ferris, "Dilemmas of Third World Refugee Policies: Mexico and the Central American Refugees" in Rogge, *Refugees, A Third World Dilemma*, 163–65.

44. Dan Greenway, "Prospects for the Resettlment of Afghan Refugees in Pakistan" in Rogge, *Refugees, A Third World Dilemma*, 193.

45. Land has been reserved for Fijians, despite the fact that some one-half of the population is composed of Indians. According to Mayer, land could be leased to Indians but only at exorbitantly high rents, thus effectively preventing their long-term sustenance from the land (Adrian C. Mayer, *Indians in Fiji* [London: Oxford University Press, 1963], 62).

46. It was expropriated under the pretext that it actually did not belong to them. Native populations could not produce evidence of property rights, such as deeds to the land, registered with local authorities and stamped in ink on paper.

47. Some within their communities feel that no private Maori should sell his land, because it needs to be kept in trust for future generations. The nineteenth century had many injustices when it came to Maori treatment, and land is at the core of disputes today.

48. In 1984, the military government had started repopulating the lands with other peoples, claiming that the land had been voluntarily abandoned Roman Krznaric, "Guatemalan Returnees and the Dilemma of Political Mobilization" *Journal of Refugee Studies* 10, no. 1 (1997), 62, 64.

49. John R. Rogge, *Too Many, Too Long: Sudan's Twenty-Year Refugee Dilemma* (Totowa, N.J.: Rowman and Allenhed, 1985), 119.

50. They assumed that Indians both wanted to become farmers and were capable of doing so. This policy of allocating property rights was

superceded by the Indian Reorganization Act of 1934 that formally ended the allotment period and prevented any more reservation lands from being allocated to private peoples. Vine Deloria, Jr. and Clifford M. Lytle, *American Indians, American Justice* (Austin: University of Texas, 1983), 9.

51. Quoted in Fergus M. Bordewich, *Killing the White Man's Indian*, 126.

52. Julie Peteet, "Identity Crisis: Palestinians in Post-War Lebanon" (U.S. Committee for Refugees, *World Refugee Survey 1997*), 38.

53. Incidentally, these lands later became thriving farming communities.

54. Howard Adelman, "The Concept of Legitimacy Applied to Immigration," in *Legitimate and Illegitimate Discrimination: New Issues in Migration*, ed. Howard Adelman (Toronto: York Lanes, 1995), 50.

55. *The Economist* (October 21, 2000) 56.

56. Pacheco, *Nicaraguan Refugees in Costa Rica*, 39–41.

57. Paul Hochenos, *Free To Hate* (New York: Routledge, 1993), 217–18. The Romas in the Czech Republic are often sent to school for the handicapped because they rarely have mastery of the national language (Jonathan fox and Betty Brown, "The Roma in the Postcommunist Era" in *Peoples versus States*, ed. Robert Ted Gurr [Washington, D.C.: United States Institute of Peace, 2000] 145). This is similar to the persistence of forced sterilization policies directed towards the Roma during the communist period, despite its public repudiation. Such discrimination continues, despite its official repudiation. During the time of communism when requirements for primary education were strictly enforced, social workers sometimes ensured that Roma children went to school. In the post-Communist period, mandatory education is not strictly enforced.

58. While education for encampment residents is under the direction of the Palestinian Authority, other Palestinians are subject to discrimination. Indeed, according to Rabinowitz, schools catering to Palestinian communities are run by a section of the Ministry of Education, quite separate to that which operates schools for Israelis. Dan Rabinowitz, "National Identity on the Frontier: Palestinians in the Israeli Education System" in *Border Identities*, eds. Thomas M. Wilson and Hastings Donnan (Cambridge: Cambridge University Press 1998), 146.

59. Arzt, *Refugees into Citizens*, 46.

60. *Economist,* January 13, 2001, 46.

61. de Voe, "Keeping Refugee Status," 57.

62. Why do countries want to do this? Such interference is deemed necessary because the demand for exit visas would overwhelm the labor market, triggering a shortage of workers and an upward pressure on wages. Moreover, when educated people emigrate, the harm to the economy is even greater due to the loss of human capital. When fertile young people emigrate, there is a potential demographic cost as the country is robbed of their offspring, (in other words, future workers). When workers emigrate, the government suffers the loss of their tax revenues; when healthy individuals emigrate, the investments of the health system have been lost, and so forth.

63. Those who stay within the Tamil zone, and are not housed with relatives, live in "welfare centres," mostly in public buildings such as schools or temples. Joke Schrijvers, "Fighters, Victims and Survivors: Constructions of Ethnicity, Gender and Refugeeness Among Tamils in Sri Lanka" *Journal of Refugee Studies* 12, no. 3 (1999), 311.

64. At the same time, Thailand was creating closed camps for its Laotian refugees. Bousquet, "Living in a State of Limbo," 39.

65. See *The Economist,* January 13, 2001, 46.

66. Refer to Article 14b of the regulation. See Ahmed Karadawi "The Problem of Urban Refugees in Sudan" in Rogge, *Refugees, A Third World Dilemma,* 126.

67. Arzt, *Refugees into Citizens,* 46.

68. Peteet, "Identity Crisis," 36.

69. Arzt, *Refugees into Citizens,* 46.

70. Pacheco, *Nicaraguan Refugees in Costa Rica,* 17–18.

71. In order to work outside the camp, a person has to be granted a work permit. Those are granted for one month, and then the person loses rights to assistance for one month. However, the job may only last one week; nevertheless, assistance cannot be adjusted accordingly, it is lost for the entire month.

72. Brubaker claims that the *jus sanguinis* concept of citizenship and national identity in Germany gave rise to immigration system based on temporary rotation of labor and social segregation, while the *jus soli* concept of citizenship in France drove preferences for permanent settlement and assimilation. It was only in 1999, under intense pressure, that Germany allowed ethnic Turkish newborns to acquire German citizen-

ship (no similar steps have been taken by Italy and Sweden, where the *jus sanguinis* principal still prevails). Rogers Brubaker, *Citizenship and Nationhood in France and Germany* (Cambridge, Mass.: Harvard University Press, 1992).

73. Gwenn Okruhlik, "Citizenship and Inequality: The Political Economy of Ethnicity" paper presented at the annual meetings of the *International Studies Association*, Chicago (February 2001), 2.

74. Peteet, "Identity Crisis", 39.

75. Neighboring Bhutan was not so tolerant, demanding allegiance to the state by forcing Tibetan refugees to take citizenship or leave. Thousands left rather than relinquish their Tibetan refugee status. de Voe, "Keeping Refugee Status", 56.

76. Rogge, "When is Self-Sufficiency Achieved?", 89.

77. *The New York Times* (December 27, 1995 and January 7, 1996).

78. *The Economist*, September 9 (2000, Survey Australia) 12.

79. Proof of civilized life included severing relations with their tribes. Deloria, Jr. and Lytle, *American Indians, American Justice,* (Austin: University of Texas, 1983), 223.

80. There is ample variation among the tribes with respect to the criteria they use. For example, the Cherokee constitution explicitly excludes Blacks and mulattos. Bordewich, *Killing the White Man's Indian*, 41.

81. H. L. Seneviratne and Maria Stavropoulou, "Sri Lanka's Vicious Circle of Displacement" in *The Forsaken People, Case Studies of the Internally Displaced,* eds. Roberta Cohen and Francis M. Deng (Washington, D.C.: Brookings Institution Press, 1998), 372.

82. The study of interethnic relations in general has been neglected by economists, since they are perceived to fall in the domain of anthropologists, political scientists, and sociologists. Gary Becker published a study on the economics of discrimination which can apply to gender and ethnic groups. This highly controversial work focused attention on gender and race in the economy (Gary Becker, *The Economics of Discrimination* [Chicago: University of Chicago, 1957]). Research by Michael Wyzan on the economic aspects of differential treatment of ethnic groups and that of Thomas Sowell on preferential policies around the world begin to fill the void in the literature. Michael Wyzan ed., *The Political Economy of Ethnic Discrimination and Affirmative Action* (New York: Praeger, 1990); Thomas Sowell, *The Economics and*

Politics of Race: An International Perspective (New York: W. Morrow, 1983).

83. Sometimes, when internal administrative boundaries coincide with ethnic boundaries, the policies take on a different form. Preferential policies may entail above-average contribution to the national budget, insufficient benefit from the national budget, unfavorable terms of trade resulting from price manipulation, unfavorable regulation pertaining to investment and foreign inflows of resources, etc. They may all elicit a sense of economic injustice, depending upon the relative economic position of a region. Relatively low-income regions might attribute their relatively inferior economic position to inadequate and insufficient preferential policies that might have led to unfair practices and exploitation of their resources. Relatively high-income regions may perceive themselves as the economic backbone of the state, while their neighbors drain their resources and restrain their growth. Thus, states with wide regional disparities in income constitute a ripe environment for perceptions of injustice at all levels of income.

84. Hochenos, *Free To Hate*, 221.

85. *The New York Times*, May 31, 1994.

86. Bill Frelick, "The Year in Review" U.S. Committee for Refugees, *World Refugee Survey* (1997), 18.

87. Michael Dravis, "Burundi in the 1990s" in *Peoples versus States*, ed. Ted Robert Gurr (Washington, D.C.: United States Institute of Peace, 2000), 191.

88. Rogge, *Too Many, Too Long*, xvi.

89. If there is no scarcity, then there is no problem. While there is scarcity in all goods in society, there must be limited access and attainability. Hoetink describes this condition as one that competition comes from scarcity that is both objective and subjective; it is not only are all economic goods scarce (in the objective sense) but members of society must perceive them as such (subjective). Harmannus Hoetink "Resource Competition, Monopoly, and Socioracial Diversity" in *Ethnicity and Resource Competition in Plural Societies*, ed. Leo Despres (The Hague: Mouton Publishers, 1975), 10.

90. This also occurs in multiethnic states, in which the dominant group promotes its own culture by suffocating that of the marginalized group (for example, in Indonesia, the Chinese are not allowed to celebrate

their New Year [the celebration has been banned since 1967]. The *New York Times* [February 7, 2000], in Japan, the Governor of Tokyo publicly referred to people of Chinese and Korean descent as "shangoku-jin" a derogatory term with xenophobic connotations used as a sharp insult (Adding insult to injury, the comment was made in reference to the Governor Shintaro Ishihara's perceived need to ready the military and riot police because these immigrant groups were likely to riot in the aftermath of a major earthquake. The *New York Times* [April 11, 2000]).

91. Residents of Indian reservations currently enjoy a unique kind of autonomy that enabled their empowerment during the 1990s. At that time, Indians realized they could make their own economic decisions independent, and despite, of White man. Bordewich provides numerous examples. He says, "In Connecticut and elsewhere, tribes were exploiting a principle of sovereignty unknown to the average American in order to build gambling casinos that sucked colossal sums of money from neighboring regions. Landowners in southern California discovered that they had virtually no way to prevent the miniscule Campo Bank of Indians from building a huge commercial waste facility on top of their watershed. New Mexicans found that they were equally helpless in the face of the Mescalero Apaches' determination to establish a nuclear waste facility on their reservation outside Alamogordo. In some states, Indian claims to land, water, and fishing rights and their demands for the return of sacred lands posed seismic threats to local economies, including, most prominently, the entire Black Hills region of South Dakota." Bordewich, *Killing the White Man's Indian,* 11–12.

92. According to the reports, speculators sequestered the Seneca headmen in a local hotel and gave them alcohol until they signed the agreement. Fergus M. Bordewich, *Killing the White Man's Indian: Reinventing Native Americans at the End of the Twentieth Century* (New York: Anchor Books, Doubleday, 1996), 9–10.

93. William Saffran, "Nations, Ethnic Groups, States and Politics: A Preface and an Agenda" *Nationalism and Ethnic Politics* 1, no. 1 (spring 1995), 2.

94. However, even in societies in which the democratic tradition reigns, evidence of discriminatory policy is not far in their history. Given

that history, a sense of collective guilt seems to prevail and to underlie laws that protect indigenous peoples and even grant them rights other ethnic groups do not share. Such developments in the United States and New Zealand have resulted in cries of injustice from other immigrant and minority groups who perceive themselves "less protected" than the native populations.

5

ENCAMPMENTS IN THE INTERNATIONAL ECONOMY: THE EFFECT OF GLOBALIZATION

Globalization has become a controversial concept. Global links of all kinds are sought out by some and viewed with suspicion by others. Globalization is simultaneously touted as a panacea for all countries seeking economic growth and maligned as a curse by all peoples who feel exploited. This contradictory response to globalization has been characterized by Friedman as the collision of lexuses vs. olive trees,[1] by Barber as jihads vs. McWorlds,[2] and by Coclanis and Doshi as the Davos Man vs. *orang ulu.*[3] While globalization is a lot of things to a lot of people, there continues to be controversy over what it really is.

The strictest definitions of globalization emphasize internationalization and technological change. According to Jay Mandle and Louis Ferleger, globalization entails two phenomena: "technological change in the processing and dissemination of information related to finance and production" and "the international spread of the technical competence necessary to use these advances efficiently."[4] According to Daniel Gaske, globalization entails two major changes: a shift to high technology, human-capital based production and the globalization of economic decisions (especially with respect to trade, investment, corporate decision making, and technology).[5] While it might be argued that previous historical periods also had internationalization and technological change, this current one is different in two ways.[6] First, both the volume and the nature of international economic interaction is different from before (Slater has said that in the current era of globalization, not only has the sheer magnitude of flows of capital, goods, services, and labor increased but the speed, pervasiveness and impermanence of international transactions have also become apparent).[7] Second, the degree and the intensity with which the world is tied together into a single marketplace is different now from previous historical periods (according to Friedman, the number of people who are affected by globalization and who partake in it is greater than ever before. As a result, he defines globalization as "the inexorable integration of markets, nation-states and technologies to a degree *never witnessed before*" [emphasis added]).[8]

The overall consensus is that globalization is like a spreading fog that is covering greater and greater territories of the world and larger and larger numbers of people. More than ever before, the world truly seems small, with shrinking distances and expanding interdependencies.[9] What are the implications of this for displaced people in encampments? In order to answer that question, we must move beyond the strictest definitions of globalization and explore some of its concomitants. We must understand how participation in the global economy has decreased the power of state governments; how the role of international organizations has increased; how Western (read stronger) economies have advocated the spread of "universal values"; and how advances in technology have increased the economic role of ethnic diasporas. This chapter explores three ways in which globalization, broadly defined, affects permanent encampments. First, it assesses the way in which the spread of universal values affects the lives of displaced persons. Second, it explores the way in which international agencies and nongovernmental organizations play a large role in the lives of encampment residents. Third, it describes the potent role of diasporas (who retain their ties to their conationals, even those in encampments) and the way in which globalization has strengthened their role. Finally, the following question is posed in this chapter: Does globalization affect encampments differently in extroverted and introverted states?

UNIVERSAL VALUES

"Today's human rights abuses are tomorrow's refugee movements." Thus starts the chapter on human rights in an annual report by the UNHCR.[10] It follows that an emphasis on the protection of human rights will result in a decrease in population displacements and, by extension, a decrease in encampments. Hence, a focus on human rights is a form of preventive action. Since many displaced people are aided by Western states (either through funding of relief agencies or through the provision of asylum), human rights protection is aggressively pursued by those states. Emphasis on such rights has come to be associated with globalization.

In fact, globalization has come to be associated with more than just human rights, it has come to be associated with a set of values that the west likes to call "universal values". In its narrowest definition, universal values refer to the protection of human rights. However, a broad interpretation is more common, one that includes respect for the individual, private property, and democratic principles. Leading Western states have introduced legislation and encouraged other countries to uphold their principles and laws. These are explained below.

The broad category of human rights law provides guarantees for the fundamental rights of all human beings. The International Bill of Human Rights is composed of the Universal Declaration of Human Rights (1948), the International Covenant on Civil and Political Rights (1966), and the International Covenant on Economic, Social and Cultural Rights (1966). These include the so-called negative rights (no one should be subjected to torture, arbitrary interference with family, home or privacy, and arbitrary deprivation of property) as well as affirmative rights (such as, the right to an adequate standard of living, to liberty, and to security of person).[11] Additional guarantees are provided by the Convention Against Torture and Other

Cruel, Inhuman or Degrading Treatment or Punishment; the International Convention on the Elimination of All Forms of Racial Discrimination; the Convention on the Rights of the Child; and the International Convention on the Protection of the Rights of All Migrant Workers and Members of Their Families.[12] With specific reference to human and minority rights, in 1992 the UN General Assembly adopted the "Declaration on the Rights of Persons Belonging to National or Ethnic, Religious and Linguistic Minorities."

These laws have all been invoked when the international community intervened on humanitarian grounds in the domestic affairs of sovereign states. Indeed, the UN Security Council passed Resolution 688 in 1991, insisting that the Iraqi government allow access to international humanitarian efforts, showing that the international community is willing to put the concept of national sovereignty and noninterference in domestic affairs to second place. Moreover, on two occasions in 1999, the international community intervened on humanitarian grounds—in Kosovo and in East Timor.[13] In this way, the Western world, spearheaded by the United States, has transformed its views on individual rights into a set of "universal values" that it asserts is not location-specific. Because of the end of the cold war, Western states have been able to impose their values as well as their view of governance, without worrying about the marginalized, nonaligned, and socialist states.

However, these universal values are far from being universally upheld, and the activist policy of the United States is not universally appreciated. With respect to the former, it is clear that not all scholars agree with the concept of the universality of human rights. Adamantia Pollis and Peter Schwab questioned whether human rights were relevant to non-Western societies or socialist ideologies by arguing that economic, cultural, and collective rights had as much validity and legitimacy as individual civil and political rights.[14] Individual culture does matter, as Harrison and Huntington stress in their book entitled *Culture Matters*. They discuss how values inherent in a specific culture shape its progress and development.[15] It is in that context that proponents of Asian values invoked the Confucian tradition and claimed that its social and cultural legacy differed from that of the

West, making Western concepts largely irrelevant for their context.[16] Indeed, they argue that alternative views on human rights and social responsibilities are equally valid. As such, proponents of this view are cultural relativists *par excellence*.[17]

With respect to the activist nature of western policy pertaining to human rights, numerous countries across the globe see its demerits as outweighing its merits, identify its imperialist properties, and highlight its similarities to religious proselytizing. Until recently, the voting majority in the UN was made up of authoritarian states that resisted efforts to seriously monitor and enforce human rights.[18] Even now, numerous states resist such policies and laws. Globalization, with its emphasis on human rights, is seen, across the globe, as forcing the world to adopt American practices (Lester Thurow writes how even the Europeans call the American brand of globalization "cowboy capitalism").[19]

Whether focusing on the concept of universal values or on American activism in spreading them, many nonadherents are appalled by what they considered to be hypocritical policies on the part of many Western states. It is not too far in their histories, they like to remind the world, that the states most concerned with human rights were themselves abusers of human rights. Indeed, the expulsion of some 10 million Germans from East Europe after World War II in what was Europe's largest case of ethnic cleansing was sanctioned by the winning powers, including the United States. Similarly, government sponsored displacement of native populations in Canada, Australia, and the United States would be grounds for indictment at the world court today).[20]

The above discussion portrays a world in which the dominant powers (all extroverted states) espouse a package of values they believe are (or should be) shared universally, while nondominant (introverted) states resist the notion altogether. The debate on values and their universality rages among academics, policy makers, leaders, and the media. While few of those consider the implications for displaced persons, they are, in fact, very important for the lives of displaced persons and the conditions of their encampments. Some of these are described next.

Human Rights

The right to liberty, a minimum standard of living, and security of person are the most basic of human rights, extended to all whether they are displaced, refugees, migrants, minorities, and the like.

Refugee Rights

These refer explicitly to displaced persons that are outside their home states. They include the right to a minimum basic set of relief goods (such as food, housing, clothing) as well as protection. In addition, the International Labor Organization defines and monitors the observance of rights of migrant workers, demanding for them entitlements from their host countries, and, thus, protecting them.[21]

Minority Rights

While the 1948 Universal Declaration on Human Rights has no reference to minorities, in 1992 the UN General Assembly adopted the "Declaration on the Rights of Persons Belonging to National or Ethnic, Religious and Linguistic Minorities."[22] This document provides a broad mandate that states protect their minorities and give them rights to participate in decision making, promote education in their tongue, and enjoy their culture. The protection of minority rights ensures that minority ethnic groups are treated according to a set of prescribed principles. Since encamped persons are usually of a different ethnic group than the state's leadership, international laws pertaining to minorities are very relevant. The imposition of full rights and equality of all citizens, irrespective of ethnic orientation, has softened the blow of internally displaced peoples in several ways. It limits what the ruling ethnic group can do to its displaced minorities and it increases the options of minorities to stay within the state or to go. If they stay, they have more protection; if they go, they go from a position of strength. With respect to the majorities, the imposition of rules pertaining to minority rights may, in effect, dampen their efforts to keep the displaced minorities low on the pecking order (since they would be under the watchful eye of the international community, thereby making their goal more unattainable).

The Sacredness of the Family

The Universal Declaration on Human Rights also underscores the sacredness of the family and emphasizes the importance of its unity. Family unity is considered a fundamental right. This issue is especially relevant for encampments because families are often broken up in the course of involuntary displacement. While efforts are made to unite nuclear and extended families in encampments, it is not always possible or feasible due to obstacles set up by both home and host states.

The Right to Exist as a Nation

Indisputable in theory, the right to exist as a nation has all too often been disputed in practice. It entails acknowledgment of a people's right to a political expression of their group identity. This has been found unpalatable by Israelis and Palestinians, who are still grappling with the concept of each others existence. The Romas in Eastern Europe are using the universal right to exist as a nation as the basis of their demands for nationhood. The right of native Americans to exist as a group has been spearheaded by the Native American Rights Fund.[23]

The Right to Return

The Universal Declaration on Human Rights states that everyone has the right to leave any country and to return to his country. This was adopted the year after the partition of Palestine into a Jewish and Arab state. In 1993, the Arusha Accords, signed between the President of Rwanda Habyarimana and the RPF brought the war to an end and ensured the right of the diaspora to return home. The right to return is a cornerstone of the Dayton Peace accords that ended the war in Bosnia. The right of return remains a crucial issue in the peace negotiations between Israel and the Palestinian Authority.[24]

The Right Not to Be Involuntarily Moved

The inverse of this right is the right not to be involuntarily expelled, namely the right not to be involuntarily evicted (namely, ethnically cleansed). The expulsion of masses is prohibited by international law. The Nuremberg Charter of 1945 makes mass deportation a crime against humanity, and the 1949 Geneva Convention Relative to the Treatment of Civilians in Time of War also prohibits forcible transfers, mass or individual.[25] The forced return of refugees, known as *refoulement* is also now illegal by international conventions.[26]

The Right to Compensation

While no specific law pertains to the right to compensation, other accumulated legislation points to the responsibility of the expelling state to provide compensation.[27]

As noted above, regulations pertaining to universal values in general, and human rights in particular, are not taken seriously by all host and home country leaders. The mere existence of encampments, and the ongoing discussions pertaining to repatriation, compensation, reunification, and integration are all indicators that the above rights have not been honored. Some countries simply eschew these rights by not signing the obligatory documents. Alternatively, their representatives sign them but their domestic policies fail to reflect any of the international norms pertaining to human and civic rights or acceptable social behavior. More often than not, there is not even the pretense of going along with Western views. For displaced persons, ignoring the above rights translates into the perpetuation of poverty at the bottom of the pecking order with no recourse to any legal system.

Incidentally, there is some evidence that displaced persons have learned to make the debate about human rights work to their advantage. Krznaric found that some encampment residents have responded to their interactions with international organizations and NGOs by what he called "the appropriation of a new language of rights."[28] Their new empowerment, stemming from knowledge about their international rights, was also described by Pritchard. He found that "contact with the UNHCR and other NGOs gave refugees access to a transnational political 'space'. The refugees' effective appropriation of such universalistic discourses as human rights in their organized struggles to return suggests that these organizations have acted as agents of change."[29] Finally, Stepputat, in his study of Guatemalan refugee returnees, also found that they drew heavily on the human rights discourse.[30]

THE ROLE OF INTERNATIONAL AGENCIES

International organizations are a conduit for the spread of universal values to encampments as well as to host and home countries. In the current era of globalization, there has been an increase in both the number and the role of international organizations, thereby facilitating the enforcement of protection of rights and liberties of displaced people.

With respect to the increase in the number of international organizations, globalization has played an important part insofar as it entailed an erosion of state boundaries and a decline in state sovereignty.[31] To fill part of the vacuum, superstates, in the form or international organizations, have emerged.[32] According to Allen Scott, these consist of "institutional arrangements within which individual countries essentially give up elements of their national sovereignty in exchange for wider access to markets and resources in a context of strong legislatively based guarantees of cooperation."[33] He continues by saying that the trend is "a relentless erosion of the borders between individual national economies and a shift in the pattern of world development from a network to interacting national economies toward a single globally integrating economic system".[34] There were as many as 5,401 international intergovernmental associations in 1994, and 31,085 nongovernmental international associations, a twenty-five-fold increase since 1960.

With respect to the role of these organizations, changing world conditions have necessitated an expansion. With special reference to encampments, the mere increase in displaced populations, as well as the

world's awareness of them, has resulted in the mobilization of attention and aid in their favor. The number of organizations that provide
humanitarian assistance to camps has increased. Indeed, aid from
UNHCR, the World Food Programme, and the International Committee of the Red Cross is now supplemented with assistance from
the United Nations Children's Fund (UNICEF), the United Nations
Development Programme (UNDP), the World Health Organization
(WHO), and the International Organization for Migration. In addition, specialized organizations increasingly provide a watchful eye to
ensure that authorities are respecting the rights of the displaced. In
that way, the involvement of organizations such as Amnesty International, the UN High Commissioner for Human Rights, and Helsinki
Watch has increased and evolved. This expansion in the role of international organizations has been identified by Cohen and Deng, who
report that international organizations come to the aid of humanitarian disasters now in ways they never did before.[35]

Nongovernmental organizations have also been on the rise, ensuring the protection of human rights by their presence, advocacy, and
direct action.[36] NGOs are often more effective than international
agencies because they answer to no home government (although
they do need permission of host governments). Moreover, unlike the
larger, more cumbersome and bureaucratic international organizations, they are flexible, fast, courageous, and willing to take risks.
They are willing to cooperate with governmental bodies, and have
done so effectively in numerous instances.[37] Their success was highlighted by the former Secretary General of the United Nations,
Boutros Boutros Ghali, who said "NGOs were more important in Somalia than the agencies of the United Nations."[38]

THE ROLE OF DIASPORAS

It has been said that "you can take a Palestinian out of Palestine but
you can't take Palestine out of a Palestinian." This phrase, applicable
to any displaced ethnic group, explains the emotional bond between
people and their ancestral territory that survives both temporal and

spatial distance. Indeed, both voluntary and involuntary migrants retain ties to their lands over time and across continents. This characteristic of diasporas underlies much of their behavior and attitude
towards their encamped conationals.

Diasporas, as international organizations, can be a conduit for the
spread of universal values.[39] In the current era of globalization, they,
too, have increased in number and expanded their role. Indeed, with
voluntary and involuntary migrations across borders on the rise,
there has been an increase in diasporas of virtually all ethnic groups
(since 1959, the diaspora of Rwandan Tutsis has grown to one million
people. Some 800,000 Tamils are estimated to be in the diaspora, in
India, Australia, Western Europe, and North America. Nearly 3 million Palestinians live in Arab countries, Europe, and the Americas).
Moreover, their presence in both their home and host states has increased. They now affect policies in both home and host states and
play an important role in promoting political and economic change.

With reference to encampments, the diaspora can promote political
change by spreading Western values and persuading multiethnic countries across the globe to adopt minority rights.[40] Diasporas residing in
the West promote the spread of Western values to their home countries
because they "speak both languages." This nonliteral interpretation of
language encompasses all aspects of culture. Since diasporas have sensitivity to home cultures, they are better positioned to guide the penetration of Western values. As Yossi Shain has shown, diasporas residing
in the West, especially in the United States, have already been instrumental in bringing Western ideas pertaining to democracy, human
rights, and respect for minorities back to their home countries.[41] Functioning as a conduit, these former immigrants can help transform interethnic relations in their home countries and, in the process, promote
interethnic harmony (for example, Palestinians in the diaspora have
been instrumental in providing political support for their encamped
conationals by forming lobby groups in their host countries).

Diasporas also promote economic change. They support encampment survival and development by sponsoring infusions of capital.
The greater their emotional or political ties to encampments, the
greater their commitment to assist. Yossi Shain presents evidence of

diasporic groups in the United States sending home states remittances that play a major part in the economic and political development at home. This is true among the Koreans, Greeks, Mexicans, Arabs, Israelis, etc.[42] Remittances that directly benefit encampments are also common. Rogerson and Letsoalo found that the principal source of household income in South African townships was the remittances of long-term labor migrants.[43] That income, in turn, is used to participate in economic activities that stimulate economic development in the homelands. Also, Saharawi refugee camps in Algeria have benefited from the remittances of Polisario personnel in foreign embassies as well as students who study abroad and then stay abroad.[44]

This transfer of capital is neither new nor surprising. Immigrant groups in the United States have traditionally sent money to their home states to support family members as well as political causes. Very often, the distinction between helping out ones family and helping a political cause is very small. Tamils raise money and send it to their countrymen in Sri Lanka, money that is used to support the war effort and aid those displaced by the war (it has been claimed that one bank in Jaffna takes in $350 million per year).[45] Similarly, there is evidence of Eritreans, Kurds, and Palestinians in the United States raising money for political causes in their home states.

Has globalization affected the way in which diasporas interact with their home states and ethnic groups? The answer is unequivocally yes. Diasporas make use of the internet, the telephone, newspapers, and inexpensive travel to keep up with events in their home countries. The new technology has helped diaporas keep in touch with their homelands and their displaced populations. Eritreans, Tamils, and Congolese are among those who use the internet to get information about their displaced and fighting conationals.[46]

Moreover, immigrants today are not the immigrants of old, who never set foot on their home soil again, who forbade their children to speak their native tongue in order to speed up integration into host culture. Instead, the new diaspora lives with one foot in one country and the other in its home state. It has loyalties in both locations and it participates in the economy and the political system in both locations. Its people perceive themselves as nationals of the home state and citizens of the host country. In other words, when immigrants become citizens of their new country, they do not leave their nationality behind. When they acquire host country citizenship, their sense of belonging to the state increases, as does their capacity and incentive to participate in its culture. They also want to exert their power, express their opinion, and influence policy. The electoral system, newly opened to naturalized immigrants, allows them to do this. It empowers them. The evidence from the United States is clear: the newly empowered groups using the electoral system to exert their influence include the Cubans, Haitians, Koreans, Chinese, Vietnamese, Dominicans, Mexicans (they supercede the traditional groups, namely the Italians, Poles, Greeks, Jews, and Germans). According to Yossi Shain, these groups have been successfully empowered: "one of the signs that an ethnic group has achieved a respectable position in American life is its acquisition of a meaningful voice in U.S. foreign affairs."[47] Despite such involvement in their host states, they do not forget their home country and their home peoples. Some have argued that they keep in touch with their homeland as ambassadors of peace. Nicholas Negroponte has said that children of the future will not know what nationalism is because their primary loyalties will lie with the international community that they access through the internet.[48] For the same reasons, Michael Detrouzos has said that the internet will bring computer-aided peace.

Thus, the diaspora is for encampments what stem cells are for human bodies.[49] Just like stem cells represent the ability of the human body to regenerate itself, so, too, the diaspora has the ability to regenerate the ethnic group it left behind. By reinventing itself, it invigorates the entire ethnic group. Such invigoration is particularly important in encampments, which by virtue of their isolation and status lag behind in dynamism and creativity. By using their position outside the country to press for political concessions, economic transfusions, respect for human rights, and democratic practices inside the camps, diasporas are the stem cells of encampments.[50]

ENCAMPMENTS AND GLOBALIZATION IN
INTROVERTED AND EXTROVERTED STATES

In chapter 2, it was proposed that encampments in extroverted countries have greater links to the global economy than encampments in
introverted states. This chapter explored three components of this
link: universal values, international agencies, and diasporas. Although
direct trade is also a link to the international economy, it is omitted
from this study because it is so rare (the export of Saharawi carpets
and rugs to Spain and France is the exception to the rule).[51]

While extroverted and introverted countries are at odds about numerous aspects of globalization, none are as explosive as universal
values and human rights. The extroverted liberal, Western democracies have been at the forefront of the movement to acknowledge,
respect, and protect people in general, and displaced minorities in
particular. With their liberal views and democratic values, extroverted countries have spearheaded the effort to reverse undemocra-
tic trends. They are using globalization as a conduit for the spread of
economic, political, and humanitarian changes. They are ensuring
that, over the long run, Western values of human rights and minority
protection do indeed become universal. They do this through their
political, economic, and social institutions that are rooted in the concept of civil and human rights. In introverted states, these institutions are missing.

It follows that countries in which political values and political culture are liberal, and where there is respect for human and minority
rights, are more likely to treat their minorities better than countries
where such liberal values are absent. In a liberal democracy, minorities and displaced peoples are more able and likely to interna-
tionalize their concerns. They are more able because international
agencies exist that are sympathetic to their cause; they are more
likely because they actually think they might succeed in achieving
recognition and having their concerns heard. They have recourse to
international organizations that can monitor the satisfaction of their
demands.[52] There is no doubt international organizations (such as
the United Nations bodies, nongovernmental agencies, and repre-

sentations of Western governments) play an important role in minority protection worldwide. However, the restrictions placed on their activities are greater in introverted states than in extroverted ones. The internationalization of minority concerns also takes place via connections with diaspora communities that are condoned in liberal democracies. Such connections allow newly naturalized and newly empowered ethnic groups to retain strong ties to their home countries that, in turn, ensure that their nationals are treated well.[53] When properly harnessed, the emotional ties that bind diasporas have the power to make constructive changes at the level of the encampments. But not all diasporas can do this. Those residing in extroverted countries are more likely to be actively involved with their ethnic compatriots in encampments than those who live in introverted states. In the former, they are more likely to have computer links, travel, and media exposure, thereby enabling greater contact than in introverted states. Thus, advances in technology and the spread of information, so fundamental to globalization and to extroverted states, have altered the very nature of exchange and communication between the diaspora and the encampments.

NOTES

1. Thomas Friedman, *The Lexus and the Olive Tree* (New York: Anchor Books, 2000).

2. Benjamin Barber, *Jihad vs. McWorld* (New York: Times Books, 1995).

3. The Davos Man refers to the global economic and business elite that participates in the World Economic Forum held in Davos, Switzerland. *Orang Ulu* is a term used in Malaysia and Indonesia to refer to traditional, country folk. Peter A. Coclanis and Tilak Doshi, "Globalization in South East Asia" in *Dimensions of Globalization*, ed. Louis Ferleger and Jay R. Mandle (The Annals of the American Academy of Political and Social Science, 570, July 2000), 50.

4. Jay R. Mandle and Louis Ferleger, "preface" in *Dimensions of Globalization*, eds. Louis Ferleger and Jay R. Mandle (The Annals of the American Academy of Political and Social Science, 570, July 2000), 8.

5. Daniel Gaske, *Understanding U.S. and Global Economic Trends*, 2nd Edition (Dubuque, Iowa: Kendall/Hunt Publishing, 1999), 121–23.

6. Indeed, the growth and development of countries has been tied to the international economy for centuries, as witnessed the role of global trade in eighteenth century imperialism, dependency relations in the twentieth century, export promotion policies of the 1980s and 1990s, and so forth. (It must be noted, however, that the degree of global integration has not grown constantly over the past century. Indeed, high trade barriers of the 1920s and 1930s prevented that, along with immigration controls, bans on foreign investments in some countries, and bans on cultural exchanges. Many of these interferences, politically induced, reduced the potential of international exchange during this century.) Some claim that this period is no different from others. See article by Louis Echitelle in the *New York Times* (1998) cited in Mandle and Ferleger, "preface," 8.

7. See Peter Slater, *Workers without Frontiers. The Impact of Globalization on International Migration* (Boulder, Colo.: Lynne Reinner, 2000), 6–8.

8. Friedman, *The Lexus and the Olive Tree*, 9.

9. This is clearly illustrated by the Asian financial crisis of the 1990s, when external shocks reverberated quickly across the globe and the social and economic consequences were fast, painful, and all too easily transmitted across countries.

10. UNHCR, *The State of the World's Refugees* (New York: Oxford University Press, 1995), 57.

11. These are described in Francis M. Deng, "Protecting the Dispossessed" *Brookings Occasional Paper* (Washington, D.C.: Brookings Institution, 1993), 5.

12. For detail on international and European covenants, see David Jacobson, *Rights across Borders* (Baltimore, Md: Johns Hopkins University Press, 1997).

13. President Clinton referred to the refugees streaming out of Kosovo and justified his NATO-led bombing campaign by saying "ending this tragedy is a moral imperative." Cited in Roger P. Winter, "The Year in Review" USCR, *World Refugee Survey 2000*, 14. While the suffering of the Kosovo population is undeniable, such words and their ensuing action must have sounded hollow to the displaced peoples across the globe, whose plight is magnified and has continued for decades. The scale of the international response, and the hundreds of millions of dollars spent on Kosovo refugees, led some aid workers to call it "almost an obscenity" (Winter, 18).

14. Adamantia Pollis and Peter Schwab, "Human Rights: A Western Construct with Limited Applicability" in *Human Rights, Cultural and Ideological Perspectives*, ed. Adamanta Pollis and Peter Schwab (New York: Praeger Publishers, 1979).

15. Lawrence E. Harrison and Samuel P. Huntington, eds. *Culture Matters* (New York: Basic Books, 2000).

16. See Fareed Zakaria, "A Conversation with Lee Kuan Yew," and Kim Dae Jung, "The Myth of Asia's Anti-Democratic Values" *Foreign Affairs Agenda 1995* (New York: Council on Foreign Relations, 1995).

17. This includes leaders of states such as Singapore, Malaysia, China, and Indonesia.

18. Gideon Gottlieb, *Nation against State* (New York: The Council on Foreign Relations Press, 1993), 31.

19. Lester C. Thurow, "Globalization: The Product of a Knowledge-Based Economy" in Ferleger and Mandle, *Dimensions of Globalization*, 27.

20. It was with Thomas Jefferson, one of the most revered early statesmen in the United States, that the idea of the systematic Indian removal originated (he even contemplated a constitutional amendment about it. The amendment would have provided for the exchange of Indian land east of the Mississippi for tracts within the newly acquired Louisiana Purchase.) Fergus M. Bordewich, *Killing the White Man's Indian: Reinventing Native Americans at the End of the Twentieth Century* (New York: Anchor Books, 1996), 43.

21. While a transnational regime for minority rights does exist in the 1990s, it is relatively weak. It is really a code of good behavior, as states are merely encouraged to comply, with no effective means of imposing sanctions on members who breach the standards (See Hugh Maill, "introduction" in *Minority Rights in Europe*, ed. Hugh Maill [New York: Council on Foreign Relations, 1994], 3). Moreover, while Europe professes to have respect for human and minority rights, and countries of western Europe have even gone to war against Yugoslavia ostensibly to protect the human rights of Kosovo Albanians, there are gaping holes in their policies. The glaring example of the Roma, 8 million stateless people across Europe whose plight is worsened by open discrimination against them in all aspects of their lives. They suffer from violence from both ends of the spectrum—the police as well as the skinheads. The new Europe has shown little interest in breaking the cycle of isolation and prejudice and poverty that the Roma face. The Roma experience is a Pan European problem and its overdue lack of solution makes western minority and human rights a Swiss cheese policy. Nev-

ertheless, Europe does have a policy of protecting minority rights and it is more respectful of human rights than most places across the globe.

22. In between these two documents, there were several covenants on civil, political, economic and social rights, which said that violation of human rights is a matter of international concern (especially article 27 of the International Covenant on Civil and Political Rights). Then, the 1975 Helsinki Final Act involved the eastern bloc in the adherence to these principles.

23. The Native American Rights Fund is the largest and oldest national interest law firm that addresses the rights of tribes to exist, to be independent, and to preserve their tribal practices. Vine Deloria, Jr. and Clifford M. Lytle, *American Indians, American Justice* (Austin: University of Texas, 1983), 156–57.

24. Palestinians claim that they have the right, supported by international laws, to return to their homeland. Israel refuses to recognize that right because it views the implementation of such a return as changing the Jewish character of Israel. President Clinton's peace proposals of 2000 involve the right of Palestinians to return to Palestinian homelands, namely still-to-be-created Palestinian lands in West Bank and Gaza. Yasser Arafat is reluctant to accept such a deal because Palestinians view the right to return as their individual right, not a collective right that can be signed away by a leader.

25. Donna E. Arzt, *Refugees into Citizens* (New York: Council on Foreign Relations, 1997), 67.

26. Countries have been getting around the law against *refoulement* by creating safe havens in the countries of conflict. For example, the international community did so in Iraq with the Kurds, and thus allowed Turkey to close its border to them. The United States did something similar with the Haiti population, and created a safe haven both within the island as well as on its base in Guantanamo Bay in Cuba. Counter this with the demands made by Macedonia, during the exodus of Kosovo Albanians in 1999, of "one in/one out."

27. Arzt, *Refugees into Citizens*, 71.

28. Roman Krznaric, "Guatemalan Returnees and the Dilemma of Political Mobilization" *Journal of Refugee Studies* 10, no. 1 (1997), 71.

29. D. Pritchard, "The Legacy of Conflict: Refugee Repatriation and Reintegration in Central American" in *Central America: Fragile Transition*, ed. R. Seider (London: Macmillan Press, 1995) cited in Krznaric, "Guatemalan Returnees and the Dilemma of Political Mobilization, 71.

30. Finn Stepputat, "Repatriation and the Politics of Space: The Case of the Mayan Diaspora and the Return Movement" *Journal of Refugee Studies* (7, nos. 2/3, 1994), cited in Krznaric, "Guatemalan Returnees and the Dilemma of Political Mobilization," 70.

31. There is a trend toward countries giving up their sovereignty over some issues to the governance by a supranational body. Marco Martiniello points out the intricacies for Europeans who are European Union citizens, and the fact that their national governments had to give up a certain kind of control over its own citizens. Marco Martiniello, "Citizenship of the European Union" in *From Migrants to Citizens, Membership in a Changing World*, ed. T. Alexander Aleinikoff and Douglas Klusmeyer (Washington, D.C.: Carnegie Endowment for International Peace, 2000). Soysal identified "post-national membership" configurations and described the emergence of transnational actors, discourses, and policy levels. While he was discussing immigration in particular, his framework is also applicable for other areas Yasemin N. Soysal, *Limits of Citizenship: Migrants and Postnational Membership in Europe* (Chicago: Chicago University Press, 1984). Miriam Feldbaum defines two terms often used in this discourse. Transnational "has been used to describe emergent institutional settings where the locus in which authority resides or policy is formulated or decisions are implemented goes beyond the national level. . . . Transnational norms refers to emergent norms, pressures or rationales driving policy decisions of implementation that are decoupled from the sole logic of the national state and territory." Miriam Feldbaum, "Managing Membership: New Trends in Citizenship and Nationality Policy" in *From Migrants to Citizens, Membership in a Changing World*, eds. T. Alexander Aleinikoff and Douglas Klusmeyer (Washington, D.C.: Carnegie Endowment for International Peace, 2000), 490.

32. Allen J. Scott, *Regions and the World Economy: The Coming Age of Global Production, Competition, and Political Order.* (Oxford: Oxford University Press, 2000), 10. Participation in the global economy decreases the power of state governments to control their own economic destinies (as the total economic destiny becomes global). According to Scott, this global destiny is partially but imperfectly regulated by a system of international contractual regimes, understandings, and organizations led by the plurination (as represented by a group of multination blocs, such as EU, NAFTA, ASEAN, CARICOM, APEC, and MERCOSUR).

33. Scott, *Regions and the World Economy*, 42

34. Scott, *Regions and the World Economy*, 41.

35. Roberta Cohen and Francis M. Deng, *Masses in Flight* (Washington: Brookings Institution, 1998), 8.

36. Leon Gordenker and T. G. Weiss, "Pluralizing Global Governance: Analytical Approaches and Dimensions" in *NGOs, the UN and Global Governance*, eds. T. G. Weiss and L. Gordenker (Boulder: Lynne Rienner, 1996). The most important NGOs that work with the displaced populations include CARE USA, Caritas Internationalis, International Federation of Red Cross and Red Crescent Societies, International Islamic Relief Organization, Jesuit Refugee Service, Lutheran World Federation, Medecins Sans Frontiers, OXFAM, World Council of Churches, World Vision, Human Rights Watch, World Wide Fund for Nature International, and International Alert.

37. An example of successful cooperation is in Tanzania: the UNHCR, the Tanzanian government, and the Lutheran World Federation/Tanganyika Christian Refugee Service came up with a tripartate approach to burden sharing of refugees and encampments. See Charles P. Gasarasi, "The Tripartite Approach to the Resettlement and Integration of Rural Refugees in Tanzania" in *Refugees, A Third World Dilemma*, ed. John R. Rogge (Totowa, N.J.: Rowman & Littlefield, 1987), 101.

38. Ted Robert Gurr, *Minorities at Risk* (Washington, D.C.: United States Institute for Peace, 1993), 187.

39. The term diaspora comes from the Greek for "dispersal" and connotes just that, people dispersed outside their national borders. There are several well-known cases of diasporas in modern times, including the Germans in Eastern Europe, the Jews in the United States, the Chinese in Southeast Asia, and the South Asians in East Africa. The Romas are also dispersed, although, unlike the others, they do not have a home state. Then there are other diasporas that differ from the classical ones described above. According to Michael Mandelbaum, "The older 'classical' diasporas of Jews, the Chinese, the Indians and the Germans were created when people moved. The new diasporas [including the Hungarian, Russian, Serb, and Albanian] were created when borders moved." Michael Mandelbaum, "introduction" in *The New European Diasporas, National Minorities and Conflict in Eastern Europe*, ed. Michael Mandelbaum (New York: Council on Foreign Relations Press, 2000), 2.

40. It is because of the big role played by the diaspora that host governments are often threatened. For this reason, some outlaw any contacts with diasporas. For example, after Museveni came to power in Uganda, the lead-

ership in Rwanda outlawed contact between the Tutsis and their diaspora. Thus, rather than the Tutsi diaspora being a source of progress, contact with it went underground. This was because the leadership was threatened since large numbers of Tutsi refugees fought in Museveni's army. Philip Gourevitch, *We Wish To Inform You that Tomorrow We Will Be Killed with Our Families* (New York: Picador USA, 1999), 73.

41. Yossi Shain, *Marketing the American Credo Abroad* (Cambridge: Cambridge University Press, 1999). However, in addition to playing a role in opportunities for interethnic harmony, diasporas can also be a part of the danger. One example that comes to mind is the role played by the Croatian diasporas in the United States and Germany in bringing to power the nationalist government of Franjo Tudman.

42. Shain, *Marketing the American Creed Abroad*, chapters 3, 5, especially pages 170–71.

43. C. M. Rogerson and Em. M. Letsoalo, "Resettlement and Under-Development in the Black 'Homelands" of South Africa" in *Population and Development Projects in Africa*, eds. John I. Clarke, Mustafa Khogali, and Leszek A. Kosinski (Cambridge: Cambridge University Press, 1985), 189.

44. *The Economist,* November 4, 2000, 52.

45. *The Economist,* August 19, 2000, 26.

46. *The Economist,* August 19, 2000, 27.

47. Shain, *Marketing the American Creed Abroad*, x. While Nathan Glazer and Daniel Patrick Moynihan have stated that ethnic influences have become very important determinants of policy in the United States (Nathan Glazer and Daniel Patrick Moynihan, eds. *Ethnicity: Theory and Experience* [Cambrdge, Mass.: Harvard University Press, 1975], 23–24) this view is countered by Alexander De Conde who argues that immigrant groups have little real power, despite the fact that it looks like they do (Alexander DeConde, *Ethnicity, Race and American Foreign Policy: A History* [Boston: Northeastern University Press, 1992], 200).

48. *The Economist,* August 19, 2000, 11.

49. Stem cells are a nondifferentiated glob of cells that divide randomly and blossom into nerve and muscle cells, becoming are a source of replacement for dead or dying cells.

50. There are exceptions to this. For example, the African American community, that might otherwise be involved in pressing for humanitarian aid in African countries, has been dormant and has failed to act as a stem cell for encampments across Africa. In part, this is due to the fact that it is

the most marginalized population group in U.S. society. Also, its domestic problems are overwhelming and have left little time, resources, and inclination for overseas problems).

51. Angharad Thomas and Gordon Wilson, "Technological Capabilities in Textile Production in Saharawi Refugee Camps" *Journal of Refugee Studies* 9, no. 2 (1996), 186.

52. A seeming contradiction warrants explanation. It may seem that the links between encampments and international organizations are greater in introverted states since they are poorer and less able to provide for refugees. These camps require attention and humanitarian assistance that they get from the international community. Thus, it would seem that role of international organizations is higher in introverted states. However, this is only a short-term phenomena. In the long run, in the lifetime of permanent encampments, international aid tends to dry up.

53. They very often have dual citizenship and multiple loyalties. Sometimes, they have voting rights in home and home countries (such as the U.S. citizens from the Dominican Republic, Mexico, and, soon, even Israel). They are the diasporas, who, according to Fred Riggs, encompass communities whose members live informally outside a homeland while maintaining active contacts with it, and some variations thereof (Fred W. Riggs, "Diasporas and Ethnic Nations" paper presented at the annual meetings of the International Studies Association [Los Angeles, March 2000], 3). Yossi Shain defines them as "a people with a common ethnic-national-religious origin who reside outside a claimed or an independent home territory" (Shain, *Marketing the American Creed Abroad*, 8). They have one foot in their home country, one foot in the host. They have citizenship in one country but often nationhood in another. Indeed, the national identity of a community may be very different from the statehood identity.

6

THE PERSISTENCE OF
NATIONALISM AND CONFLICT

Despite overwhelming evidence of political, economic, and social change across the globe, some ethnic groups continue to engage in violent interactions with each other. They battle over the same issues that their forefathers battled over a decade or a century ago. At the core of such disputes is the interethnic competition for resources.[1] The resources may have changed and the rules of the competition may have been adjusted to accommodate for new conditions, but the essential goals, as well as manifestations of the struggle, have not changed significantly over the past century.

Implicit in the above paragraph is a relationship between four variables: ethnicity, nationalism, economics, and conflict. This chapter analyzes these four variables and their relationships in the context of encampments, as well as their home and host countries. It addresses the role economics plays in matters of ethnicity and nationalism. Furthermore, it describes how encampments are subject to the confluence of three nationalisms: the one that festers within the encampment itself, the one that exists within the host state, and, finally, the one that prevails in home states and continues to affect encampment residents. Finally, this chapter explores

the differences between nationalism and its expressions in introverted and extroverted states.

THE ECONOMY, NATIONALISM, AND ETHNIC CONFLICT

The relationship between ethnicity and nationalism has been discussed in chapter 1 and warrants no further elaboration here. However, the economic roots of nationalism and the relationship between
nationalism and economics are relevant for the study of encampments, and thus need some attention.

In an earlier work, the author suggested that the state of the
economy can lead to and can accentuate feelings of ethnic loyalty
and group distinctiveness. In other words, it can stimulate feelings
of nationalism.[2] Given that nationalism is the political expression of
ethnic sentiments, its link to interethnic competition for economic
resources is indisputable. Nationalist feelings by definition contain
elements of interethnic competition because of the underlying motivation to pursue ends that will enhance a group's overall well-being, position, and advantage within society. A group's well-being is
simultaneously political, cultural, and economic (indeed, it is hard
to distinguish between the desire for national control of resources
among the inhabitants of diamond-rich Yakutia [in Russia] and the
pride in their culture and the desire to see their people in power).
Thus, nationalism is simply a coherent manifestation of interethnic
competition.[3]

In the course of such interethnic competition, the critical consideration among populations is the perception of economic injustice. Such perceptions exist both with respect to objective macro-
conditions (such as poverty), as well as policy aimed at rectifying
those conditions (such as antipoverty programs for targeted ethnic
groups). People perceive injustice because they believe they are
making above-average contributions (to the national budget), receiving insufficient benefits (from the national budget), facing unfavorable terms of trade resulting from price manipulation, are
subject to unfavorable regulation pertaining to investment and for-

eign inflows of resources, and so on.[4] Perceptions of economic injustice mingle with ethnic, religious, and cultural factors to fuel nationalist ideology.

While not all nationalism necessarily results in conflict, it does so sufficiently to produce an abundant literature explaining the emergence of interethnic conflict.[5] Several bodies of theory have addressed the link between nationalism, economics, and conflict at length. The human ecology theories are based on newcomers (such as incoming migrants) and the niches they find for themselves.[6] If migrants have economic opportunities, then inequalities between them and the host population decreases and the potential for conflict diminishes. Numerous offshoots of the niche idea developed, including Frederick Barth's contention that ethnic and racial violence follows when niches overlap.[7] Other theories, based on economic inequalities, suggest that conflict arises between regions and ethnic groups because one is consistently at the core and dominates those on the periphery.[8] Other economic theories focus on dual labor markets and middle man minorities, in which ethnic conflict arises because some minorities have managed to create (or exploit) a niche in the economy, much to the anger of the dominant ethnic group.[9] Donald Horowitz's contribution to the literature states that conflict results from a "modernization gap" between ethnic groups that have developed at different rates.[10] Competition theories focus on conflict that erupts from interethnic competition. Among these, Susan Olzak claims that the factors that raise the levels of competition among race and ethnic groups increase the rates of ethnic collective action. Conflicts erupt when ethnic inequalities and racially ordered systems begin to break down, as due to economic change.[11]

The above discussion is relevant for encampments and their host communities in several ways. First, competition for resources characterizes encampment life. While camps compete with each other for limited host and international resources, the most ferocious competition takes place within the encampment, among its residents. They compete with each other for allocations of food, business opportunities, preferable housing, and jobs. They also compete with the neighboring community for employment, food, markets, etc. Since they are the newcomers, it is they who are attempting to create new niches for themselves. To the extent that they spill into niches of the neighboring host communities, conflict ensues. Second, in the process of competition, encampment residents perceive economic injustice due to insufficient infusions from the host/international community. At the same time, host states feel economic injustice because they feel encampments are an unfair drainage of their resources. Thus, both among encampments and host communities, perceptions of economic injustice are not hard to find. Third, given that the host economy remains the core and the encampment remains the periphery, the relationship between them is one of inequality and is therefore predisposed to conflict. Therefore, niche encroachment, perceptions of economic injustice, and inequality reinforce each other as they spin into a spiral of escalating tension, distrust, and conflict.

The fundamental characteristics of encampments, namely uprootedness, poverty, scarcity, and isolation, are conducive to producing active and strong nationalist feeling among the residents. Encampments bring out the worse elements of nationalism. They enable fringe, extremist sentiments to become mainstream, both within the camp and outside. From within, encampments are viewed as prisons that only combative behavior has a chance of breaking; from outside, they are viewed as an eyesore, a drain of resources, and an impediment to the development of neighboring host areas.

HOMO HIERARCHICUS

Interaction between encampments and host states, already volatile and difficult, is further complicated by ethnic factors. Displaced persons are usually of a different ethnic/national/religious group than home and host majorities. As a result, it is difficult to divorce the ethnic dimension from overall camp/host interactions.[12] All too easily, conflict between encampments and host/home communities becomes interethnic conflict.

Such conflict is rooted in hierarchical relations between ethnic groups. In multiethnic states, often some ethnic groups are ranked higher than others in some real or imagined hierarchy.[13] They view themselves, and are viewed by others, as better, smarter, richer, more competent, more accomplished, and more powerful. As a result, they believe they are more deserving. In the words Srdjan Bogosavljevic, they believe they "have the right to more sunshine."[14] In some multi-ethnic states, such hierarchy is written into the constitution (see chapter 4), it is embedded in laws and implemented with supporting policies. Alternatively, hierarchy is simply known. Ethnic bias is passed on from generation to generation in spoken and unspoken ways. The existence, persistence, and prevalence of such hierarchies led Louis Dumont to coin the phrase *homo hierarchicus* in reference to multiethnic societies.

Homo hierarchicus is an underlying feature in encampment conflicts. Whether it is ensconced in laws or whether it is simply known, hierarchical structure is part of the baggage involuntary migrants carry when they are displaced. There are numerous examples of encampments that do not shed their pre-camp hierarchies. For example, in Rwanda, the Tutsis are at the top of the ethnic hierarchy (with their herdsmen background and aristocratic pretensions that were strengthened by the status accorded to them by the Belgian colonial rulers). They are followed by the Hutus, traditionally cultivators, and lastly by the Pygmies, who in times of monarchy were the court jesters.[15] In times of conflict, involuntary migration and encampment, this hierarchy does not crumble. There is evidence, for example, that the Pygmies are considered so low in the ethnic hierarchy that they were enlisted by Hutu militias as rapists to add a greater measure of degradation to the violation of Tutsi women.[16] Similarly, in Sri Lanka, the hierarchy is very clear: the Sinhalese are at the top (they comprise 74 percent of the population and are mostly Buddhist), followed by the Tamils (some 18 percent and mostly Hindu), and, finally, the Muslims, or Moors (7 percent, all Muslim). Among the Tamils, there is a further hierarchical subdivision: the original residents of the island are higher in the hierarchy than the newly arrived plantation Tamils who were brought in as laborers in the nineteenth century.[17] To the extent that these people all end up in encampments together, their relative position in the hierarchy is maintained.

Homo hierarchicus is also evident in government assistance to internally displaced populations. According to Ted Robert Gurr, "governments are usually willing to assist persons belonging to the same ethnic group as the dominant one in the government: for example, ethnic Russians in Russia, ethnic Georgians in Georgia, ethnic Azerbaijanis in Azerbaijan or Bosnian Muslims in government controlled parts of Bosnia. Others sometimes find themselves badly neglected."[18] When they are of the same ethnic group, government resources are stretched in order to provide assistance (as, for example, the Croatian government did for displaced Croats from Bosnia, but not for displaced Muslims).

Homo hierarchicus is also reflected in host country policy in general, and refugee policy in particular. Not all ethnic groups are equally welcome. For example, refugees in Thailand are enumerated by ethnicity and treated in accordance to their status in the ethnic hierarchy: Vietnamese come first, followed by the Lao and the Chinese.[19] Also, under the rule of Idi Amin, Uganda's refugee policy was not universally applicable. While Asians (even with citizenship papers) were expelled in 1972, Rwandan refugees were allowed to settle on unoccupied land.[20]

Finally, *homo hierarchicus* even permeates the terminology used to refer to displaced peoples and, in turn, affects the conditions of their encampment. The example from Burundi is poignant. There, different terms have been used to officially describe the country's uprooted population: Tutsis are said to be "displaced" while Hutus are said to be "dispersed."[21] This distinction reflects a politicization of the displacement crisis as it labels involuntary migrants by their ethnicity. That, in turn, facilitates disparities in assistance and protection (displaced Tutsis get protection from the Burundi military, others do not. Moreover, the camps for the Tutsis have been created where there is better access to assistance while the Hutu camps tend to be more remote).

INTERETHNIC CONFLICT AND ENCAMPMENTS:
THE CONFLUENCE OF THREE NATIONALISMS

Nationalism is fueled by interethnic economic competition (and the concomitant perceptions of economic injustice). It is also fueled by ethnic hierarchical structures (and their concomitant ranking of rights and benefits of ethnic groups). As both economic competition for scarce resources as well as ethnic hierarchies are found in encampments, host countries, and home states, it follows that nationalist sentiment is likely to be present. When it is, the ensuing confluence of nationalisms in camps, host states as well as home countries, constitutes a potent mix that easily escalates into conflict.

Such conflict rarely stays passive for long. More often than not, violence is present and characterizes camp/host relations. What often begins as microlevel harassment of encampment residents turns into street fighting and verbal abuse. Soon, the conflict escalates into riots, antiminority legislation, pressures for involuntary migrations, and so on. Governments and targeted ethnic groups engage in a retaliatory spiral of confrontational measures. Spurred on by the international community's current focus on minority rights, encampment residents pursue their demands as never before.[22] Leaders react in a knee jerk fashion, often aggravating the volatile atmosphere and the precarious overall balance between groups. They introduce yet more policies, progressively more restrictive and discriminatory in nature.

Because conditions for the escalation of violence are present, the need for security of encampments is great. It has been argued that the most important task for host authorities and the international community is to provide security.[23] Cohen and Deng report "internally displaced persons have regularly pointed out that security is as important to them as food. Providing food and supplies without attending to protection can undermine assistance programs and even lead to situations in which the victims become the "well-fed dead."[24] Bill Frelick said international organizations "feed the hungry, clothe the naked and watch them die."[25]

Nationalism and Conflict in Encampments

Displaced persons in encampments have economic, political, and social demands. Among the former is their desire to have more economic opportunities to improve their lives. Among their political demands, displaced people desire to return to their homelands or find a permanent home elsewhere.[26] Among social demands, displaced people want the right to stop being invisible. They reject their marginalization as stateless and homeless citizens and want to be acknowledged with respect.[27]

Given little hope for achieving these goals by peaceful means, many encampments have become a source of violent rebel activity. Aristide Zolberg called such encampments refugee-warrior communities[28] in which residents use their warrior skills to promote violence against host and home states. According to international law, this is a contradiction in terms. The purpose of camps is to provide humanitarian assistance or to help people establish settlements in which to live. No provisions are made for political activism among encampment residents. Yet it persists. All too often, encampment residents make incursions into their home state for political reasons. In Afghani refugee camps, the mujahedin are trained and their operations are based. In Palestinian camps, the Intifada grew and developed. Nicaraguan contras have lived in camps with refugees. The Hutu camps in Goma were centers of criminal activity.[29] Guatemalan camps in Chiapas have been accused of housing guerrillas, or at least leftist sympathizers.

Not all encampment violence is political in nature and is aimed at home states. There is ample evidence of violent, poverty-induced crime as camp residents make incursions into host communities. In the United States, crime rates by the Native American population tend to be higher, on a per capita basis, than among other groups. In the Czech Republic, crime by Romas jumped during the 1990s to new levels: according to Paul Hochenos, "although Roma make up only two percent of the Czech population, they accounted for 11 percent of all crimes and fifty percent of crimes such as pick-pocketing and burglary."[30] In South Africa, there has been a dramatic increase in crime since the mid-1980s, most of which is committed by Blacks. The murder rate is one of the highest in the world, and cases of robbery, rape, assault, housebreaking, and vehicle hijackings hit record highs in the early 1990s.[31]

In addition to political and economic crime committed by encampment residents against home states and their host communities, there is also violence within encampments among displaced residents. This usually takes the form of poverty-induced petty crimes or crimes of passion. Harassment of fellow refugees also occurs (Ted Robert Gurr found this among the camps in the West Bank and Gaza. He said that those "who are allowed to work in Israel are often the target of discrimination and harassment at home by fellow Palestinians" because work is only available to those who are "trustworthy").[32]

Nationalism and Conflict in Host States

Host states are often intolerant of their refugees and internally displaced peoples for a variety of economic, political, and social reasons. Among the former, the most important is the perception that the cost of encampments is greater than the benefit. Given scarce resources, host governments and their populations resent the drain of money that is necessary to ensure survival of encampments. With respect to the political source of intolerance, host authorities and populations are leery of the empowerment that international organizations bestow upon refugees. Among the social sources of intolerance, ethnicity of the displaced populations plays a fundamental role. To the extent that they are not of the dominant host majority, displaced persons are the convenient targets of xenophobia and chauvinism.

Intolerance of displaced peoples easily translates into violence. This includes both spontaneous as well as organized efforts to harass and ultimately dislocate encampment residents. Some examples follow.

In the Czech Republic, the first president of the Republican Party, Miroslav Sladek, publicly offered a new Alfa Romeo sports car to the first police force that rid its town of Romas.[33] In Lebanon, Palestinians were often harassed, culminating in the massacring of hundreds of encampment residents (in the Sabra and Shatilla refugee camps) by Phalangist militiamen in 1982.[34] The Kibeho massacre in Rwanda, in which several thousand Hutus were killed by the Rwandian army, became the largest known killing in an encampment setting known to date.[35] Genocide was said to be "an exercise in community building . . . killing Tutsis was a political tradition in postcolonial Rwanda; it brought people together."[36] This continued in their refugee encampments. Indeed, the Hutu leaders who led the genocide against the Tutsis continued their operations in the refugee camps in the Congo, using civilians as human shields, expropriating the flow of international assistance, and finally killing as many as 10,000 camp residents.[37] In the Sudan, government planes deliberately bombed encampments with displaced peoples, government soldiers attacked them on the ground, and rebel troops ambushed them. In 1994-1995, 60,000 residents of one encampment were forced to flee once again due to a government military offensive.[38] Africa Watch has reported that government has burned and bulldozed the homes of some 500,000 residents in the vicinity of Khartoum.[39] Moreover, after 1983, when Islamic Sharia was introduced, the southern Christians, most of whom are residents in northern encampments, were subject to inhumane treatment: flogging, amputation of limbs, and stoning to death. In Burundi, the government-run radio urged Tutsis to attack their Hutu neighbors. Those in encampments were fair play. As a result, when Hutu refugees were invited to return to their homes after land reforms in 1972-1973, they believed that they were being made to live in groups so that they could be killed more easily.[40]

Nationalism and Conflict in Home States

People who were involuntarily displaced and subsequently encamped have lingering issues with their home authorities. The lack of resolution of these issues reinforces potent emotions and results in the perpetuation of nationalist sentiment and conflict.

One of these lingering issues is the role played by home authorities in the displacement process. In most cases of involuntary migration, cleansing the country of target minorities (i.e., ethnic cleansing) was an explicit or implicit goal of the authorities. Involuntary displacement was usually followed by the state-sanctioned destruction of homes and villages in order to eliminate the economic or emotional pull they might exert on the migrants (this formula was applied to the Kurds in Turkey,[41] the Mayan peasants in Guatemala,[42] and the Karen in Myanmar,[43] among others). Needless to say, such displacement and concomitant destruction fosters anger and frustration coupled with a sense of injustice and a desire for revenge. When properly harnessed by ethnic political leaders, these feelings are a potent source of nationalist sentiment that can be used to develop a cadre of refugee-warriors. As long as the goals of refugee-warriors are to return to their countries and reclaim their lands, home country governments are justified in perceiving a threat from the encampments.

Another lingering issue is compensation for lost property. Involuntary migrants demand that they be compensated for the lands, livestock, businesses, and homes they were forced to abandon when they fled. Home authorities are disinclined to comply. All to often, they question whether displacement even occurred, claiming instead that involuntary migrants were in fact voluntary migrants. Unwillingness to acknowledge the problem and engage in negotiation produces frustration among camp residents that is often expressed with violence.

NATIONALISM IN INTROVERTED AND EXTROVERTED STATES

It was suggested in chapter 2 that permanent encampments located in extroverted states are less prone to nationalism and its violent manifestation (both within the camp as well as in host and home states) than those in introverted states. The reasons for this reside in economic and political differences between states at different tiers.

Economic Differences

Extroverted states tend to be more developed and have higher rates of long term economic growth than introverted states. How does that affect nationalism in the encampments? In order to answer that question, a slight regression into academic literature is necessary. There is a consensus among scholars that the relationship between economic decline and ethnic awareness is direct. In other words, the greater the deterioration and stagnation of an economy, the greater the efforts of minority ethnic groups to differentiate themselves from the majority or dominant group.[44] This rise in ethnic awareness and nationalism is due to the rise in interethnic competition, which increases during periods of economic decline (since decline upsets the balance of employment, distribution of resources, education opportunities, and economic advantages). The more economic conditions deteriorate, the more ferocious interethnic competition becomes, and the more it fuels nationalist ideology.

In applying this argument to encampments, it follows that the severe drop in economic conditions of displaced peoples affects their group awareness and their nationalist sentiment. When displaced peoples are encamped, the decline in standards of living that they experience, and the poverty they find themselves in, highlights group differentiation, stimulates economic competition, and results in nationalist tendencies. An extroverted, more developed country is wealthier and more able to offset the decreases in poverty by financial support to the encampments. A less developed introverted country, strapped for cash, is less likely to do so, thereby perpetuating exactly those conditions that foster nationalism.

Political Differences

Intolerance towards displaced populations is often reflected in discriminatory policies, such as those described in chapter 4. Such policies provide a catalyst for interethnic conflict because of their very nature. When they are adopted, minority ethnic groups respond by turning inward, accentuating their differences and strengthening their bonds. The groundwork is laid for group mobilization and for the articulation of the boundaries of their "differentness." At the same time, discriminatory policies discourage intergroup contact (and, according to Lake and Rothchild, barriers are erected to further communication and conflict resolution).[45] A legal framework that allows discrimination in the workplace, the capital market, the educational system, and so forth, affects the target population economically, socially, and politically. As a result, such government policy may spark discontent and fear and lead to violent interethnic conflict. In the words of Olson and Pearson, "policy providing systematic advantage to certain groups, or that are designed to disadvantage others, can be viewed as a catalyst for violence."[46] Their research shows that multiethnic states with discriminatory policy are more likely to experience violence in the form of riots or ethnically related civil war than states that do not adopt such policy.[47] Their conclusions are supported by Ted Gurr's research, according to which minorities that engage in violent rebellion are often discriminated against politically, economically, and culturally.[48]

In liberal democracies, where human and minority rights are respected, discrimination is less overt and more subdued due to human and minority rights legislation than in introverted countries where no such legislation exists. As a result, nationalist sentiment leading to conflict between displaced persons and host populations is less likely to develop in extroverted states. When it does, it is less likely to be as strong or last as long as in introverted states.

In conclusion, it is clear that extroverted and introverted states do not share the same experience: interethnic conflict is longer, deeper, and more violent in countries that are not liberal democracies and that are at lower levels of development. This does not imply that interethnic conflict does not occur in highly developed democracies. However, minorities have more recourse to protective institutions since extroverted states, by definition, tend to have political rules and regulations that protect the human, ethnic, and minority rights of camp residents. Thus, the confluence of nationalism at the level of the encampment, the host state, and the home country is less harmful in extroverted than in introverted states.

NOTES

1. See Milica Z. Bookman, *The Demographic Struggle for Power* (London: Frank Cass, 1997).

2. Milica Zarkovic Bookman, *Economic Decline and Nationalism in the Balkans* (New York: St. Martin's Press, 1994).

3. Simply but not exclusively. Indeed, nationalism is a manifestation of other factors also.

4. It is clear that economic exploitation may be perceived by populations in regions that are more or less developed relative to the nation, as is evident in Italy (Lombardy as well as the Mezzogiorno), India (Punjab as well as Kashmir), the former Yugoslavia (Slovenia as well as Macedonia), and in the former USSR (Lithuania as well as Turkmenia). The high-income, subnational regions such as Lombardy, Punjab, Slovenia, and Lithuania experienced tax revolts, reflecting a dissatisfaction with what they perceived to be unfair drainage of their resources, while the less developed regions lobbied for increased "spread effects" of national development, as well as for a change in the redistributive policy.

5. See the literature survey provided by David A. Lake and Donald Rothchild, eds. *The International Spread of Ethnic Conflict: Fear, Diffusion and Escalation* (Princeton: Princeton University Press, 1998), chapter 1.

6. See, for example, Robert Park and E. W. Burgess, *Introduction to the Science of Sociology* (Chicago: Chicago University Press, 1921); Amos Hawley, *Human Ecology* (New York: Ronald Press, 1950).

7. Frederick Barth, "Ecological Relationships of Ethnic Groups in Swat, North Pakistan," *American Anthropologist* 58, (1956).

8. See for example, Michael Hechter, *Internal Colonialism* (Berkeley: University of California Press, 1975).

9. Edna Bonacich, "A Theory of Ethnic Antagonism: The Split Labor Market," *American Sociological Review* 37, (1972); Edna Bonacich, "A Theory of Middleman Minorities," *American Sociological Review* 38, (1973).

10. Donald Horowitz, *Ethnic Groups in Conflict* (Berkeley: University of California Press, 1985).

11. Susan Olzak, *The Dynamics of Ethnic Competition and Conflict* (Stanford: Stanford University Press, 1992), 2-3.

12. In those multiethnic societies where substate divisions are drawn according to ethnic, religious, or linguistic lines, the distinction between ethnic and regional economic competition is often blurred. In other words, it is difficult to determine just how much competition between peoples is due to their ethnicity and how much to their regional affiliation. For example, when Slovenes and Punjabis (in the former Yugoslavia and India, respectively) competed for resources with other constituent regions in their federations, it was hard to decipher if they were competing on the basis of their

regional or ethnic affiliation. A similar situation arose in the Soviet Union, Czechoslovakia, Canada, and Spain. Why is it important to identify the basis of the competition? Because when ethnic or religious distinctions coincide with regional administrative boundaries, then the soil is fertile for the emergence of a nationalist and, perhaps, even separatist movement. When ethnic and administrative boundaries do not coincide, then interethnic competition is merely regionalism. In that case, competition cannot spill over into demands that are nationalist in origin or aspiration (in the United States and Italy, for example, there is no nationalist sentiment because there is no association between ethnic identity and the region).

13. Hierarchy in ethnic groups should not be confused with the pecking order discussed in chapter 4.

14. Srdjan Bogosavljevic, *Bosna I Hercegovina Izmedu Rata I Mira* (Belgrade: Dom Omladine, 1992).

15. The Pygmies were the original inhabitants of Rwanda, and their descendents today are called the Twa peoples. They account for some 1 percent of the population.

16. Philip Gourevitch, *We Wish to Inform You that Tomorrow We Will Be Killed with Our Families* (New York: Picador USA, 1999), 8.

17. Among the Tamils, there is further hierarchy. The Sri Lanka Tamils claim greater longevity on the island (and are concentrated in the north) and the Indian (or plantation) Tamils arrived in the nineteenth century as labor imports by the British; they are concentrated in the in the east. These sociocultural distinctions are brought to the encampments. Joke Schrijvers, "Fighters, Victims and Survivors: Constructions of Ethnicity, Gender and Refugeeness among Tamils in Sri Lanka" *Journal of Refugee Studies* 12, no. 3 (1999), 310.

18. Robert Ted Gurr, *Minorities at Risk* (Washington, D.C.: United States Institute of Peace, 1993), 53.

19. Netnapis Nakawachara and John Rogge, "Thailand's Refugee Experience" in *Refugees, A Third World Dilemma*, ed. John R. Rogge (Totowa, N.J.: Rowman & Littlefield, 1987), 272.

20. The Obote government, on the other hand, had confined the refugees to their encampments, even those who had settled outside for a period of years. See Aristide R. Zolberg, Astri Suhrke, and Sergio Aguayo, *Escape from Violence: Conflict and the Refugee Crisis in the Developing World* (New York: Oxford University Press, 1989), 67-68.

21. U.S. Committee for Refugees, "Burundi: A Patchwork of Displacement" in. *The Forsaken People, Case Studies of the Internally Displaced,*

eds. Roberta Cohen and Francis M. Deng (Washington, D.C.: Brookings Institution Press, 1998), 19.

22. According to Stanley Hoffman, "international law, in what amounts to a revolution, has been giving [activists of all kinds] rights against their governments. It is they who destroy states, overthrow regimes and benefit from the new information technology." The *Miami Herald*, January 23, 2000.

23. It is often difficult to provide security when it is the host state that is perpetuating it.

24. Roberta Cohen and Francis M. Deng, *Masses in Flight* (Washington, D.C.: Brookings Institution, 1998), 10.

25. Bill Frelick, "Assistance without Protection," U.S. Committee for Refugees, *World Refugee Survey* (Washington, D.C.: Immigration and Refugee Services of America, 1997), 24.

26. Since obstacles prevent their return, camp residents take steps to keep the goal of repatriation alive in their hearts and minds. For this reason, the Polisario leaders of the Saharawi named all four camps in Algeria after Western Saharan towns of El Ayoun, Smara, Auserd, and Dakhla.

27. This need was described by Donna Arzt in her discussion of the Is-raeli/Palestinian conflict as the concept of "identity, community and nation-hood, motivated by fierce, ancient and primordial forces of human dignity, protection, and survival, and expressed in the modern vocabulary of sover-eignty, statehood and citizenship." Donna E. Arzt, *Refugees into Citizens*, (New York: Council on Foreign Relations, xi.

28. Zolberg, Suhrke, and Aguayo, *Escape From Violence*, 275-78.

29. Encampment residents in Goma, a few miles across the border in the Congo, were Hutus who fled retribution for their genocide against the Tut-sis. Many of the camp leaders were associated with the murderous Hutu Power political group. Within weeks of their arrival, they began to organize bands of encampment residents who would conduct bloody cross-border raids on Rwanda. Gourevitch, *We Wish To Inform You*, 167.

30. As a result, the Skinheads that attack the Romas are viewed favorably by the majority population because they play the role of social protectors from criminals. Paul Hochenos, *Free to Hate* (New York: Routledge, 1993), 221.

31. Hein Marais, *South Africa Limits to Change* (London: Zed Books, 1998), 109.

32. Gurr, *Minorities at Risk*, 222.

33. Hochenos, *Free to Hate*, 226.

34. This included women and children, and occurred under the eye of the Israeli Defense Force troops. See Gurr, *Minorities at Risk*, 237.

35. Incidentally, this massacre took place with international humanitarian staff present, but no one was authorized to stop the violence. Gourevitch, *We Wish To Inform You*, 177-78.

36. Philip Gourevitch, *We Wish To Inform You*, 95-96.

37. Such activity led Bill Frelick to say that the word "refugee" didn't even apply to these people and, in fact, they should have been called hostages or captives held against their will in camps. Moreover, he suggested that what they encountered in Congo (Zaire) was not asylum but rather "psuedo-asylum": "on the surface, it looked like true asylum: governments making available parcels of their territory to serve as temporary havens for neighbors in need . . . but things were not what they seemed. Refugee camps are supposed to be protected areas where those who fear persecution and violence can find safety. These camps, however, were dominated by the very brutal thugs who had butchered and hacked their way through a killing spree inside Rwanda in 1994". Bill Frelick, "The Year in Review" U.S. Committee for Refugees, *World Refugee Survey* (Washington, D.C.: Immigration and Refugee Services of America, 1997), 15.

38. Frelick, "The Year in Review," 44.

39. AfricaWatch, *Sudan: Refugees in Their Own Country* (Washington, D.C.: Human Rights Watch, 1992).

40. U.S. Committee for Refugees, "Burundi: A Patchwork of Displacement" in *The Forsaken People, Case Studies of the Internally Displaced*, ed. Roberta Cohen and Francis M. Deng (Washington, D.C.: Brookings Institution Press, 1998), 25.

41. In Turkey, the government displaced Kurds and burned their villages. The two to three million displaced persons are uprooted due to conflict between the government and the Kurdish Workers Party that began in 1998. Much of it was due to the government's deliberate attempt to depopulate villages. Just since 1992, some 2000 Kurdish villages have been destroyed. Gurr, *Minorities at Risk*, 48.

42. In Guatemala, violence against the Mayan peasants began a few decades ago, culminating in the period between 1979-1983, when government soldiers burned some forty villages. By the end of 1995, the National Council of the Displaced in Guatemala reports estimates of the number of people displaced as between 200,000 to 1.5 million. Gurr, *Minorities at Risk*, 65.

43. In Myanmar, as many as 500,000 Karen are displaced or refugees at the end of 1999 (30 percent of the Karen population); in the Shan state, the

army forced 300,000 Shan to move or to relocation sites; and 40,000 to 50,000 Mons have been displaced from the Mon state by the authorities. The system is always the same: expanded military control is accompanied by forced labor, extortion, confiscation of land, and religious persecution. In other words, an effort to rid the country of non-Burmese (USCR, *World Refugee Survey*, 134. The Thai government had tolerated the refugees from Burma, who lived quietly in camps assisted by a variety of NGOs (Thailand is not a signatory to the UN conventions on refugees, and does not allow the UNHCR to operate within its borders). However, in the mid-1990s, it toughened its stance toward the refugees because it improved its relations with the military leaders. One form that took is forced deportations, closing borders, and refusal to give refugee status to those who cross over, thus relegating them to illegal status and preventing them from living in encampments.

44. Miroslav Hroch found this in nineteenth-century Europe, Beth Michneck in pre-breakup USSR, and Anthony Birch in Bangladesh (Miroslav Hroch, *Social Preconditions of National Revival in Europe* [Cambridge: Cambridge University Press, l985]; Beth Michneck, "Regional Autonomy, Territoriality, and the Economy," paper presented to the American Association for the Advancement of Slavic Studies, Washington, October l990; Anthony Birch, *Nationalism and National Integration* [London: Unwin Hyman, l989].) In addition, Christine Drake claims that poverty of some regions and their populations, especially relative to others, "was a major underlying cause of the civil war in Sudan, and it had a definite role in the breakup of Pakistan into Pakistan and Bangladesh. Within Indonesia, too, several of the regional rebellions experienced since independence have had economic grievances at their root". Christine Drake, *National Integration in Indonesia: Patterns and Policies* (Honolulu: University of Hawaii Press, l989), 145.

45. David A. Lake and Donald Rothchild, "Ethnic Fears and Global Engagement: The International Spread and Management of Ethnic Conflict" Policy Paper #26, *Institute on Global Conflict and Cooperation* (Berkeley, CA: University of California) 1996.

46. Marie L. Olson and Frederic S. Pearson, "Policy-Making and Discrimination: Forecasting Ethnopolitical Violence" paper presented to the annual meetings of the International Studies Association (Los Angeles, March 2000), 3.

47. They also claim that more democratic multiethnic states are less likely to adopt discriminatory policies than less democratic states. Finally,

they found that discriminatory policy changes are more likely to result in violence when the disadvantaged group is large in proportion to other groups in the state. Marie L. Olson and Frederic S. Pearson, "Policy-Making and Discrimination: Forecasting Ethnopolitical Violence" paper presented to the annual meetings of the International Studies Association (Los Angeles, March 2000).

48. Ted Robert Gurr, "A Risk Assessment Model of Ethnopolitical Rebellion: Applied to Asian Minorities in the late 1990s" paper presented at the workshop on Crisis and Conflict Early Warning Systems, CIDCM, University of Maryland, November 14-16, 1996, cited in Marie L. Olson and Frederic S. Pearson, "Policy-Making and Discrimination: Forecasting Ethnopolitical Violence" paper presented to the annual meetings of the International Studies Association (Los Angeles, March 2000), 6.

⑦

CONCLUSION

It is better to be an involuntarily displaced person in an extroverted country than in an introverted one. In other words, it's better to be an encampment resident in a highly developed, liberal democracy than in a dictatorial, less-developed state. In order to substantiate this assertion, this chapter ties together qualitative arguments presented in chapters 3-6 with the quantitative information presented in chapters 1-2.

The implications of the above assertion are also discussed in this chapter. Specifically, since not every displaced person can be encamped in a developed liberal democracy, what relevance does the comparison between introverted and extroverted host states have for the majority of involuntarily displaced persons?

BRINGING THE HOME STATE BACK IN

While the preceding chapters focused on the tier of the host state, the tier of the home state is not negligible.[1] It, too, influences the livelihood of encampment residents in numerous ways. It determines the chance of repatriation, the extent to which compensation will be made for confiscated property, and the likelihood that refugees will be allowed to retain their citizenship. Moreover, it determines whether countries will even engage in negotiations pertaining to their displaced populations. The tiers of home and host states of displaced groups are listed in table 7.1.

By considering the tier of both home and host states, the most desirable combination can be identified (these are presented in table 7.2).

Table 7.1. Refugee Encampment Residents by Tier of Host and Home States

Encampment Residents by Ethnicity	Host State Tier	Home State Tier
Saharawis	Low Introverted	High Introverted
Aborigines	High Extroverted	High Extroverted
Azeris	High Introverted	Low Introverted
Tutsis	Low Introverted	Low Introverted
Natives (Canada)	High Extroverted	High Extroverted
Christian Blacks (Congo)	Low Introverted	Low Introverted
Indians (Nicaragua)	Low Extroverted	Low Introverted
Greeks	Low Extroverted	Low Extroverted
Romas	Low Extroverted	Low Extroverted
Vietnamese	High Extroverted	Low Introverted
Tibetans	High Introverted	High Introverted
Kurds (from Iraq in Iran)	High Introverted	Low Introverted
Afghanis (in Iran)	High Introverted	Low Introverted
Palestinians (in Israel)	Low Extroverted	Low Extroverted
Palestinians (in Jordan)	Low Extroverted	Low Extroverted
Palestinians (in Lebanon)	High Introverted	Low Extroverted
Indians (Guatemala)	Low Extroverted	High Introverted
Maori	High Extroverted	High Extroverted
Afghanis (in Pakistan)	Low Introverted	Low Introverted
Irian Jayas	Low Introverted	High Introverted
Chechens	Low Extroverted	Low Extroverted
Somali clans	Low Introverted	Low Introverted
Blacks (Zulu, Lhasa, etc.)	Low Extroverted	Low Extroverted
Tamils	High Introverted	High Introverted
Eritreans	Low Introverted	Low Introverted
Christian Blacks (in Sudan)	Low Introverted	Low Introverted
Hutus (from Burundi)	Low Introverted	Low Introverted
Karen, Mon, Karenni	Low Extroverted	Low Introverted
Kurds (in Turkey)	High Introverted	High Introverted
Christian Blacks (in Uganda)	Low Introverted	Low Introverted
Natives (U.S.)	High Extroverted	High Extroverted

Note: the order of the ranking is as follows—high extroverted, low extroverted, high introverted, low introverted
Source: table 1.1

Table 7.2.   Ranking of Home/Host Tier Combinations

	Host INTROV	Host EXTRO
Home INTROV	Worst	Second Best
Home EXTRO	Third Best	Best

Encampment residents in extroverted states, who were displaced from extroverted states, are best off. Residents in introverted states who were displaced from introverted states are least well off. Within those two extremes are populations whose home and host states belong in different tiers. Among those two possibilities, it is more important that the host country be extroverted than the home country, simply because the conditions and prospects for the permanent encampment are most dependent on the host state.

THE CAPACITY AND INCENTIVE IN EXTROVERTED AND INTROVERTED STATES

Why is it preferable to be displaced from an extroverted state and encamped in an extroverted state? Because extroverted states have both the capacity and the incentive to adequately deal with issues pertaining to their permanent encampments. A more developed country has the resources for greater public services and welfare programs, and it has a political culture that both condones and tolerates the redistributive powers of the state to financially support displaced populations. Therefore, a liberal industrial democracy has both the capacity (that comes from its high level of development) as well as the incentive (that comes from its political values and culture) to seek mutually acceptable resolutions to displacement and encampment dilemmas. In introverted states, both the capacity and the incentives are lower.

Thus it comes as no surprise that encampment residents, as migrants in general, prefer to move to extroverted states rather than to introverted ones. Indeed, it is easy to understand why East Europe's biggest and most mistreated minority, the Roma, have been emigrating in large numbers, not to neighboring countries (such as Greece, Turkey, or Poland) but rather to Canada and the United States.[2] It is easy to understand why Indonesians, Chinese, and Malaysians would like to enter Singapore, where the government prides itself on its ability to provide its citizens with the five "Cs" (car, condo, credit cards, cash and career with a multinational).[3] The United States, also, despite its three "Gs" (guns, ghettoes, and gated communities[4]) continues to attract migrants in pursuit of the American Dream. There, even encampments have become attractive (the number of Americans claiming to be Indians on the United States census forms has tripled to more than 1.8 million since 1960.[5] This has coincided with a rise in the reservation population).

Capacity

In the concluding sections of chapters 3-6, the superior capacity of extroverted states to address encampment issues was highlighted. Without using the term "capacity," it was claimed that extroverted states were more capable than introverted states of providing financial resources for camp development, as well as greater opportunities for displaced peoples. Extroverted states can do this because they have higher incomes and have experienced greater economic development. Their market systems create conditions for the proliferation of growth. They are fully integrated into the global economy in which their leadership position enables them to take advantage of all possibilities for further growth. As noted in chapter 2, a high GDP per capita tends to be accompanied by forward and backward linkages that permeate all sectors and regions of the economy. Growth is diffused across cities and rural areas. Infrastructure, such as roads and electricity, is not limited to the capital and its environs. Some of this will spill over into the encampments. Indeed, it follows that the geographical setting of encampments, be they rural, suburban, or urban, is more developed and therefore more conducive to generating income and propelling growth than in introverted states. In those, income levels are low, and development levels are also low. Income and growth tends to be concentrated in the urban areas while the countryside, where the majority of encampments are located, tends to have dismal conditions with respect to infrastructure, employment, and standards of living. As in extroverted states, this spills over into encampments.

It follows from the above that extroverted countries have the economic capacity to use public funds for encampment assistance. They have macroeconomic policies that can transfer money and assets to encampments. Through taxation, the public sector funds education, health care, medicines, income-generating projects, and start-up grants. Extroverted states have a high income base that can sustain fiscal policy. By contrast, introverted countries with lower incomes have less scope for generous public programs that benefit encampments.

Incentive

A free market economy tends to go hand in hand with liberal, Western-style democracy. While there are exceptions, notably highly developed and politically repressive Singapore and South Korea, academic literature, as well as empirical evidence, has supported the link between a laissez-faire economic organization and a democratic political system.

Liberal democracies have based their institutions on civil and human rights. These rights are protected by law and prevent discrimination on grounds of personal characteristics such as race, ethnicity, religion, gender, and age. Rules pertaining to these rights govern the housing market, the job market, the capital market, and the product market. The explicit expression of civic and human rights, such as the Bill of Rights in the United States, serves an important role in liberal democracies: it is the ultimate equalizer. Since all people have the same rights by law, the legal system can be viewed as an ethnostabilizer. Such ethnostabilizers are built into the political system and they prevent the institutionalization and the formalization of discrimination against ethnic groups when competition between groups escalates and pressures for discriminatory policies mount. Ethnostabilizers, then, are background rules and regulations that are dormant when not needed, but that automatically become activated to protect citizens of all ethnic backgrounds if and when interethnic animosities emerge.

The existence of domestic ethnostabilizers implies that interethnic competition is less likely to be deep and persistent among ethnic groups that are equally protected by the law. These ethnostabilizers serve to dissipate animosities between people who, while hierarchically ranked in income, education, occupation, etc., are equal under the rule of law.

Moreover, numerous liberal political systems have accommodated their permanent encampments by providing them with rights and power. In the United States, the Indian Self-Determination Act of 1975 initiated a shift of authority to tribal governments that is still ongoing.[6] The Status peoples of Canada had less autonomy than the native peoples of the United States, although 1991 was a year of change. At that time, the government recognized the right of 140,000 native peoples in the Ontario province to be self-governing and to grant self-government and land rights to 17,500 Inuit of the North-west Territories (one fifth of all Canadian territory).[7] The Aborigines of Australia were under the jurisdiction of states until 1967, when aboriginal affairs were transferred to the federal government, thereby ensuring consistent treatment while enlarging the scope of their benefits. The Maoris of New Zealand, who fared better than other indigenous peoples, were able to resist the newcomers, were able to keep much of their land, and were given representation in settlers' parliament as early as 1867.[8]

The experience of extroverted states indicates an interesting phenomenon. Those countries that have given up some of their own sovereignty to various forms of international partnerships are exactly the ones that accommodate selected domestic ethnic groups by granting them limited sovereignty. By contrast, introverted countries are much too insecure in their own sovereignty to grant another ethnic group semisovereign rights.

The above discussion raises the question of whether comparing the political rights of indigenous populations in extroverted countries with refugee camps is valid. What is the usefulness of discussing encampments in extroverted countries since they only exist as reservations for native peoples? Indeed, refugee encampments in North America and Western Europe are short term holding stations where people await dispersal, resettlement, and integration. In response, it is important to note that native lands in countries such as the United States, Canada, Australia, and New Zealand have been around for over a century. As such, they have had time to develop into what they are today, along with home states. Conditions in native lands weren't always good. In fact, before their home countries became as politically accommodating as they currently are, native populations lived in dismal conditions. The forcible removal of American Indians into reservations is ethnic cleansing *par excellence* and the genocide of the Aborigines in Australia bespeak of horrors shared by some of today's displaced peoples in introverted states. Yet, it is relevant and important to study these cases because they point out the direction for the future. *Indeed, to the extent that permanent encampments as institutions survive, the example of extroverted states is relevant.* A discussion of the future of permanent encampments follows.

IMPLICATIONS FOR PERMANENT ENCAMPMENTS

If extroverted states have greater capacity and incentive to provide a superior economic, political, and social life for their encamped populations, then where does that leave encampment residents in introverted countries? Are they just doomed to perpetual inferiority, low living standards, and the absence of rights?

Some scholars contend that the geopolitical and geoeconomic settings of a country determine its future prospects as well as the fate of its peoples. Dannensprecher invoked geography to describe the development patterns of post-Communist Eastern Europe.[9] Jeffrey Sacks used geography to explain differences in wealth and poverty across the globe.[10] In addition to such geographical determinism, scholars such as Lawrence Harrison and Samuel Huntington have advocated cultural determinism according to which one's culture determines the nature of one's economic activities.[11] Applying the concept of determinism to encampments implies that displaced persons have little choice as to where they find themselves, and there is little they can do to change their fate because it is tied to the fate of their host country. The fate of introverted states is not as pleasant as that of extroverted states. Thus, geographical and cultural determinism dooms introverted states to perpetual inferiority.[12]

While geographical and cultural determinism may provide an appropriate framework for explaining differences among states, its implications for encampments are not encouraging. Geographical determinism implies that change is not possible; cultural determinism implies that change is not likely. Such a view results in a defeatist attitude among those who might be tempted to change the conditions of encampments. Such a view exonerates host and home countries, as well as international organizations, from actively seeking to change conditions in encampments. Such a view condones their passivity.

By contrast, a more positive and constructive approach to long-term encampments is warranted. Such an approach is rooted in the *realpolitik* view that a gap between countries will always exist. Indeed, there will always be richer and poorer countries; there will always be differences between introverted and extroverted countries. However, what follows from that assertion need not be negative, but, rather, can be creative, energetic, and constructive. The goal should not be to equalize all states (an unattainable, and according to some, an undesirable goal)[13] but rather to raise the standard of living in the poorer, more introverted group. While working patiently on the root of the problem (namely, the festering interethnic struggle that caused the displacement in the first place), it is necessary to focus on more immediate issues. These issues include providing greater economic opportunity for displaced peoples in encampments while ensuring some respect for their rights. In other words, making encampments more accommodating, hopeful, and pleasant.

In order to focus on those issues, introverted states must undergo a transformation. In other words, they must take on some of the characteristics of extroverted states.

How can that be achieved? How can the plethora of introverted countries become more like extroverted countries? If we accept the strength of geographical and cultural determinism, then how can these countries overcome the obstacles to change and become more extroverted? Also, if we accept the strength of the distrust and apprehension of the global economy that define introverted states, then how can they overcome the obstacles they themselves raised?

The answer lies in money and globalization. If the economic benefit is sufficiently clear and large, then introverted countries that resist change can be convinced to modify their goals, policies, and behaviors.

The Role of Globalization and International Economic Integration

Globalization can be a source of change in introverted countries. Philip Curtin pointed out that global diffusion has always been a source of innovation in the course of human history.[14] Moreover, Robert Holton has argued that throughout history, societies have depended on intercultural borrowing and exchange.[15] Therefore, this current period of intense globalization, in which social, political, and economic ideas are traded and diffused, in which they touch more people in society than any other, has the potential to portend great changes across the globe. These changes include political liberalization and increased attention to human and civil rights. With reference to displaced persons, these changes include the proliferation of political values and liberties that affect permanent encampment residents, the opportunities they have, and the treatment they receive.

The way introverted countries treat or mistreat their inhabitants has come under new scrutiny by the international community. This extends to internally displaced persons as well as refugees. The western community has taken on a proactive position and encourages states with displaced peoples to adopt minority protection norms and institute mechanisms for respecting their rights. It has gentle and not-so-gentle forms of persuasion at its disposal. Extroverted states are using their economic power to induce introverted states to adapt. While numerous ways may exist, economic pressures are the most convincing. Indeed, it is money that speaks the loudest and reaches the farthest. Leaders across the globe are sensitive to money issues since they are so closely related to economic growth, political power, status in the world community, etc. As Kaplan points out, "it is much more important nowadays for the leader of a developing country to get a hearing before corporate investors at the world economic forum than to speak before the U. N. General Assembly."[16] Therefore, money could be used as a carrot as countries are rewarded with financial benefits in exchange for imposing minority legislation and respecting minority rights. These benefits may include access to international sources of capital, encouragement of foreign investment, participation in international decision-making processes, and access to resources and trade. Through these avenues, the West can encourage domestic policies that are based in their own norms of human rights and views of proper interethnic behavior.[17] The introduction of such conditionality in economic relations might serve to alter refugee-insensitive regimes. Such a discriminating system of support of those states that show respect for the rights of their displaced populations might carry the message clearly and, in the long run, fundamentally alter interethnic relations. According to Carol Lancaster, U.S. foreign policy must be redesigned to take into consideration both the changing post-Cold War world as well as American values. She views foreign aid as the main tool, both carrot and stick, to enable the United States to meet its challenges: to provide peace and to enable the spread of globalization (and temper its costs). Foreign aid that is linked to western values and humanitarian goals is the vehicle to that.[18] Similar policy is already implemented in Europe. As a result, Turkey faces a dilemma (Eric Rouleau describes how, in order to be considered for the European Union membership, it must conform to the European standards of human rights and democracy. However, that entails all but rewriting the constitution to acknowledge the existence of their minorities, Kurds in particular).[19] Also, as a result, the Czech Republic introduced minority legislation (namely, the Czech Refugee Act, which was the first to be established by a central European state. This new legislation is intended to harmonize Czech standards with those of EU states). Across the world, in Indonesia, the United States and others have threatened to postpone a grant of 5.6 billion unless refugee camp issues are resolved.[20] Bolivia's funding is also under review, resulting in major concessions to its Indian population.[21] China was rejected from the World Trade Organization on grounds of human rights.[22]

Linking loans and other forms of assistance to good behavior, democratic changes and the respect for human rights has been welcomed and supported by UNHRC. It has led to their assessment: "The political and economic changes that have taken place in African states such as Malawi, Mozambique and Zambia, for example, would almost certainly not have taken place so quickly without this kind of pressure."[23] The UNHCR recognizes that by making host countries more responsive to Western pressures for a universal outlook on human rights, positive benefits trickle down to displaced persons in general, and encampments in particular. Moreover, the watchful eye of international organizations on the lookout for human rights incursions resulted in some behavioral changes. Gourevitch reports how, in Rwandan jails, there were daily killings of prisoners until the Red Cross began registering people. Then the killing became more difficult because "the regime wanted to keep a good international image."[24]

Extroverted states get away with applying pressure because many introverted countries have an ambivalent attitude towards globalization. On the one hand, they are aware that, in the late twentieth century, high rates of economic growth tend to be associated with a global presence and participation in the international economic relations. In some parts of the world, "becoming global" has replaced the development mantra of the 1960s and 1970s, namely "becoming modern."[25] The experience of the four Dragons of Asia (Singapore, Hong Kong, Taiwan, and South Korea), especially with respect to the success of their export promotion policies that catapulted them into the global economy, has served as a pointer for many achievement-oriented states. But it is not just high rates of economic growth that poor countries aspire to. It is a broader goal: it is political, social, and cultural integration with some global common denominator. Countries that trade, exchange, and invest across state boundaries also tend to have governing policies that are receptive to manifestations of global culture, as well as populations that seek greater exposure to different cultures. This has recently been highlighted by the opening of a Starbucks Coffee shop inside the Forbidden City in Beijing. The *New York Times* comments, "If ever there was an emblem of the extremes to which globalization has reached, this is it: mass market American coffee culture in China's most hallowed historic place. Even a McDonald's in the Kremlin would not come as close."[26]

On the other hand, introverted states that jump on the globalization bandwagon have to give up some of those very characteristics that keep them introverted. Globalization threatens the local culture, production methods, and choices. Global participation increases economic competition and political awareness. It can topple governments. Hence, many introverted states endure a love/hate relationship with globalization while they analyze the costs and benefits of their participation.

If they give in to the unrelenting quest for economic growth and head in the direction of extroverted states, then a convergence of tiers is likely to occur. A benefit of this convergence is the exposure to greater democracy and respect for rights that displaced populations in introverted countries would have. Another benefit is the decrease in interethnic conflict. Indeed, if the economic development and liberal democracy of extroverted countries are conducive to protecting ethnic groups (be they minorities or majorities), then it bodes well for world efforts to quell interethnic conflicts. When countries "speak the same language," they are more likely to discuss those thorny issues that produced involuntary displacement in the first place. Their communication might be more than a dialogue between the deaf. While even optimists will concede that universal democratization and economic growth is at best a long-run goal, to the extent that it promotes interethnic harmony, it is worth pursuing.

Thus, rather than say that globalization indicates the end of geography,[27] it is more appropriate to say that globalization indicates the beginning of a new kind of geography, one in which introverted countries take on characteristics of extroverted countries as a result of economic pressures and incentives.

The Future of Permanent Encampments and the Permanent Encampments of the Future

The discussion about which tier of states has the capacity and incentive to provide a superior economic and political environment for its encampments skirts the question of whether encampments should even exist. Indeed, why not dismantle them altogether? Why not resolve the underlying problem that leads to their existence and why not simply disperse the concentrated populations? All these are valid questions that numerous scholars, leaders, and media have raised over the years.

Alas, permanent encampments are here to stay. Permanent encampments are a fact of life that is unlikely to change in the near future because they are the result of intractable dilemmas. Encampments have existed throughout history, as have ethnic groups who were either targets of displacement or who engaged in displacement. At the current time, there is no evidence of a decrease in involuntary displacements. To the contrary, there has been an increase. Widespread famines and environmental disasters continue to cause unprecedented numbers of refugees to relocate; wars and secessions are inducing voluntary and involuntary migrations as people of varying ethnic groups adjust to new leaders and new borders.[28] Some communities continue to live with the threat of expulsion for generations (the UNHCR cites the Romas in the Czech Republic, the Rohingyas in Myanmar, and the ethnic Russians in Estonia and Latvia).[29]

Not only is there no indication that the number of displaced people will decrease but there is also no indication that permanent encampments will close due to a better solution. Displaced peoples are concentrated into encampments because it is the simplest way to provide short-term aid and, over the long run, the simplest way to postpone a proactive solution. Host and home countries, as well as international organizations, are at a loss to find mutually acceptable solutions to encampments. Political, economic, social, and cultural factors play a role in preventing or postponing decisions and actions. In addition, displaced persons themselves sometimes share the blame for the lack of a solution.

They reject host country resettlement or third country asylum because they want to return to their homelands, refusing to accept that their promised land is no longer promised to them. Alternatively, they refuse to return to their homelands, where economic conditions are worse than in the encampments. Sometimes, displaced persons reject home and host state offers of assimilation because they want to retain their identities, keep their collective goals alive, and accept solutions on their terms (Anne Fadiman said "*involuntary migrants*, no matter what pot they are thrown into, tend not to melt."[30] [emphasis added]). Finally, encampment residents sometimes hold out for the asylum country of choice. Indeed, the "magnet effect" continues to attract refugees who hope they can use encampments to immigrate to Western states.

Without any reason to believe that population displacement will cease, encampments will not be formed, and permanence will not creep up on them, it is time to accept the reality of permanent encampments. It is time to acknowledge that settlements of displaced persons are, in fact, durable solutions rather than merely extended asylum. Permanent encampments are the nonsolution solution. It is time to accept them for what they are and to legitimize them. It has been said that the world needs to do more than send blankets, beans, and bandages to encampments.[31] Indeed, it needs to send political, economic, and social acceptance. Permanent encampments are fundamentally political constructs and, as such, they require political legitimization as to the durable solution that they, in fact, are. They need to be demystified and deconstructed and accepted as the only feasible solution at any given time. Given the lack of agreement between displaced people, host states, home states, and third country asylum states as to the best solution for displaced migrants, permanent encampments should be accepted as the second best solution while the search for the best continues. And continues.

The recommendation made above is summarized as follows: the world community should accept the reality of permanent encampments. It should strive to improve their economic and political conditions, achieve a mutually beneficial *modus vivendi* between camp residents and host countries, and minimize interethnic conflict both inside and outside the encampments. It can best achieve those goals by inducing introverted states to adopt characteristics of extroverted states, especially those that directly affect displaced populations. Globalization, when properly harnessed, has the ability to induce such a transformation. While much of the literature pertaining to encampments is pessimistic and negative, suggesting that they should be dismantled and their residents dispersed, this study instead suggests that they, in fact, are the only concrete solution, *ceteris paribus*.

NOTES

1. Refugee encampments are a transborder issue, involving at least a home and host state. The UNHCR states that "refugee problems are by definition transnational problems, which cannot be resolved by means of uncoordinated activities in separate countries" (UNHCR, *The State of the World's Refugees* [New York: Oxford University Press, 1995], 49). In his study of refugees, Aristide Zolberg emphasized the need to address involuntary population movements transnationally. He said, "law is founded on the notion that the world is divided into a finite set of states with mutually exclusive jurisdiction over segments of territory and clusters of population" (Aristide Zolberg, Astri Suhrke, and Sergio Aguayo, *Escape from Violence: Conflict and the Refugee Crisis in the Developing World* [New York: Oxford University Press, 1989], vi). However, encampment issues are rarely limited to the confines of a single country. Instead, at the minimum, they involve at least two countries (home and host—intermediate and third country) and, at most, the entire international community (namely, the international institutions that have been developed to deal with involuntary displacement and subsequent encampment). Also, when one encampment in one host country is used as a staging ground for guerilla warfare into the home state (such as Hutu refugees in Goma in Congo raiding neighboring Rwanda), then the conflict becomes transborder and a regional issue, not just internal. Therefore, whether we are studying a single country in which populations have been involuntarily displaced or whether our scope includes a multitude of states, it is clear that issues pertaining to encampments spread beyond the borders of the camp.

2. Given their unemployment rates of 80-100 percent (as, for example, in Slovakia), their dismal housing, education, and health care, they are looking

to emigrate. There has been a large exodus, since around 1997, when it became clear that the new democracy of Eastern Europe was not meant for all citizens and that their condition, *en masse,* deteriorated clearly since the demise of Communism. During the Communist times, the ideology of full employment made it illegal for adults to be unemployed unless they were disabled or engaged in otherwise productive activity. Under those conditions, the Roma were employed. During the post-Communist period, discrimination against them prevented their employment since preference was given to migrants from Ukraine and other former soviet states. At first, most Roma emigration was to Canada, although Britain and the United States were also favored. It is estimated that some 20 percent of the Roma from the Czech republic left since 1997, and many thousands have left from Slovakia, Romania, and Hungary. *New York Times,* April 2, 2000.

3. *New York Times,* September 19, 1999.

4. This term was coined by a Canadian politician. *Economist,* July 24, 1999, Canada Survey, 3.

5. Fergus M. Bordewich, *Killing the White Man's Indian: Reinventing Native Americans at the End of the Twentieth Century* (New York: Anchor Books, 1996), 18.

6. In 1934, the Indian Reorganization Act halted the conversion of reservations into private property of individual Indians, reversed the doctrine of assimilation (which was the cornerstone of government policy since 1880), and committed the federal government to strengthening the tribes. The Navahos, the largest and one of the most successful tribes, have their own representative council and flag, schools and colleges, police force, and a complete administrative system. In 1991, George Bush described tribes as "quasi-sovereign domestic dependent nations," whose "government-to-government relationship is the result of sovereign and independent tribal governments being incorporated into the fabric of our Nation." The Bush administration introduced the "self-governance" initiative according to which tribes may manage federal Indian programs themselves, without the oversight of the Bureau of Indian Affairs. Bordewich, *Killing the White Man's Indian,* 112.

7. As a result, indigenous peoples will have rights and status comparable to those of provincial governments. The recent establishment of the territory of Nunavut as a province represents the culmination of such policy. Until 1991, while they enjoyed some special legal standing and some privileges, control of their land, schools, and economic activity was in the hands

of the provincial governments and the federal Department of Indian and Northern Affairs. They also have fewer land rights and less self-government. Ted Robert Gurr, *Minorities at Risk* (Washington, D.C.: United States Institute of Peace, 1983), 166-67.

8. They fared so well mostly as a result of their relative size and the high degree of complexity and organization in their political and social systems at the time of European arrival. Gurr, *Minorities at Risk*, 162-63.

9. See, for example, Wolfgang Dannensprecher's paper presentation at the meetings of the Association for Nationality Studies (New York, April 2000).

10. Jeffrey Sacks said that tropical ecozones are poorer than temperate ecozones. He was quoted in the *New York Times*, January 13, 2001.

11. Lawrence E. Harrison and Samuel P. Huntington, eds. *Culture Matters: How Values Shape Human Progress* (New York: Basic Books, 2000).

12. Such a view is supported by evidence from Africa, where most encampments are located. Recently, President Clinton wanted to make positive economic changes on the continent, banking on Uganda, Rwanda, Ethiopia, and Eritrea to turn the tide of poverty and underdevelopment, unstable governments, and corrupt bureaucracies. Yet, during the two years between his first and second trip (1998 and 2000), all four states have gone to war. Such a realization prompts Westerners to further support geographic determinism and view Africa as hopeless.

13. Some theories of economic development are based on the idea of social and economic inequality that prods one group to perform in order to keep its privileged place in society. See the discussion of the heroic entrepreneur in Bengamin Higgins, *Economic Development* (New York, 1957) chapter on Schumacher.

14. Philip Curtin, *Cross-Cultural Trade in World History* (New York: Cambridge University Press, 1984).

15. Robert Holton, *Globalization and the Nation-State* (London: Macmillan, 1998).

16. Robert Kaplan, *The Coming Anarchy* (New York: Random House, 2000), 80.

17. It is difficult to make this argument devoid of value judgements. The bias reflected here, and shared by other Western scholars, is that the West can contribute to overall modernization and improvements in standards of living by exporting its notions of freedom, equality, and adaptability. By

opening up a country, citizens' freedom of choice and movement is increased. They become more exposed to other ways through increased access to information, and they begin to compare their own economic social and political limitations, inequalities, and injustices. The new scrutiny will result in reevaluation and change.

18. Carol Lancaster, "Redesigning Foreign Aid" *Foreign Affairs* (Sept-Oct 2000), 74-76.

19. Eric Rouleau, "Turkey's Dream of Democracy" *Foreign Affairs* (Nov/Dec 2000).

20. *New York Times,* October 10, 2000.

21. *New York Times,* October 7, 2000.

22. For years, the United States government delayed china's acceptance into the WTO. However, in 2000, the U.S. senate finally approved "permanent normal trade relations," paving the way for WTO acceptance (with minor changes in both positions that would allow the saving of face). *New York Times,* September 20, 2000. Michael Santoro's study of Chinese human rights and the motives of global capitalism underscores the lack of a facile solution to the dilemma between human rights or expanded commerce, worker protection or globalization. Michael A. Santoro, *Profits and Principles, Global Capitalism and Human Rights in China* (Ithaca, N.Y.: Cornell University Press, 2000).

23. UNHCR, *The State of the World's Refugees,* 40.

24. Philip Gourevitch, *We Wish to Inform You that Tomorrow We Will Be Killed with Our Families* (New York: Picador USA, 1999), 91.

25. Alex Inkeles and David Horton Smith, *Becoming Modern: Individual Change in Six Developing Countries* (Cambridge, Mass.: Harvard University Press, 1974).

26. *New York Times,* November 25, 2000.

27. R. O'Brien, *Global Financial Integration: The End of Geography* (London: Pinter, 1992).

28. In addition to involuntary displacement, differences in human capital needs are causing workers to relocate voluntarily in order to maximize their employment options, wage differentials are attracting workers from low income to high income regions, and movements of enterprises in search of profit maximization induce workers to follow.

29. UNHCR, *The State of the World's Refugees,* 67.

30. Some residents in permanent encampments are resisting assimilation, that's why they are displaced. This includes the Hmong, who fled

China because they didn't want to assimilate, and then Laos for the same reason. Unlike migrants who would love to come integrate into the United States, they came so they could resist integration. Anne Fadiman, *The Spirit Catches You and You Fall Down* (New York: Farrar, Strauss and Giroux, 1997), 183.

31. This term was used by Philip Gourevitch in *We Wish to Inform You*, 170.

SELECTED BIBLIOGRAPHY

Adelman, Howard, ed. *Legitimate and Illegitimate Discrimination: New Issues in Migration.* Toronto: York Lanes Press, 1995.

Adelman, Howard and J. Sorenson, eds. *African Refugees: Development Aid and Repatriation.* Boulder, Colo.: Westview Press, 1994.

AfricaWatch, *Sudan: Refugees in Their Own Country.* Washington, D.C.: Human Rights Watch, 1992.

Ager, Alastair, ed. *Refugees, Perspectives on the Experience of Forced Migration.* London: Cassel Publishers, 1998.

Ake, C. *Democracy and Development in Africa.* Washington, D.C.: Brookings Institution, 1996.

Aleinikoff, T. Alexander and Douglas Klusmeyer, eds. *From Migrants to Citizens, Membership in a Changing World.* Washington, D.C.: Carnegie Endowment for International Peace, 2000.

Allen, T. and H Morsink, eds. *When Refugees Go Home.* Trenton, N.J.: Africa World Press, 1994.

Anand, Dibyesh. "(Re)Imagining Nationalism: Identity and Representation in Tibetan Diaspora in South Asia." *Contemporary South Asia* 9, no 3, (2000).

Anaya, James. *Indigenous Peoples in International Law.* New York: Oxford University Press, 1996.

Angrist, Joshua D. "The Palestinian Labor Market between the Gulf War and Autonomy." *MIT Department of Economics Working Paper* #98-05, 1998.

Archer, Fiona. "Current and Future Land Use in the Namaqualand Rural Reserves." Cape Town: Surplus People Project, 1995.

Arzt, Donna, E. *Refugees into Citizens*. New York: Council on Foreign Relations, 1997.

Baitenmann, H. "NGOs and the Afghan War: the Politicization of Aid." *Third World Quarterly* 12, no 1, (1990).

Bascom, Johnathan. "Internal Refugees: The Case of the Displaced in Khartoum." In Richard Black and Vaughan Robinson, eds. *Geography and Refugees*. London: Belhaven Press, 1993.

Bell-Fialkoff. Andrew, *Ethnic Cleansing*. New York: St. Martin's Griffin 1999.

Betts, Tristan. "Zonal Rural Development in Africa." *Journal of Modern African Studies* 7, no 1 (1969).

Black, Richard and Thomas Mabwe. "Planning for Refugees in Zambia, The Settlement Approach to Food Self-Sufficiency." *Third World Planning Review* 14, no. 1 (1992).

Black, Richard and Vaughan Robinson, eds. *Geography and Refugees*. London: Belhaven Press, 1993.

Bookman, Milica Z. *Ethnic Groups in Motion: Migration and Economic Competition in Multi-Ethnic States*. London: Frank Cass, 2002.

Bookman, Milica Z. *The Demographic Struggle for Power*. London: Frank Cass, 1997.

Bordewich, Fergus M. *Killing the White Man's Indian: Reinventing Native Americans at the End of the Twentieth Century*. New York: Anchor Books, 1996.

Bousquet, Gisele. "Living in a State of Limbo: A Case Study of Vietnamese Refugees in Hongkong Camps." In *People in Upheaval*, edited by Scott M. Morgan and Elizabeth Colson. New York: Center for Migration Studies, 1987.

Bowles, Edith. "From Village to Camp: Refugee Camp Life in Transition of the Thailand-Burma Border." *Forced Migration Review* 2, 1998.

Bramwell, A., ed. *Refugees in the Age of Total War*. London: Unwin Hyman, 1988.

Brettel, Caroline and James Frank Hollifield, eds. *Migration Theory: Talking across Disciplines*. New York: Routledge, 2000.

Burr, Millard, *Khartoum's Displaced Persons: A Decade of Despair*. Issue Brief, Washington, D.C.: U.S. Committee for Refugees, 1990.

Camus-Jacques, Genevieve. "Refugee Women: The Forgotten Majority." In *Refugees and International Relations*, edited by Gil Loescher and Laila Monahan. Oxford: Oxford University Press, 1989.

Castles, S. and M. J. Miller. *The Age of Migration: International Population Movements in the Modern World*. London: Macmillan, 1993.

Cernea, Michael M., ed. *The Economics of Involuntary Resettlement*. Washington, D.C.: World Bank, 1999.

Chambers, R. "Hidden Losers? The Impact of Rural Refugees and Refugee Programs on Poorer Hosts." *International Migration Review* 20, 1986.

———. *Settlement Schemes in Tropical Africa*. New York: Praeger, 1969.

Chan, K.B. and D. Loveridge. "Refugees in Transit: Vietnamese in a Refugee Camp in Hong Kong." *International Migration Review* 21, 1987.

Cohen, Felix S. *Handbook of Federal Indian Law*. Albuquerque: University of New Mexico Press, 1942.

Cohen, J.D. "Psychological Adaptation and Dysfunction among Refugees." *International Migration Review* 15, 1981.

Cohen, Roberta and Francis M. Deng. *Masses in Flight: The Global Crisis of Internal Displacement*. Washington, D.C.: Brookings Institution, 1998.

Cohen, Roberta and Francis M. Deng, eds. *The Forsaken People: Case Studies of the Internally Displaced*. Washington, D.C.: Brookings Institution, 1998.

Cook, Cynthia C., ed. *Involuntary Resettlement in Africa*. Washington, D.C.: World Bank, 1994.

Crisp, Jeff. "Who Has Counted The Refugees? UNHRC and the Politics of Numbers." *New Issues in Refugee Research*, Working Paper no. 12, UNHRC Policy Research Unit, June 1999.

Dawood, Zohra. "Race and Space: Dispossession through the Group Areas Act." Surplus People Project Research Paper, Cape Town, 1994.

De Voe, Dorsh Marie, "Keeping Refugee Status: A Tibetan Perspective." in *People in Upheaval*, edited by Scott M. Morgan and Elizabeth Colson. New York: Center for Migration Studies, 1987.

Deloria, Vine, Jr. and Clifford M. Lytle. *American Indians, American Justice*. Austin: University of Texas Press, 1983.

Deng, Francis M. *Protecting the Dispossessed*. Washington, D.C.: The Brookings Institution, 1993.

Deng, Francis M., Sadikiel Kimaro, Terrence Lyons, Donald Rothchild, and I. William Zartman. *Sovereignty as Responsibility*. Washington, D.C.: Brookings Institution, 1996.

Desbarats, Jaqueline. "Forces of Dispersal and Forces of Concentration in Refugee Resettlement." In *Refugees, A Third World Dilemma*, edited by John D. Rogge. Totowa, N.J.: Rowman and Littlefield, 1987.

Despres, Leo, ed. *Ethnicity and Resource Competition in Plural Societies*. The Hague: Mouton Publishers, 1975.

Diehl, P. F., ed. *The Politics of Global Governance: International Organizations in an Independent World*. Boulder, Colo.: Lynne Rienner, 1997.

Dukic, Natali and Alain Thierry. "Saharawi Refugees: Life After the Camps." *Forced Migration Review* 2, 1998.

Fadiman, Anne. *The Spirit Catches You and You Fall Down*. New York: Farrar, Strauss and Giroux, 1997.

Farr, Grant M. "Definitions of Legitimacy: Afghan Refugees in Pakistan." In *Legitimate and Illegitimate Discrimination: New Issues in Migration*, edited by Howard Adelman. Toronto: York Lanes Press, 1995.

Ferleger, Louis and Jay R. Mandle, eds. *Dimensions of Globalization*. The Annals of the American Academy of Political and Social Science 570, July 2000.

Ferris, E. *Beyond Borders: Refugees, Migrants and Human Rights in the Post-Cold War Era*. Geneva: World Council of Churches Publications, 1993.

Fleras, Augie and Paul Spoonley. *Recalling Aotearoa. Indigenous Politics and Ethnic Relations in New Zealand*. Oxford: Oxford University Press, 2000.

Franck, Thomas, "Are Human Rights Universal?" *Foreign Affairs* 80, 1, 2001.

Freedom House. *Freedom in the World: The Annual Survey of Political Rights and Civil Liberties, 1998–1999*. New York: Freedom House, 1999.

Frelick, Bill. *The Wall of Denial: Internal Displacement in Turkey*. Washington, D.C.: U.S. Committee for Refugees, 1999.

Friedman, Thomas L. *The Lexus and the Olive Tree*. New York: Anchor Books, 2000.

Gerner, Deborah J. *One Land, Two Peoples. The Conflict over Palestine*. 2nd edition, Boulder, Colo.: Westview Press 1994.

Goose, Stephen D. and Frank Smyth, "Arming Genocide in Rwanda." *Foreign Affairs*, 73 no. 5, 1998.

Gourevitch, Philip *We Wish to Inform You that Tomorrow We Will Be Killed with Our Families*. New York: Picador USA, 1999.

Gordenker, Leon. *Refugees in International Politics*. New York: Columbia University Press, 1987.

Gurr, Ted Robert. *Minorities at Risk: A Global View of Ethnopolitical Conflicts*. Washington, D.C.: United States Institute of Peace, 1993.

Hathaway, J. *The Law of Refugee Status*. Toronto: Butterworths, 1991.

Haines, C.W. "The Pursuit of English and Self-Sufficiency: Dilemmas in Assessing Refugee Programme Effects." *Journal of Refugee Studies* 1, no. 3/4, 1988.

Hammar, Tomas. "Immigration Regulation: The Cost to Integration." In *Legitimate and Illegitimate Discrimination: New Issues in Migration*, edited by Howard Adelman. Toronto: York Lanes Press, 1995.

Hammond, J. "War Uprooting and the Political Mobilization of Central American Refugees." *Journal of Refugee Studies* 6, no. 1, 1993.

Hansen, A and O. Smith, eds. *Involuntary Migration and Resettlement: the Problems and Responses of Dislocated People*. Boulder, Colo.: Westview Press, 1982.

Harrell-Bond, B. E. *Imposing Aid: Emergency Assistance to Refugees*. Oxford: Oxford University Press, 1986.

Harrison, Lawrence E. and Samuel P. Huntington, eds. *Culture Matters: How Values Shape Human Progress*. New York: Basic Books, 2000.

Helton, Arthur C. and Natalia Voronina. *Forced Displacement and Human Security in the Former Soviet Union: Law and Policy*. Ardsley, N.Y.: Transnational Publishers, 2000.

Hitchcox, Linda. *Vietnamese Refugees in Southeast Asian Camps*. New York: St. Martin's Press, 1990.

Hochenos, Paul. *Free to Hate*. New York: Routledge, 1993.

Holton, Robert. *Globalization and the Nation-State*. London: Macmillan, 1998.

Horowitz, Donald. *Ethnic Groups in Conflict*. Berkeley: University of California Press, 1985.

Human Rights Watch. *Helsinki Watch Annual Report*. Various years.

Hyndman, M.J. "Refugee Self-Management and the Question of Governance." *Refuge* 16, no. 2, 1997.

Jacobson, David *Rights across Borders*. Baltimore, Md.: Johns Hopkins University Press, 1997.

Johnson, T. "Eritrean Refugees in Sudan." *Disasters* 3, no. 4, 1981.

Joly, Daniele. *Haven or Hell: Asylum Policy in Europe*. London: Macmillan, 1996.

———. *Refugees, Asylum in Europe*. Boulder, Colo.: Westview Press, 1992.

Kaplan, Robert. *The Coming Anarchy*. New York: Random House, 2000.

Kibreab, G. "Eritrean Women Refugees in Khartoum, Sudan, 1970–1990." *Journal of Refugee Studies* 8, no. 1, 1995.

———. "The Myth of Dependency Among Camp Refugees in Somalia." *Journal of Refugee Studies* 4, no. 6, 1993.

Krznaric, Roman. "Guatemalan Returnees and the Dilemma of Political Mobilization." *Journal of Refugees Studies* 10, no. 1, 1997.

Kulchyski, Peter, ed. *Unjust Relations. Aboriginal Rights in Canadian Courts.* Oxford: Oxford University Press, 1994.

Laber, Jeri. "The Hidden War in Turkey." *The New York Review of Books*, June 23, 1994.

Lake, David A. and Donald Rothchild, eds. *The International Spread of Ethnic Conflict: Fear, Diffusion and Escalation.* Princeton: Princeton University Press, 1998.

Lancaster, Carol. "Redesigning Foreign Aid." *Foreign Affairs*, Sept-Oct 2000.

Lawless, R and L. Monahan, eds. *War and Refugees: The Western Sahara Conflict.* London: Pinter, 1988.

Lee, Luke, T. "Internally Displaced Persons and Refugees: Toward a Legal Synthesis?" *Journal of Refugee Studies* 9, no. 1, 1996.

Lintner, Bertil, "Drugs and Economic Growth, Ethnicity and Exports." In *Burma, Prospects for a Democratic Future*, edited by Robert I. Rotberg. Washington, D.C.: Brookings Institution 1998.

Loescher, G. *Beyond Charity: International Cooperation and the Global Refugee Crisis.* Oxford: Oxford University Press, 1993.

Loescher, G. and L. Monahan, eds. *Refugees and International Relations.* Oxford: Oxford University Press, 1989.

Messina, C. "From Migrants to Refugees: Russian, Soviet and Post-Soviet Migration." *International Journal of Refugee Law* 5, no. 4, 1994.

Mittleman, J.H., ed. *Globalization: Critical Reflections.* Boulder, Colo.: Lynne Rienner, 1996.

Money, Jeanette. *Fences and Neighbors: The Political Geography of Immigration Control.* Ithaca, N.Y.: Cornell University Press, 1999.

Morgan, Scott M. and Elizabeth Colson, eds. *People in Upheaval.* New York: Center for Migration Studies, 1987.

Morawska, Eva. "Intended and Unintended Consequences of Forced Migrations: A Neglected Aspect of East Europe's Twentieth Century History" *International Migration Review* 34, no. 4, 2000.

Mtango, Elly-Elikunda. "Military and Armed Attacks on Refugee Camps." In *Refugees and International Relations*, edited by Gil Loescher and Laila Monahan. Oxford: Oxford University Press, 1989.

Nagel, Stuart S. and Amy Robb, eds. *Handbook of Global Social Policy.* New York: Marcel Dekker, 2000.

National Land Committee and Surplus People Project. "Closing the Door: The Implication and Implementation of the 1993 Land Legislation." Cape Town, 1994.

Nattrass, Nicoli. "Wage Strategies and Minimum Wages in Decentralized Regions: The Case of the Clothing Industry in Phuthaditjhaba, South Africa." *International Journal of Urban and Regional Research* 24, no. 4, 2000.

O'Brien, R. *Global Financial Integration: The End of Geography.* London: Pinter, 1992.

Olzak, Susan. *The Dynamics of Ethnic Competition and Conflict.* Stanford: Stanford University Press, 1997.

Pacheco, Gilda. *Nicaraguan Refugees in Costa Rica: Adjustment to Camp Life.* Washington, D.C.: Center for Immigration Policy and Refugee Assistance, Georgetown University, 1989.

Palmer, Geoffrey and Matthew Palmer. *Bridled Power, New Zealand Government Under MMP.* Oxford: Oxford University Press, 1994.

Peteet, Julie. "Identity Crisis: Palestinians in Post-War Lebanon." U.S. Committee for Refugees, *World Refugee Survey*, 1997.

Picciotto, Robert, Warren van Wicklin, and Edward Rice, eds. *Involuntary Resettlement, Comparative Perspectives.* World Bank Series on Evaluation and Development 2, New Brunswick: Transaction Publishers, 2001.

Pilkington, Hilary and Moya Flynn, "From 'Refugee' to 'Repatriate': Russian Repatriation Discourse in the Making." In *The End of the Refugee Cycle?* edited by Richard Black and Khalid Koser. Oxford: Berghahn 1999.

Pollis, Adamanta and Peter Schwab, eds. *Human Rights, Cultural and Ideological Perspectives.* New York: Praeger, 1979.

Preston, R. "Refugees in Papua New Guinea: Government Response and Assistance, 1984–1988." *International Migration Review* 26, no. 2, 1992.

Pritchard, D. "The Legacy of Conflict: Refugee Repatriation and Reintegration in Central America." In *Central America: Fragile Transition,* edited by R. Sieder. London: Macmillan, 1995.

Proudfoot, M. J. *European Refugees 1939–1952: A Study of Forced Population Movement.* London: Faber and Faber, 1957.

Punjabi, Riyaz. "Forced Migrations in South Asia: The Dilemma of Security of the State and the Rights of Migrants." Paper presented at the annual meetings of the International Studies Association, Chicago, February 2001.

Ramirez, Mario A. *Refugee Policy Challenges: The Case of Nicaraguans in Costa Rica*. Center for Immigration Policy and Refugee Assistance, Georgetown University, 1989.

Refugee Policy Group. *Older Refugee Settlements in Africa*. Final Report, Washington, D.C., 1985.

Richmond, Anthony. *Global Apartheid: Refugees, Racism and the New World Order*. Oxford: Oxford University Press, 1995.

――――. *Immigration and Ethnic Conflict*. London: Macmillan 1988.

Rizvi, G. "The Afghan Refugees: Hostages in the Struggle for Power." *Journal for Refugee Studies* 3, no. 3, 1990.

Rogers, R. and Emily Copeland. *Forced Migration: Policy Issues in the Post-Cold War World*. Medford, Mass.: The Fletcher School of Law and Diplomacy, Tufts University, 1993.

Rogerson, C.M. and Em. M. Letsoalo. "Resettlement and Under-Development in the Black 'Homelands' of South Africa." In *Population and Development Projects in Africa*, edited by John I. Clarke, Mustafa Khogali, and Leszek A. Kosinski. Cambridge: Cambridge University Press, 1985.

Rogge, John R. *Refugees, A Third World Dilemma*. Totowa, N.J.: Rowman & Littlefield, 1987.

――――. *Too Many, Too Long: Sudan's Twenty-Year Refugee Dilemma*. Totowa, N.J.: Rowman and Allanheld, 1985.

Rolfe, Chris, Clare Rolfe, and Malcolm Harper. *Refugee Enterprise, It Can Be Done*. London: Intermediate Technology Publications, 1987.

Rowse, Tim. *Obliged to be Difficult, Nugget Coomb's Legacy in Indigenous Affairs*. Cambridge: Cambridge University Press, 2000.

Schrijvers, Joke. "Fighters, Victims and Survivors: Constructions of Ethnicity, Gender and Refugeeness among Tamils in Sri Lanka." *Journal of Refugee Studies* 12, no. 3, 1999.

Scott, Allen J. *Regions and the World Economy: The Coming Age of Global Production, Competition, and Political Order*. Oxford: Oxford University Press, 1998.

Shain, Yossi. *Marketing the American Credo Abroad*. Cambridge: Cambridge University Press, 1999.

Sharp, Andrew. *Justice and the Maori*. Second Edition, Oxford: Oxford University Press, 1997.

Shaw, Malcolm. *Title to Territory in Africa: International Legal Issues*. Oxford: Clarendon, 1986.

Simmons, A.B., ed. *International Migration, Refugee Flows and Human Rights in North America*. New York: Center for Migration Studies, 1996.

Slater, Peter. *Workers without Frontiers: The Impact of Globalization on International Migration*. Boulder, Colo.: Lynne Reinner, 2000.

Sowell, Thomas. *The Economics and Politics of Race: An International Perspective*. New York: W. Morrow, 1983.

Smyser, W.R. "Refugees, a Never Ending Story." *Foreign Affairs*, Fall 1985.

Stepputat, Finn. "The Hard Road to Self-sufficiency." *Refugees* 80, 1990.

———. "Repatriation and the Politics of Space: The Case of the Mayan Diaspora and the Return Movement." *Journal of Refugee Studies* 7, no. 2/3, 1994.

Surplus People Project. *Forced Removals in South Africa: General Overview*. Volume 1 of the Surplus People Project Report, Cape Town, 1983.

Thomas, Angharad and Gordon Wilson. "Technological Capabilities in Textile Production in Saharawi Refugee Camps." *Journal of Refugee Studies* 9, no. 2, 1996.

UN High Commissioner for Refugees. *The State of the World's Refugees*. New York: Oxford University Press, various annual editions.

U.S. Committee for Refugees. *World Refugee Survey*. Washington, D.C.: Immigration and Refugee Services of America, various annual editions.

Wearne, P. *The Maya of Guatemala*. London: Minority Rights Group International, 1994.

Weaver, J. "Searching for Survival: Urban Ethiopian Refugees in Sudan." *Journal of Developing Areas* 22, 1988.

Weiss. Thomas G. and Cindy Collins. *Humanitarian Challenges and Intervention*. 2nd edition, Boulder, Colo.: Westview Press 2000.

Wiener, Myron. *The Global Migration Crisis: Challenge to States and to Human Rights*. New York: HarperCollins, 1995.

Williams, Walter. *South Africa's War against Capitalism*. New York: Praeger, 1989.

Wilson, Thomas M. and Hastings Donnan, eds. *Border Identities*. Cambridge: Cambridge University Press, 1998.

Wolf, Martin. "Will the Nation-State Survive Globalization?" *Foreign Affairs* 80, no. 1, 2001.

Zakaria, Leila F. and Samia Tabari. "Health, Work Opportunities and Attitudes: A Review of Palestinian Women's Situation in Lebanon." *Journal of Refugee Studies* 10, no. 3, 1997.

Zayonchkovskaya, Zhanne, Alexander Kocharyan, and Galina Vitkovskaya, "Forced Migration and Ethnic Processes in the Former Soviet Union." In *Geography and Refugees,* edited by Richard Black and Vaughan Robinson. London: Belhaven Press, 1993.

Zetter, Roger. "The Greek-Cypriot Refugees: Perceptions of Return under Conditions of Protracted Exile." *International Migration Review* 23, no. 2, 1994.

Zetter, Roger. "Refugees and Forced Migrants as Development Resources: the Greek-Cypriot Refugees from 1974." *Cyprus Review* 4, no. 1, 1992.

Zolberg, Aristide, Astri Suhrke, and Sergio Aguayo. *Escape from Violence: Conflict and the Refugee Crisis in the Developing World.* New York: Oxford University Press, 1989.

INDEX

ABOUT THE AUTHOR

Milica Z. Bookman is a professor of economics at St. Joseph's University in Philadelphia. She was educated at Brown University, London School of Economics, and Temple University. She is the author of numerous articles and seven books, including, most recently, *Ethnic Groups in Motion* and *The Demographic Struggle for Power*.